PENTECOSTALISM in ASIA:
Its Theology and Mandates

WONSUK MA

APTS Press Occasional Papers Series Book 4

WIPF & STOCK · Eugene, Oregon

Wipf and Stock Publishers
199 W 8th Ave, Suite 3
Eugene, OR 97401

Pentecostalism in Asia
Its Theology and Mandates
By Ma, Wonsuk

Softcover ISBN-13: 979-8-3852-7619-6
Hardcover ISBN-13: 979-8-3852-7620-2
eBook ISBN-13: 979-8-3852-7621-9
Publication date 2/3/2026
Previously published by APTS Press, 2026

This edition is a scanned facsimile of the original edition published in 2026.

Dedicated to

Woolim and Boram,
our two sons,
who have been journeying with us
to discover what it means to be Pentecostal in Asia

CONTENTS

Publisher's Preface

to the Occasional Paper Series

This book is the fourth volume in the *APTS Press Occasional Papers Series.* The first three books are *Pentecostals and the Poor: Reflections From the Indian Context* by Ivan Satyavrata, *For All Peoples: A Biblical Theology of Missions in the Gospels and Acts* by Craig S. Keener, and *The Versatility of Paul: Artisan Missioner, Community Developer, Pastoral Educator* by Robert Banks. All are available through our website, www.aptspress.com.

The purpose of this series is to produce smaller books comprised of articles that deal with theological, anthropological, and missiological issues relevant to serving God in Asia. From time to time, other disciplines may also be included. As the title suggests, the books will be published as articles of interest to our readers become available.

For further information on this series or other works of the APTS Press, including our journal, the *Asian Journal of Pentecostal Studies*, please contact us through the website.

Sincerely,

The Publisher

Acknowledgments

A book with this long span of making (from 2005 to 2025) has had many hands involved, perhaps too many to name them all. Here are a few that I would like to mention.

Asia Pacific Theological Seminary in the Philippines was the birthplace of my lifelong interest in Asian Pentecostal studies. Through my quarter-century teaching in the seminary community, I developed not only courses and programs relevant to the subject but also my knowledge. Therefore, it is fitting that the oldest chapter was first published in the seminary's journal, and the latest chapters were lectures delivered to the seminary community. For the 2023 Annual William Menzies Lectureship, our hosts were Dr. Jun Kim, its academic dean, and his wife, Jane. The Kims, along with the entire seminary community, extended their warm reception with their iconic generosity and kindness. With my entire family, who enjoyed our time there, I want to thank them.

APTS Press deserves separate mention. Dave Johnson, the press director, guided me with professionalism and passion, sprinkled with his big laughter. I want to thank this special long-time colleague. The Press's editing and production teams fine-combed the manuscript, spotting missing information, and suggesting better readings for the final production. They indeed drastically improved my presentation, although I still bear the final responsibility for any typos or misinformation.

Two close friends also read parts or the whole of the manuscript in various stages, and for this assistance, I want to thank Judy Gilliland, my mission colleague, and Jaime Riddle, my current assistant at Oral Roberts University, who also created the index and also proofread the final version.

I am extremely honored by the gracious forewords by two global Christian leaders. Billy Wilson, representing 570 million Spirit-empowered believers worldwide, reflects on Asian Pentecostalism from his extensive knowledge of global Pentecostal-Charismatic Christianity. As he also serves as the President of Oral Roberts University, Tulsa, Oklahoma, USA, where I teach, this book is a small contribution to his passion for Spirit-empowered scholarship. Additionally, Hwa Yung offers his informed and cautionary affirmation of the unique role of Asian Pentecostal Christianity. As a friendly and Spirit-filled outsider, his foreword points Pentecostals towards future tasks. In the recent Lausanne Congress IV (2024), both leaders spoke powerfully on the work of the Holy Spirit in mission and evangelization. I am privileged to have these two global leaders gracing the book.

I also want to thank the publishers of my previous studies for their kind permission to include them in this book. They are *Asian Journal of Pentecostal Studies*, Regnum Books, WCC Publications, Langham Literature and Langham Global Library, and Cambridge University Press. The details of the original publication information are found in the relevant chapters. The original studies have been updated and revised for the book.

This book is affectionately dedicated to my two sons, who spent their growing years in the Philippines with us. As a struggling Korean missionary family, they journeyed with us in deepening our appreciation for the Holy Spirit's work in the Asian cultural and religious context.

Summer 2025

Foreword One

Asia is the last frontier of Christian mission, with only 8.2 percent of its 4.62 billion people evangelized as of 2020.[1] The continent that birthed Christianity has struggled to move forward for two millennia and currently has the lowest proportion of Christians. And yet, this is not the end of the story. Between 2000 and 2020, Asia also experienced the second-highest growth rate of the Christian faith. Closer scrutiny suggests that East and Southeast Asia may now hold the highest potential for Christian growth between 2020 and 2050.

Navigating this tension, Wonsuk Ma contends that Asian Christianity will indeed lead the next era of global Christian growth. As a Distinguished Professor of Global Christianity, former Director of the Oxford Centre for Mission Studies, and one of the *50 Pentecostal and Charismatic Leaders Every Christian Should Know,*[2] Ma is highly qualified to make this claim. Using growth data, he argues that Asian Pentecostalism is the key variable that will make the difference inside the Asian church and beyond. I fully concur with his argument for two reasons.

First, Spirit-empowered Christianity is the fastest-growing and largest active Christian segment in the world. The Catholic Church holds the most adherents,[3] but in the United States, they are approximately three times less active than Pentecostals and

[1]Todd M. Johnson and Gina A. Zurlo, *World Christian Encyclopedia*, 3rd ed. (Edinburgh: Edinburgh University Press, 2020), 4.

[2]Dean Merrill, *50 Pentecostal and Charismatic Leaders Every Christian Should Know* (Minneapolis: Chosen, 2021).

[3]With 1.24 billion globally as of 2020, in Johnson and Zurlo, *WCE*, 6.

Charismatics.[4] When we start applying percentages like these to global numbers, we find that Spirit-empowered Christians are indeed the largest active Christian faith family on the earth.[5] It is this fact, coupled with East and Southeast Asia's outstanding Pentecostal growth rate, that puts their region forward as the greatest growth engine for global Christianity in the next era.

Second, Spirit-empowered believers are committed and effective evangelists. I have personally seen and facilitated this in my leadership of Empowered21, a global network of Spirit-empowered churches, organizations, and leaders. In 2023, I launched the EveryONE initiative with the bold vision of making sure everyone on earth has an opportunity to hear and respond to the gospel before Pentecost 2033, which marks the 2000th anniversary of Christ's resurrection, outpouring of the Spirit, and birth of the church. Ma takes up this vision, discussing Asian reception and agency in the task at hand. He affirms the missiological pneumatology of Spirit-empowered Christianity as "Spirit-empowered for witnessing" based on Acts 1:8. He describes how Spirit-empowered believers are wired to be evangelists par excellence. He further engages ecumenism by positing unique contributions of Spirit-empowered theology to the church at large.

---

[4]See 17 percent activity rate for weekly Mass attendance in the USA, in Jonah McKeown, "By the Numbers: How the Catholic Church Has Changed During Pope Francis' Pontificate," *National Catholic Register,* March 13, 2023. Alternatively, 29 percent is reported in Pew Research Center, "10 Facts about U.S. Catholics" (March 4, 2025). For USA Pentecostal-Charismatics, see 66 percent attending church weekly or more, in Pew Research Center, "Spirit and Power—A 10-Country Survey of Pentecostals" (October 5, 2006).

[5]Active Catholics would number approximately 248 million out of 1.24 billion adherents globally (20%), while active Spirit-empowered Christians would number 425 million out 644 million adherents (66%) globally.

Ultimately, Ma presents a well-argued case that a new era is dawning for Asian Pentecostalism to live up to the mandates of the time. The research is inspiring, challenging, and provocative—a must-read not only for every Spirit-empowered believer but also for every Christian committed to the Great Commission.

William M. Wilson
President, Oral Roberts University
Chair, Empowered21 and the Pentecostal World Fellowship

Foreword Two

Some twenty years ago, in a discussion with an American scholar who was enthusiastically expounding how Pentecostalism began at the Azusa Street Mission in 1906, the question was raised by some present about Pentecostalism's multiple origins. The scholar, who did not seem to understand the question, perhaps deemed it irrelevant or simply ignored it. As an Asian Christian, I found this and other similar experiences rather condescending, reinforcing the prevailing tendency for historical interpretations to be more often than not Western-centric. Thankfully, the world of scholarship is changing, and increasingly, a global perspective is being set forth.

For this reason, Wonsuk Ma's book on Asian Pentecostalism is to be hugely welcomed. Much of the study is focused on East and Southeast Asia, with a special emphasis on China, Korea, and the Philippines. But it also spreads its wings wider to interact with Pentecostalism in other parts of the world, as well as with Christian movements outside the Pentecostal stream. It touches on a whole variety of issues confronting the church, both in Asia and the world today. These include how we understand the Holy Spirit and his "signs and wonders," Pentecostalism as a religion of empowerment for the poor and marginalized, the challenge of socio-political transformation, the theology of blessing and its flip side, the prosperity gospel (the gospel of need versus the gospel of greed), contextualization, what Pentecostalism can contribute to the growth of the church globally, and others.

In this foreword, I would like to make three comments to help in our reflections on the subject. First, on the basis of hard statistics, Ma argues that it is the Pentecostal stream of Christianity that has been the fastest growing in the past decades and will continue to be in the coming years. This is not surprising given the words of the risen Christ in Acts 1:8, "You will receive power when the Holy Spirit has come upon you, and you will be my witnesses . . . to the ends of the earth." What is beyond doubt is that it is those segments of the global church that have taken seriously the empowering of the Holy Spirit that are most effective in the proclamation of the gospel today. This is of special significance for the church in Asia, where some 90 percent of the population has yet to respond to the gospel. But Ma goes further to argue that, given the high proportion of Pentecostals in the Asian church and that China, Korea, and the Philippines are three of the largest missionary-sending churches globally today, Asian Pentecostalism may well be the main engine of growth for global Christianity in the coming years. If this is true, then the Asian church must take this challenge seriously.

The second comment relates to the first. Ma is aware of some of the major issues plaguing Pentecostalism in Asia. Nevertheless, his prognosis about the future of Pentecostalism is optimistic—Pentecostals usually are! As one who shares his belief that the global church urgently needs to recover the power of the Holy Spirit in its life and mission, I am in broad agreement with him.

However, there are two caveats. First, despite the contributions that Pentecostalism has made to ecumenism to date, the fact remains that Pentecostals have major issues with their ecclesiology(s). This may not be so with Classical Pentecostals. But the second category of Pentecostals, the Charismatics, often have ambiguous relationships with their respective denominational leadership. As for the third category of the so-called "neo-Charismatics," one can find almost any ecclesiology under the sun somewhere among them. This, then, is one of the biggest challenges facing Pentecostalism today. Unless a solidly biblical ecclesiology is formulated that provides both discipline and accountability, Pentecostalism will easily degenerate into a myriad of fissiparous groups wherein, as in the days of the judges, everyone will simply do "what is right in his own eyes (Judg 21:25)."

The other caveat relates to something not discussed in the book, the issue of discipleship. In the past hundred-plus years, there have been some amazing revivals and movements of the Spirit throughout East and Southeast Asia. But how many of these have moved on to produce strong, mature churches is uncertain. Thus, ecclesiology and discipleship are two key issues that Pentecostals have to address urgently if Pentecostalism in Asia is to help the churches reach their fullest potential for the advance of the Kingdom.

My third comment relates to the existing terminologies used in speaking of "Pentecostals" or "Pentecostals/Charismatics." This group includes three categories, namely, Classical Pentecostals (denominations traceable back to Azusa Street), Charismatics (Christians who accept the tenets of Pentecostalism but remain in older Western-originated denominations) and neo-Charismatics (a catch-all category for independent and/or Charismatic churches, and also indigenous churches birthed in the Majority World which are Pentecostal in practice). Although this seems to be the accepted categorization, I suggest that it only makes sense within a Western reading of church history. Why so?

In the Western reading of church history, Classical Pentecostalism suddenly burst forth in 1906 at Azusa Street. Then Charismatics emerged in the 1960s but remained in mainstream denominations. Finally, the awareness dawned that many groups and churches had been taking the Holy Spirit and his work seriously all over the world, sometimes way before Classical Pentecostalism emerged. Thus, all these groups were lumped together as neo-Charismatics, as if they all came after the Charismatic Renewal. It is the "neo-" in the third category that fails to do justice to what the Holy Spirit has been doing all along throughout church history.

To begin with, the revival at Pandita Ramabai's Mukti orphanage in India in 1905 was a full year before Azusa Street. In China, Pastor Hsi ([1835?]-1896) had begun operating powerfully in the gifts of the Holy Spirit two decades earlier.[1] In what sense can the term "neo-" meaningfully be used of these two and other similar historical figures? That is not all. It is increasingly recognized that the European Enlightenment led to a dominance of an anti-supernaturalism taking over in the West, with the result

[1]Mrs. Howard Taylor, *Pastor Hsi, Confucian Scholar & Christian,* rev. ed. (London: Overseas Missionary Fellowship, 1949).

that much of the historical writings passed down to us have had the supernatural elements edited out in the interest of modernity. Take the example of John Wesley. As a Methodist, I found it most distressing that earlier works on John Wesley had little to say about the supernatural in his ministry. However, it is heartening to note that scholarly writings in the past few decades have begun to do justice to the supernatural dimension of early Methodism under Wesley, the most notable being Robert Webster's Oxford dissertation, published as *Methodism and the Miraculous.*[2] But here again, the question must be asked, in what sense can the term "neo-" be applied to Wesley, as well as other historical figures who have been similarly mistreated in Western scholarship? The point is that the term "neo-Charismatic" is anachronistic and historically distorting and therefore should be replaced by something more accurate. Would "pneumatics" or "Pneumatic Christianity" be worth considering?

Thank you, Wonsuk Ma, for giving us a stimulating book about what God is doing through his Spirit in Asia and the world. May this book help us to discern more clearly the direction in which the Spirit is leading the Asian church!

Hwa Yung
Bishop Emeritus, The Methodist Church in Malaysia

---

[2]Robert Webster, *Methodism and the Miraculous: John Wesley's Idea of the Supernatural and the Identification of Methodists in the Eighteenth Century* (Lexington, KY: Emeth Press, 2013).

Abbreviations

AJPS	*Asian Journal of Pentecostal Studies*
APS	Asian Pentecostal Society
APTA	Asia Pacific Theological Association
APTS	Asia Pacific Theological Seminary
CCR	Catholic Charismatic Renewal
CGI	Church Growth International
CCA	Christian Conference of Asia
GCF	Global Christian Forum
HDI	Human Development Index
ISEC	*Introducing Spirit-Empowered Christianity*
NGOs	Non-Governmental Organizations
NIDPCM	*New International Dictionary of Pentecostal and Charismatic Movements*
PWC	Pentecostal World Conference
PWF	Pentecostal World Fellowship
SPS	Society for Pentecostal Studies
TCTCV	*The Church: Towards a Common Vision*
TSPM	Three-Self Patriotic Movement
WAPTE	World Alliance for Pentecostal Theological Education
WCC	World Council of Churches
WCE, 3rd ed.	*World Christian Encyclopedia*, 3rd edition

Introduction

Asian Pentecostalism has been an enduring subject in my life and career. When I grew up in a small, widow-led "crying" church in a city with an overwhelming presence of Presbyterian churches (of different sub-denominations), I wondered why our church was "not in league" with other churches. I knew we were "different" without knowing why. I suspected that praying for healing and the Holy Spirit "stuff" might have been the culprit. But I also knew that in non-denominational prayer mountains, "receiving grace" means what I learned later to be the "baptism in the Holy Spirit." In my Bible college years, I became acquainted with the phenomenon of the "Full Gospel Church" led by David Yonggi Cho. In the first half of the 1970s, his church was a subject of envy for its rapid growth, but also of harsh criticism for its chaotic worship and claims of supernatural experiences. Many classmates were obsessed with church growth through impactful preaching and divine healing. However, Pentecostal churches, including Cho's, were not part of the "league" of decent churches. They were for the outcasts (or the "disinherited"). Only later did I realize that this "fringe" status of the movement was a critical part of the identity of Pentecostalism!

My further study and missionary work from the late 1970s in the Philippines added a broader, deeper, and more diverse picture of Pentecostalism. For the first time, I read literature produced by Pentecostal thinkers and practitioners from the West. It was my delight to know that Pentecostals wrote! The wider exposure meant that I also read literature critical of Pentecostal beliefs. By the time I began to teach, two realities had become clear: 1) almost all of the literature available on Pentecostalism was by Westerners, inadvertently shaping an impression that Pentecostalism is "made in the USA;" and 2) nothing was written about non-Western Pentecostalism. My students from different countries of the Asia-Pacific region were a fresh source of new knowledge. To encourage and facilitate local experiences and histories of Pentecostalism, both the Asian Pentecostal Society and the *Asian Journal of Pentecostal Studies* were launched before the turn of the century.

The Book

This book explores the critical role of context in shaping Asian Pentecostal theology and in developing its believers' identity and mandates (or mission) in Asia. With incredible socio-cultural diversity in the region, sample cases are presented at the risk of generalization. While context shapes the beliefs and daily Christian life of Pentecostals, the same context also shapes their self-understanding and life's meaning. I further aim to demonstrate the grassroots nature of Pentecostal spirituality and mission engagement.

The impetus for this book arose during the 2023 William Menzies Annual Lectureship of the Asia Pacific Theological Seminary (APTS) in the Philippines. By the gracious invitation of the director of the APTS Press, the process began. The result is nine chapters in two parts.

Part One: "Theology" includes five previously published chapters. They have been thoroughly revised and updated for this publication. Chapter 1 demonstrates the diversity of Pentecostal faith in Asia by showcasing five Pentecostal-Charismatic communities and movements in three countries. The dynamic interaction with the socio-cultural context of each movement results in a unique Pentecostal spirituality. Chapter 2 examines the process of Pentecostal theological formation and its four consequent theological outcomes, which have the unique potential to impact the Philippine context positively. Chapter 3 is on pneumatology. After mapping its current "under-construction" state, I encourage Asian Pentecostals to actively participate in the development of pneumatology. Chapter 4 addresses ecclesiology. Characterizing Pentecostal churches as a "free church," the chapter examines a megachurch and network of "underground" churches in two different settings. It again illustrates the contextual adaptation and cultural influence on the formation of local Pentecostal churches. Chapter 5 interacts with an ecumenical document on ecclesiology produced by the World Council of Churches (WCC). The church world now recognizes the sheer size of Pentecostal-Charismatic Christianity and includes it in their reflections. Although most Pentecostal churches are not members of the WCC, the latter has sought to interact with them to ensure that their efforts would be relevant to "other" churches.

Part Two: "The Mandates" includes three messages delivered at the Menzies lectureship as well as a new study prepared for the book. The theme of the lectureship was "Asian Pentecostalism: Its Locus and Call in the Global Christian Context." This part considers the context into which Asian Pentecostals are sent. Chapter 6 examines the global role of Asian Pentecostalism within the continuing growth of Christianity. Although it has the lowest rate of evangelization, the Asian church, especially the Pentecostal church, holds out promise as a vital role player. Chapter 7 surveys the Pentecostal landscape of the traditional three "families"—Classical Pentecostal, Charismatic, and Neo-Charismatic. I also inventory the unique strengths of each group in enriching the whole of Pentecostal Christianity in the region. Chapter 8 places Asian Pentecostalism in the global Christian context, identifying its role in bringing various churches together. Considering the multi-religious context of Asia, Asian Pentecostals are called to participate actively in programs to foster church cooperation and unity. Chapter 9 closes the book by studying Pentecostal engagement with social issues, presenting successful case studies, and highlighting the potential of Asian Pentecostalism in extending Christ's hand to the needy.

While the second part of the book arose from the lectureship, thus maintaining consistency, the first five chapters were originally published as stand-alone studies at different times. For this reason, despite revisions and updates, inconsistencies may be present. I am aware of at least one repetition of the Word of Life Church in two chapters. Due to the relative scarcity of publications on Chinese Christianity, particularly on the house church movement, I have used this case more than once.

Two Concepts to Clarify

Pentecostalism

The definition of Pentecostalism has been sharply debated among theologians, historians, and sociologists. In the first half of the twentieth century, the term referred to what is called "Classical Pentecostals." These denominational groups, primarily found in North America and Europe, trace their roots to the early twentieth-century Holiness-Pentecostal revival, such as that found in the Azusa Street revival (1906–1909) in Los Angeles. Their doctrinal uniqueness is found in the concept of "baptism in the Spirit," with speaking in tongues as its initial evidence. At the advent of the Charismatic movement in the 1960s among mainline churches, including the Roman Catholic Church, the defining characteristic of the movement shifted to supernatural gifts such as healing, speaking in tongues, prophecy, and others, with a reduced emphasis on baptism in the Spirit. However, with the "discovery" of indigenous Pentecostal groups worldwide, a universally acceptable definition of this fast-growing segment of Christianity has become simply unattainable unless one presents a definition too diluted to be useful.

For the present discussion, the term "Pentecostal Christianity" is used as an umbrella term encompassing the whole breadth of believers who accept the work of the Holy Spirit today. They include Classical Pentecostals, Charismatics, and Neo-Charismatics. Neo-Charismatics are Spirit-filled believers who do not belong to the first two groups. They can include Christians who accept Pentecostal beliefs and practices while attending non-Pentecostal/Charismatic churches/communities. For this book, the working definition of the term is: "A segment of Christianity which believes in and practices the availability of the supernatural gifts of the Holy Spirit today, with characteristically lively and spontaneous worship, the manifestation of spiritual gifts, and an enthusiastic Christian lifestyle and witnessing."

Asia

In this book, "Asia" refers to East and Southeast Asia for two practical reasons. The first is my familiarity with the region. As a Korean, I can attest to the similarities in East Asia. There are notable cultural values shared by East Asian nations. Also, the languages are either Chinese-based or under its strong influence. Naturally, Southeast Asian nations with sizeable Chinese populations, such as Singapore and Malaysia, maintain similar connectivity with Chinese cultural influence. My work in the Philippines included teaching students from Asia and the Pacific. My acquaintance with these countries has increased through three decades of work.

The second is a reasonable level of commonalities among countries in the region. In this most diverse and populous continent in the world, the grouping of nations is a challenge. We will consider religion as a source of "reasonable commonalities" within East and Southeast Asia. A Buddhist bloc of countries includes Cambodia, Laos, Myanmar, Thailand, and Vietnam. The Islamic group contains Brunei, Indonesia, and Malaysia. Religiously plural nations with traditional Confucian influence are China, Japan, Korea, and Taiwan. The Philippines is the only Christian-majority nation, while the religious life of North Korea is practically non-existent. Religious pluralism is a phenomenon with diverse religions present and constitutionally sanctioned. This pluralism is pronounced compared to the rest of Asia—South Asia, West Asia (or Middle East), and Central Asia. In social life, a varying degree of social pressure is understandable.

However, the "reasonable commonalities" may not be reasonable at times. The disparity among East and Southeast nations is wide, especially in forms of government, economy, history, and more. A comparison, for instance, between Singapore and North Korea in terms of economic and social life will be planets apart! This book keeps these irreconcilable differences in mind as it attempts to be relevant to most nations in the region. The study of each country is outside of the book's purview. Fortunately, several resources on Pentecostalism in Asian nations are:

- Allan Anderson and Edmond Tang, eds., *Asian and Pentecostal: The Charismatic Face of Christianity in Asia*, 2nd ed. (Oxford: Regnum Books, 2011).
- Vinson Synan and Amos Yong, eds., *Global Renewal Christianity, Volume 1: Asia and Oceania* (Lake Mary, FL: Charisma House, 2016).
- Denise A. Austin, Jacqueline Grey, and Paul W. Lewis, eds., *Asia Pacific Pentecostalism* (Leiden: Brill, 2019).

Also useful, although not on Pentecostalism, is:

- Kenneth R. Ross, Francis D. Alvarez SJ, and Todd M. Johnson, eds., *Edinburgh Companions to Global Christianity, Volume 4: Christianity in East and South-East Asia* (Edinburgh: Edinburgh University Press, 2020).

CHAPTER 1

Asian Pentecostalism In Context: A Challenging Portrait[1]

Asia is home to five major world religions and a myriad of regional, national, and local ones. As the largest continent, with almost two-thirds of the world's population, it has the widest array of cultures, histories, languages, and sociopolitical experiences. The complexity of the region makes any encounter with the host context exceptionally rich, creative, and multi-faceted. Understandably, global Pentecostalism, estimated to reach 1.032 billion by 2050,[2] finds a wide range of forms and features in Asia.

The question of who Pentecostals are, especially in the Asian context, is a challenging inquiry. The Pentecostal movement is shaped through the continual, dynamic interaction between people of the Pentecostal faith—regardless of their consciousness of being labeled as such—and their sociocultural environments. They often come from, but also unconsciously with, other religious orientations. They strongly believe in a dynamic, often supernatural experience of the person and work of the Holy Spirit in their daily lives and worship. Thus, the way this collective phenomenon of dynamic spirituality is categorized is only a secondary question. "Pentecostalism" is

---

[1]First published in *Cambridge Companion to Pentecostalism* (Cambridge: Cambridge University Press, 2014), used by permission.

[2]Unless otherwise indicated, statistical figures are taken from Todd M. Johnson and Gina A. Zurlo, *World Christian Encyclopedia*, 3rd ed. (Edinburgh: Edinburgh University Press, 2020), 26. Henceforth, *WCE*, 3rd ed.

an umbrella term that encompasses Classical Pentecostals, Neo-Pentecostals or Charismatics, and Neo-Charismatics, including indigenous and independent Pentecostals. The term may be used interchangeably with Charismatic Christianity.[3]

By the conclusion of this chapter, I will challenge the notion that Pentecostalism in Asia is a transplanted version of the Pentecostal religion "made in the USA." Clear historical links are sometimes challenging to establish, even among Classical Pentecostal groups. I will demonstrate that Pentecostalism interacts so dynamically with cultures, religions, and social issues that the result of this encounter varies significantly from one context to another.

This study begins with a picture of Asian Pentecostalism, sampled in case studies of Pentecostal-Charismatic groups from three countries. Although the samples do not include South Asia, the survey provides a reasonable sense of the Pentecostal landscape in Asia. The second part is an analysis of Asian Pentecostalism, portraying a set of traits observed in the samples and all Charismatic Christianity in Asia. I have not begun with any standard definition of Pentecostalism in Asia, against which to measure Asian Pentecostalism. Instead, from this study, I hope to develop an understanding of Asian Pentecostalism and the commonalities shared by its local expressions. The study ends with a brief reflection for the future.

Five Pentecostal Groups in Three Countries

The cases have been selected to provide a fair spectrum of Charismatic Christianity in Asia. For Korea, a well-known Prayer Mountain and a strong Charismatic Presbyterian network will illustrate the expression of indigenous Korean Pentecostalism and its spirituality in two different social contexts and periods of the nation. For the Philippines, the focus is on a vast, controversial Catholic Charismatic network, paying particular attention to their

---

[3]For a recent characterization of the Pentecostal movement, see Todd M. Johnson and Gina A. Zurlo, *Introducing Spirit-Empowered Christianity: The Global Pentecostal & Charismatic Movement in the 21st Century* (Tulsa: ORU Press, 2023). Henceforth, *ISEC*.

creative and controversial responses to their contemporary socio-religio-economic challenges. For China, two different networks are chosen, one from the pre-1949 era and the other from the post-Cultural Revolution era. They again illustrate the responses of Charismatic Christianity to different sociopolitical challenges.

South Korea

The first Western Pentecostal missionary to Korea, Mary Rumsey, began her missionary work in 1928, but many scholars claim the 1907 Pyongyang Revival began the Korean Pentecostal movement. From the beginning, the "Holy Spirit Movement," popularly known among Korean Christians, was not a denominational movement until the arrival of Pentecostal missionaries.[4] For this reason, this study will look at the indigenous stream of Pentecostalism that has played an essential role in shaping Korean Pentecostalism as it is today. Pentecostal spirituality and worship are widely spread across denominations, although their entry into common Christian life came through the "back door." It is also noticeable that indigenous forms of religiosity have been incorporated into Pentecostal practices.

Yongmoon Prayer Mountain

The first back door of Pentecostal spirituality was through the Prayer Mountains. The origin of the Korean Prayer Mountain movement is unclear, but it proliferated after the country's independence (1945). During the height of Japanese oppression of Christianity, when many churches were closed and leaders imprisoned, records reveal that Christians found mountains as handy places to spend days and nights praying.[5] Buddhists and

---

[4]See Young-hoon Lee, *The Holy Spirit Movement in Korea* (Oxford: Regnum Books, 2009); also Boo-woong Yoo, *Korean Pentecostalism: Its History and Theology* (Frankfurt: Peter Lang, 1988); and Allan Anderson, *An Introduction to Pentecostalism* (Cambridge: Cambridge University Press, 2004), 136-41.

[5]For example, Rev. Yong-do Lee, a controversial Methodist revivalist, experienced the work of the Holy Spirit on Geumgang Mountain during a ten-

Shamanists have also traditionally ascribed religious values to them.

The leader of the Prayer Mountain movement was Woon-mong Ra (1914-2009), a lay Methodist leader trained in Chinese classics.[6] He established Yongmoon-san Prayer Mountain in 1945 as well as a Protestant monastery, a convent, Bible schools, and a weekly Christian newspaper. About 10,000 Christians attended a week-long summer revival camp in this remote place during its heyday. This was an actual Pentecostal event in which topics such as healing, prophecy, miracles, and hearing God's voice were freely taught, prayed for, and experienced.

Prayer Mountains were a seedbed of Pentecostal Christianity, particularly in the 1950s and 1960s. It is important to note that these topics were not openly discussed in most churches, especially among Presbyterian churches, where supernatural manifestations were believed to have ceased at the close of the apostolic period. Some participants returned to their churches and "disrupted" normal church life by advocating charismatic gifts such as those experienced at Prayer Mountains. Later, Prayer Mountains appeared throughout the country and near urban centers, often led by students of Ra. Yeol-soo Eim estimates that by 1994, there were more than 500 of them.[7] They attracted Christians with special needs, both physical (e.g., illness) and spiritual (seeking the fullness of the Spirit). Ra remained extremely influential, although sometimes controversial, until large churches began incorporating Pentecostal messages and practices in the early 1970s. Most of them also began to open their own Prayer Mountains, such as the Choi Jashil Memorial International Fasting Prayer Mountain of the Yoido

---

day fast and prayer; see Lee, *The Holy Spirit Movement in Korea*, 51. Woon-mong Ra's first visit to Yongmoon Mountain in 1940 was similarly motivated; see Yeol-soo Eim, "South Korea," in *New International Dictionary of Pentecostal and Charismatic Movements,* edited by Stanley M. Burgess, et al. (Grand Rapids: Zondervan, 2003), 241. This dictionary is henceforth referred to as *NIDPCM.*

[6]For his life and ministry, see Chang-soo Kang, "The Analytical Study of the Life of Woon-mong Na, Indigenous Korean Pentecostal" (Th.M. thesis, APTS, Philippines, 2002); Eim, "South Korea," 241.

[7]Eim, "South Korea," 241.

Full Gospel Church in 1973. In 1979, this community established a link with the International Pentecostal Holiness Church (USA), but this partnership was short-lived. Ra's place was reduced to several institutions as fewer visitors were attracted and doctrinal controversies around his theology continued. Yet the role of the independent Prayer Mountains cannot be underestimated in spreading Pentecostal spirituality throughout Korea.

Onnuri Community Church

Since the 1970s, the Holy Spirit movement has found its main place in local churches. In this period, significant growth in Christianity occurred with the emergence of megachurches.[8] A second back door of Pentecostal spirituality persisted in local church settings through annual revival meetings. Following the pattern of the Pyongyang revival, such week-long, three-meetings-a-day events included intense spiritual experiences. The two main emphases were Bible study and prayer. However, testimonies of healings, miracles, speaking in tongues, and the like abounded. Large churches, often led by well-known preachers, incorporated Pentecostal aspects into their messages and worship, regardless of their denominational orientation. A study of megachurches in Korea, undertaken a decade ago, identified ten of fifteen as Pentecostal/Charismatic in their worship and preaching.[9]

The Onnuri Church, established in 1985 by Yongjo Ha (1946-2011), a Reverend, is a case in point. Although a part of the Presbyterian Church of Korea, the congregation exercised a powerful influence through innovative worship and mission programs. Although never explicated, some programs of the church may trace their theological influence to Pentecostalism. Its highly successful Praise and Worship program was a brilliant incorporation of the

---

[8]Young-gi Hong, "The Backgrounds and Characteristics of the Charismatic Mega-Churches in Korea," *AJPS* 3, no. 1 (Jan. 2000): 100 n. 4. Hong defines a megachurch as a congregation with a minimum of 10,000 adult members participating in Sunday worship.

[9]Ibid., 105-06.

Pentecostal worship tradition that is celebratory and participatory. Also congruent with Pentecostal traditions was the church's mobilization of the whole church for mission. Ha envisioned mobilizing 1,000 missionaries and 20,000 Christian workers.[10]

One historical link with Pentecostalism is Ha's earlier involvement with Youth With a Mission (YWAM). This large movement mobilized youth for mission, with a clear Pentecostal link through its founder. The core value of the church's ministry was encapsulated in "Acts 29." Because the Book of Acts consists of only twenty-eight chapters, this ministry asserted that "the book had not been completed and was still being written."[11] The ideal of the church, according to the church's publication, was to be "led by the Holy Spirit, with actively mobilized laity, with a deep sense of calling."[12] Until his recent death, Ha led numerous missionary campaigns in Japan and elsewhere. It is reported that the congregation has ten campuses with 75,000 members. In addition, about twenty-five network churches are in operation in Korea, with more outside the country.[13]

Thanks to the indigenous spirituality of the Holy Spirit movement in Korea, the widespread influence of Pentecostal spirituality makes it difficult to tally the number of Pentecostal/Charismatic believers in Korea. The Johnson-Zurlo team estimated 9.15 million in 2020.[14] Considering the deep-rooted Pentecostal spirituality that has permeated church life for more than a century and the various shapes and forms it takes to express itself, the larger figure appears to be more likely.

---

[10]Onnuri Community Church, *Onnuri Community Church: The First 30 Years* (Seoul: Onnuri Community Church, 2017) does not contain the words "Holy Spirit" in its headings. However, the work of the Spirit is embedded in terms such as "Acts 29," "Dancing with the Word and the Spirit," etc.

[11]"Expanding Missions with the Acts 29 Vision," in *Onnuri Community Church*, 127-32.

[12]"A Dream of 'The Church,'" in *Onnuri Community Church*, 115-17.

[13]Onnuri Church, "Campuses and Vision Churches," https://www.onnuri.org/about-onnuri/service-times/vision-campuses/ (accessed June 29, 2025).

[14]*ISEC*, 155.

Philippines

The Philippines, an island nation, had a different historical and cultural orientation from Korea and China. The more than three-century-long colonial rule by Spaniards (1565-1898) shaped diverse people groups into a nation and made the country the only dominantly Christian nation in Asia. Protestant Christianity was introduced mainly by American denominations with the American defeat of the Spanish fleet in 1898. The first North American Pentecostal missionaries arrived as early as 1926, followed by Filipino-American Pentecostals in the 1930s. The first Assemblies of God church was planted in Antique in 1928. Many of them are members of the Philippine Council, formally established in 1940.[15] The establishment of various Pentecostal denominations took place in the 1940s. Classical Pentecostalism experienced waves of revival, and Pentecostal-type worship and spirituality are widespread among Evangelical churches.

Our discussion will focus on the emergence of Charismatic Christianity in the early 1980s, although the Catholic Charismatic movement was introduced as early as 1969. The proliferation of Catholic prayer meetings and home fellowships was attributed to the social unrest under the Marcos dictatorship. The urban middle and upper classes sought their spiritual haven in mushrooming new Charismatic groups. The Roman Catholic Church issued a directive in 1983 to keep the "Born Again" (Protestant) influence away from Catholics.[16] Many groups eventually broke off and became independent "fellowships" and "family worship centers"

---

[15]See chapter 2. Also, "Philippines," *NIDPCM*, 201–07. For the Philippines Assemblies of God, see Trinidad E. Seleky, "Six Filipinos and One American: Pioneers of the Assemblies of God in the Philippines," *AJPS* 4, no.1 (2001): 119-29. Also, for more details, see Dave Johnson, *Led by the Spirit: The History of the American Assemblies of God Missionaries in the Philippines* (Pasig City, Philippines: ICI Ministries, 2009), 7-20.

[16]The Archdiocesan Office of Manila produced a booklet entitled "Guidelines for Prayer Groups" (1983) to regulate Bible study and prayer groups among Catholics.

in restaurants and hotel ballrooms.[17] However, one group grew so large that the Catholic Church had to make a special provision: the El Shaddai Catholic Charismatic Community.

Mariano "Mike" Z. Velarde (or "Brother Mike," 1939-), a realtor and businessman, acquired a radio station as part of his business dealings and began a Christian radio program in 1982. As its popularity grew, he began a monthly prayer meeting that soon began to meet weekly. *El Shaddai,* the title of the radio program, also referred to his large Catholic Charismatic network, claiming eleven million followers.[18] Its explosive growth was frequently attributed to his radical claim for healing and material blessings as an "entitlement" for committed Christians. The group's sheer size created a formidable challenge to locate suitable meeting places large enough for the still-growing crowds. The fellowship finally built its own multimillion-dollar facility called El Shaddai International House of Prayer. On any given Sunday in major Asian cities such as Hong Kong, a huge crowd of Filipino El Shaddai members (mostly women) meets in a large downtown park to celebrate their weekly mass. Because of its size, the Catholic Church's *Guidelines* published decades ago, proved inadequate for the El Shaddai. Currently, two Catholic bishops oversee Velarde and his group.[19]

The El Shaddai movement deserves a close examination for its size and impact. (Currently, there is only one scholarly monograph[20] and a handful of shorter articles available.) The most prominent point in the group's theology is God's material blessings. In the beginning, the context provided the strongest justification for

---

[17]In 1981, ten 5-star hotels in Manila regularly hosted at least one Charismatic service; see Dynnice Rosanny D. Engcoy, "A Reflection of a Missionary to the Philippines: Gary A. Denbow Interview," *AJPS* 8, no. 2 (2005): 307-26, 319.

[18]*WCE,* 3rd ed., 642, reports nine million in the Philippines and two million among overseas Filipinos in 1981. Even today, the original radio program is remembered by its name, *El Shaddai DWXI Prayer Partners Fellowship International.*

[19]Archdiocesan Office of Manila, "Guidelines for Prayer Groups."

[20]Katharine L. Wiegele, Investing in Miracles: El Shaddai and the Transformation of Popular Catholicism in the Philippines (Honolulu: University of Hawaii Press, 2006).

Velarde's preaching, as his followers were mostly the urban poor, struggling to survive each day.

In addition to the general problems associated with the so-called prosperity gospel, Velarde's flamboyant celebrity-like lifestyle contrasts with the daily context of his average members. This teaching could suggest that God can be manipulated by giving, reducing this form of Christianity into just another folk religion. Velarde's presentation of divine healing can easily slip into a folk religious mode, as he blessed objects such as handkerchiefs and tea leaves to become instruments of healing. In this way, there are similarities between the folk practices of many Pentecostals and Catholics.

Equally controversial is Velarde's political involvement. His endorsement of the morally corrupt presidential candidate Joseph Estrada in the 1998 election was a scandal, as the president was impeached and ousted from his office in 2001. Velarde translated his religious following into a political machinery by creating a political party, *Buhay Hayaan Yumabong*. The party's profile carries Catholic beliefs, including the sanctity of unborn babies.[21] Since the 2004 congressional election, the party has maintained at least two congressional seats, including that of Velarde's son. Velarde's bid for a seat was unsuccessful in the 2010 election.

The number of Pentecostal-Charismatic Christians in 2020 was 38 million. This can be broken down among three streams: 4.2% denominational Pentecostals, 70.3% Charismatics, and 25.4% Neo-Charismatics.[22]

China

Details about Chinese Christianity are difficult to ascertain, but the resurgence of Christianity after the Cultural Revolution (1966-76) has been consistently affirmed. Widely agreed upon is the presence of a number of Pentecostal elements, especially among independent church groups. Relatively younger and newer

---

[21]BuhayParty-list, "PartyProfile," http://www.buhaypartylist.com.ph/about-us/ (accessed December 27, 2011).

[22]*ISEC*, 153.

"uncles" and "aunts" have only vague connections with the pre-1949 patriarchs.[23]

Today's Chinese Christianity serves as a rare "laboratory" for the rise of indigenous Christianity, due to little external (e.g., missionary) interference. The diverse Chinese understandings of being Christian and a church, as well as the Christian response to the immediate sociopolitical context, have likely been determined by reading Scripture within their context. Some groups with varying historical connections with pre-1949 Western Pentecostal Christianity have reappeared. However, the Chinese Christianity that was slowly introduced to the outside world throughout the 1980s and 1990s mostly resembled indigenous forms of Christianity, with varying expressions of deep spiritual experiences and Pentecostal elements.[24] We will look at one group each from the pre- and the post-Cultural Revolution eras.

The Jesus Family

The Jesus Family was established in 1927 in North China, in Mazhuang, Taian County of Shandong Province, by Jiang Dianying (1890-1957). Jiang, a businessman, became Pentecostal in the 1920s through the influence of the American Assemblies of God mission in Xian. He later developed the idea of Christian community life based on the teachings of Jesus to the rich young ruler (Matt 19:16). In response to successive natural disasters in the vast area of north and central China, people were forced to look for any way to survive. Jiang founded the Jesus Family by reorganizing and renaming the Christian silk-making cooperative he had earlier organized.

---

[23]David Aikman uses these terms in *Jesus in Beijing: How Christianity Is Transforming China and Changing the Global Balance of Power* (Washington, DC: Regnery, 2003).

[24]Edmond Tang, "The Changing Landscape of Chinese Christianity," *China Study Journal* 23 (Spring/Summer 2008): 37. Also Allan Anderson and Edmond Tang, eds., "'Yellers' and Healers: Pentecostalism and the Study of Grassroots Christianity in China," in *Asian and Pentecostal: The Charismatic Face of Christianity in Asia*, 2nd ed. (Oxford: Regnum Books, 2011), 379–94.

Jiang laid out rules for a self-sufficient Christian communal life. Members gave up their properties for communal use. In the early years, families were separated into male and female dormitories. Everyone worked on farms or in light industries within the community. However, the members spent a considerable amount of time in worship and prayer each day.

Their theology centered on three major emphases: regeneration (e.g., being born again), being "filled with the Holy Spirit," and millennial eschatology. The influence of the Western Pentecostal belief in the baptism in the Spirit was apparent. They prayed for healing and practiced speaking in tongues, prophecy, and other spiritual gifts.[25] In addition, prominent among the Jesus Family members were "dancing in the Spirit" and "testimony." One could be taken into the heavenly presence of the Lord through a vision or trance, receive a direct revelation from him, and convey it to the rest of the community in "testimony."

Like many independent Christian groups, the Jesus Family maintained an expectation of the immediate return of the Lord. Its egalitarian and socially secluded communal life strongly appealed to the masses marginalized by chronic poverty,[26] although ironically, the leadership of Jiang and local family heads whom he appointed were authoritarian. It was estimated that the movement grew to more than one hundred communities throughout north and central China by 1949 with 10,000 members. The movement was disbanded in 1953, and today it survives only in Taiwan.

Born Again Fellowship

The Born-Again Fellowship is sometimes called Full Scope Church of 'Weepers'[27] or the Word of Life Church[28] of Henan Province.[29]

---

[25]Luke Wesley, *The Church in China: Persecuted, Pentecostal, and Powerful* (Baguio, Philippines: AJPS Books, 2004), 51.

[26]At least three "families" existed near large cities: Shanghai, Wuhan, and Nanjing.

[27]Aikman, *Jesus in Beijing*, 279.

[28]Wesley, *The Church in China*, 35.

[29]Often called the "Pentecostal capital of China" in Tang, "The Changing

It was one of the largest networks in China, started in the early 1980s by Xu Yongze (Peter; 1940-). An effective evangelist, he deployed teams of young evangelists within Henan and nearby provinces through his loosely networked congregations. The group grew steadily despite the repeated imprisonments of Xu and his leaders. Membership estimates differ vastly from 3 to 5 million adherents. Since Xu left China in 2001, the church has become fragmented.

The Born-Again movement shared at least three characteristics with other independent churches that have adopted varying degrees of Charismatic influence. First, suffering and healing were normative for believers. Xu, as pastor and co-worker of the famous Brother Yun, endorsed Yun's testimony of suffering and many cases of healing and miracles as authentic.[30] The network's "Statement of Faith" included a section on the Holy Spirit, including the following points: "The Holy Spirit gives all kinds of power and manifests the mighty acts of God through signs and miracles;" "Christians can experience the outpouring and the infilling of the Holy Spirit;" and "We do not forbid speaking in tongues nor do we insist that everyone must speak in tongues."[31] Prayers and claims for healing were a regular part of their worship. The prominence of healing was widespread among Chinese Christianity.[32] In regard to the latter, Fielder argued that healing is a common feature of most Chinese religions, including Taoism, and Christianity offers a functional substitute.[33]

Second, egalitarianism in ministry was common among the new independent Christian groups. As rightly observed by Fielder,

---

Landscape," 37.

[30]Xu Yongze, "Preface," in *The Heavenly Man,* Brother Yun and Paul Gattaway (Peabody, MA: Hendrickson, 2002), viii.

[31]"Chinese House Church Confession of Faith," quoted in *Inside China's House Church Network: The Word of Life Movement and Its Renewing Dynamic,* Yalin Xin (Lexington, KY: Emeth Press, 2009), 146.

[32]Caroline Fielder, "The Growth of the Protestant Church in Rural China," *China Study Journal* 23 (Spring/Summer 2008): 49. Also, Sigurd Kaiser, "The Kingdom and Power: Elements of Growth in Chinese Christianity: Some Personal Insights," *Religions & Christianity in Today's China* 2, no. 2 (2012): 42-44.

[33]Fielder, "Growth of the Protestant Church in Rural China," 49.

the new charismatically oriented congregations, especially in rural areas, adopted a simple church structure that allowed anyone to lead a congregation.[34] Women quickly rose into active leadership roles, an astonishing development given the established Christian tradition as well as Chinese cultural norms. This radical promotion of lay and women leadership made a major contribution toward the church's unprecedented growth.

Third, the affective and emotional dimension of Christian spirituality and worship was typical. Tang viewed the outbursts of emotion as one of the four main characteristics of the new Christian groups.[35] The Born-Again Fellowship, as its nickname "Weepers" suggests, was often known for weeping as a sign of genuine repentance. Although leaders denied this as a requirement for their members, to common minds, weeping attained a theological significance.[36] It is possible that the "seemingly hysterical" emotional excess,[37] among other things, caused the Born-Again Fellowship to be classified as a cult in the mid-1990s by the Chinese authorities and the official Three-Self leadership.

Figures for Christianity in China as a whole were already challenging. The Johnson-Zurlo team estimated 106 million Christian believers and 37 million Pentecostal-Charismatics for 2020.[38] Many agree that a significant portion of Chinese Christians are "renewalists," found both among registered as well as unregistered churches.[39]

What We Observe

Four defining characteristics of Asian Pentecostalism emerge from these five cases: flourishing in adverse situations, indigenous

---

[34]Ibid., 45.
[35]Tang, "The Changing Landscape," 38.
[36]Aikman, *Jesus in Beijing*, 88-89.
[37]Ibid., 279.
[38]*ISEC*, 145.
[39]For example, *WCE*, 3rd ed., 195, 198.

expressions, engagement with the wider world, Charismatic leadership, and mega-size movements.

Flourishing in Adverse Circumstances

Except for the Onnuri Church, these groups were born and continue to operate in harsh sociopolitical and economic contexts. Their spirituality was shaped by their attempts to provide spiritual community and practical ways to cope with contextual challenges. Conservative Christianity, including Pentecostalism, tends to record significant growth under adverse and harsh circumstances.

Pentecostal Christianity often counters sociopolitical and economic pressure by creating an alternative world, redirecting the church's priority attention elsewhere. In the first several decades of the twentieth century, Chinese Christianity was apolitical, with fresh memories of the Boxer Rebellion and two wars. The Jesus Family provided a practical alternative society, incorporating a strong spiritual component. It grew significantly through the war years, even though its founder had already died. Peter Xu interprets the destructive Cultural Revolution as God's tool "to destroy the old structure of the Chinese church so that he could rebuild it according to his purposes."[40]

In Korea, the Prayer Mountain movement was born shortly after the independence of the nation, which was quickly engulfed in the destruction of the Korean War. An escape to a remote mountain, away from daily routines, supplemented with otherworldly concentration and powerful spiritual experiences, provided a perfect spiritual haven. Pentecostals and Evangelical Christians were either silent or even supportive of military rulers in the 1970s and 1980s and achieved record church growth. In a sense, with its intense attention to spiritual experiences, Pentecostalism created an alternative universe from which to draw strength for daily life and beyond.

Independent Charismatic churches in the Philippines provide another case of a Pentecostal response under the political oppression of the Marcos dictatorship. Social unrest was the soil where the

---

[40]Xu, "Preface," in *The Heavenly Man*, viii.

powerful Charismatic movement was born, especially among urban professionals. The new form of spirituality not only provided a new meaning to life in the specific context but also redirected restless minds to spiritual satisfaction.

When it is not struggling with something, Pentecostalism itself struggles. When a harsh political system no longer exists and society moves beyond poverty, the movement faces a real challenge. This has been observed both in the West and in places such as Korea.

At least two examples are observable in our cases. First is the emergence of a Pentecostal interest in politics: forming political parties and/or running for elected positions, including presidential seats. The motivation is not clear: is this an outcome of a deep theological and missional reflection, a desire for recognition, or the simple realization of political potential in sheer numbers? This trend slowly spread among Pentecostal leaders in the Philippines, Indonesia, and Korea. It is worth pondering what turns Pentecostals—traditionally otherworldly and millenarian—toward politics.

The Pentecostal reaction to economic hardship is divided into two expressions. First, in earlier days, the response was more denial with a good dose of millennial eschatology and a strong emphasis on mission. The Jesus Family took a further practical step, countering the chronic hardship by establishing Christian communities. The Prayer Mountain became a spiritual haven, satisfying an escapist impulse for an "out-of-world" experience for a week or so. It is important to note, however, that Ra began as a Christian activist among poor farmers, and his original idea for the Prayer Mountain was a Christian community.

Second is the development of a theology of blessing. In Korea, the forerunner was David Yonggi Cho. His theology was shaped by the dire poverty of the postwar Korean society in the 1950s. This focus was reinforced in the early 1970s by American faith preachers like Robert Schuller and Oral Roberts.[41] The El Shaddai group offers the

---

[41]Wonsuk Ma, "David Yonggi Cho's Theology of Blessing: Basis, Legitimacy and Limitations," *Evangelical Review of Theology* 35, no. 2 (Apr. 2011): 140-159.

clearest demonstration of the prosperity gospel in Asia. As discussed, material prosperity and divine healings occupy a prominent place in Velarde's message. Material abundance often serves as a tangible sign of God's blessing, especially for those whose daily survival is an urgent need.[42]

The unusual capabiliy to contextualize has been well documented in missionary settings.[43] Pentecostals exhibited radically different responses in political and economic areas, depending on their contexts. This proves the ingenuity of Pentecostal interactions with and responses to religio-cultural and sociopolitical contexts. This further explains why Charismatic Christianity continues to evolve in different forms, expressions, and shapes. It adapts to its setting and appropriates traditional religious and cultural beliefs and symbols, as well as modern communication technologies.

Indigenous Expressions and Engagement with the Wider World

Almost all the groups studied had limited or no outside support. They were established through the vision and efforts of national leaders. Some, such as the Jesus Family and Yongmoon Prayer Mountain, exhibit forms and ethos that are close to indigenous religiosity and culture. The reading of Scripture in their own contexts, informed by their own experiences, must have given birth to their unique understanding of Christianity and its mission. Filipino Charismatic groups likewise exhibit ingenuity in responding to their contemporary challenges with openness to their indigenous religious resources.

This does not completely rule out outside influences. The impact of Western Christianity can be broadly traced, often represented by missionaries. Marie Monsen, a Norwegian missionary (1872–1962), had an abiding influence on the Xu family. This was transmitted through their generations, including to Peter and his sister Deborah. It is fascinating to observe that the

---

[42]Wiegele, *Investing in Miracles*, 6-8, 17-27.

[43]Andrew M. Lord, "The Holy Spirit and Contextualization," *AJPS* 4, vol. 2 (2001): 201-203.

influence was preserved and relayed by female members of the extended family.[44]

Christianity in China, Korea, and the Philippines adapted due to contact with American Evangelical missionaries at the turn of the twentieth century. Mark Noll argues that the forms and ethos of Christianity practiced in the United States heavily influenced the development of global Evangelicalism, including these groups.[45] In all case studies, including the Catholic Charismatic El Shaddai, their form of Charismatic Christianity resembles American Evangelicalism with its Bible-oriented, individualistic, voluntary, and pragmatic characteristics.[46] Even El Shaddai—with Velarde's prosperity preaching—appears to be more American than liturgy-based Roman Catholic. Ha's exposure to the missionary and Pentecostal ethos of Youth with a Mission is also clear.

Despite traces of external influences, none of these groups had significant missionary involvement in leadership or as a consulting influence. The closest is Gary Denbow's role in shaping the Filipino Charismatic movement in the early 1980s. However, his influence was, at best, indirect.[47] Missionary influences, as observed in the Xu family, were mainly in spiritual formation. Even Monsen's heavy emphasis on repentance and the presence of the Holy Spirit became an indigenous external form of deep emotion.[48]

Additionally, all the groups exhibited their primary concern for immediate contextual challenges as Christians. Both the Jesus Family and Yongmoon Prayer Mountain responded to extreme economic and political difficulties by proposing the idea of Christian communities. Even the more modernist Onnuri Church network effectively responded to the social and spiritual needs of

---

[44]Yalin Xin, "Deborah Xu: The Story of a Catalytic Leadership in the Chinese House Church Movement," in *Evangelical and Frontier Mission: Perspectives on the Global Progress of the Gospel*, ed. Beth Snodderly and A. Scott Moreau (Oxford: Regnum Books, 2011), 138-42.

[45]Mark A. Noll, *The New Shape of World Christianity: How American Experience Reflects Global Faith* (Downers Grove: IVP Academic, 2009), 11-12.

[46]Ibid., 120-25.

[47]Engcoy, "A Reflection of a Missionary to the Philippines," 307-26.

[48]Xin, "Deborah Xu," 138-39.

an urban middle-class, educated population. Ha's early exposure to an American Pentecostal missionary group was successfully incorporated into his organizational and theological framework, resulting in the mobilization of a significant number of the laity for missionary service.

Third, the form and content of their spirituality were not a Western import but more indigenously sourced. One of the last ambitions of Ha before his death in 2011 was to impact Japan with the gospel. His approach, often dubbed the "Korean Wave," was to harness the potential of cultural forces effectively. Ha's gospel presentation, called *Love Sonata*, was a successful, well-staged cultural form designed for the Japanese population. It resembled the popular Korean drama *Winter Sonata*, which captivated Japanese viewers in 2002.

Almost all groups studied appropriated and incorporated local sociocultural and even religious traits into their forms of Christian spirituality and life. Not all indigenous forms were without problems. The Jesus Family's community movement lived out the egalitarian Christian principle in daily living. Yet its authoritarian leadership betrayed this principle, which was in accordance with sociocultural traditions.

When the two forces of Christian and indigenous values clash, a critical role for any leader is determining how to negotiate a healthy and balanced tension. The political efforts of the two Filipino charismatic leaders may have been an attempt to formulate a Christian response to contemporary challenges. Those efforts stirred up much controversy both within and outside Christian circles.

Charismatic Leadership

In all the groups mentioned, the vision, dedication, and influence of the leaders are paramount to their network. Often, their spiritual experience has led to a radical vision of their network. One characteristic of Charismatic Christianity, especially in the non-Western world, may be the presence and role of charismatic leaders. The path of a Pentecostal network is almost always determined by the leader's understanding of self-identity, an interpretation of the times, a sense of calling, and a vision for the group.

The authority of charismatic leaders stems from their encounter with God, frequently in crisis experiences. Miraculous healing is a common experience, as seen in Velarde, Ha, Yonggi Cho, and many others. Their healing ministry has been rooted in their firm faith in the authority of the Bible and reinforced by their own experiences. Such personal encounters impact their theology and spiritual life; the theology of their networks mirrors their leaders' orientation. The emphasis of the Jesus Family on the "testimony" traces its roots to Jiang's experience-oriented spirituality, including the personal encounter and revelation he claimed to have received from the Lord. Xu's initial evangelistic experience, together with his repeated imprisonments, built his spiritual resilience. This was replicated in the militant deployment of young evangelists throughout Henan Province and beyond.

The Charismatic leaders' robust leadership was also seen in the development of their theology. Ha's total commitment to the mobilization of his church for mission is traced to his exposure to the Pentecostal value encapsulated in a "Prophethood of All Believers."[49] The professional career of Villanueva led his church to be very holistic in their missionary scope. El Shaddai's ministry includes community development, caring for the urban poor and children, the provision of medical services and education, advocacies including antipornography campaigns, and other helps—in addition to evangelism and church planting.[50] Jiang's business experience and his formation of a cooperative led him to establish Christian communities.

Ra began as a scholar of Chinese classics, and this had at least two expressions. The first was his attempts to incorporate his learning into the Christian message. Some of his theological positions created severe controversy: he considered Buddha and Confucius as prophets of God. The second was his commitment

---

[49]Roger Stronstad, *The Prophethood of All Believers: A Study in Luke's Charismatic Theology* (Sheffield: Sheffield Academic Press, 1999).

[50]Wiegele, *Investing in Miracles*, 33-35.

to literature. He began a well-known Christian weekly newspaper, which regularly carried his interpretation of current world events in the light of Scripture.

The charge that Velarde runs his ministry like a business was not without support, considering Ra's business background and entrepreneurial thinking. For example, he owned the twenty acres of land on which new facilities were built. The church paid for the land in installments.

The mobilization of the laity for ministry, an idea drawn from Classical Pentecostal tradition, is common throughout these case studies. The exception is the Jesus Family, which embodied a community-oriented lifestyle. The Born-Again group epitomized the massive mobilization of the laity for evangelistic and pastoral ministries with a minimal amount of in-house training. The Onnuri Church formalized this process with a series of training programs and an administrative structure to deploy a large number of missionary candidates from the church's vast network in Korea and overseas. Ha's systematic evangelistic campaigns in Japan were accompanied by a large number of his members providing prayer, ministry, and administrative assistance. The Prayer Mountain movement, with its general emphasis on experiences with the Holy Spirit, served as a breeding ground for lay workers for ministry. The Charismatic groups in the Philippines regularly drew their ministerial resources, including pastoral staff, from their members. To them, the sense of calling was more important than theological training. (This is often observed throughout various forms of Pentecostal churches.)

The almost unquestioned authority of charismatic leadership was also witnessed in Africa and Latin America, where cultures moved such leaders beyond the common social sphere. Their religious orientation distanced them further toward a sort of "holy" or "other world." Their behaviors were often blindly approved by their followers, even when they went against common ethical norms.[51] Often, the "independent" nature of their ministries placed the leaders outside of normal accountability structures. This is not

[51]Ibid., 37-39.

to imply that most Charismatic leaders have questionable moral standards, but rather to suggest that they are extremely vulnerable to moral and financial lures.

Mega-sizes

Megachurches or networks are almost always Pentecostal in spirituality, worship, and theology. Our survey reveals that the growth and spread of Charismatic groups gave birth to the megachurch movement. This global phenomenon was partly encouraged and fueled by the popular church growth movement (observed first by Donald McGavran and later by C. Peter Wagner). The North American movement quickly discovered that Asia was leading the race, once claiming that more than half of the world's ten largest churches were in Asia. Ra's Prayer Mountain was once one of the most renowned annual phenomena, drawing tens of thousands to this remote area of Korea. Soon, congregations with more than ten thousand members arose in large cities in Asia and elsewhere.

The five groups in this study include at least two groups not typically viewed as "churches:" the Jesus Family and the Yongmoon Prayer Mountain. The former was a membership-based community, so its limited growth is understandable. Even then, they demonstrated some Pentecostal features. At that time, David Yonggi Cho's megachurch was building its large auditorium in Seoul. Many believe that the Prayer Mountain laid a spiritual foundation by bringing traditional indigenous Pentecostal practices into the center of Christian spirituality—that is, making it a part of the "normal part" of local congregational life. Interestingly, megachurches emerged as the independent Prayer Mountain movement declined.

Some observers believe that the megachurch phenomenon was a part of urbanization. This correlation is almost certain in South Korea, where the rise of large churches through the 1970s and 1980s coincided with rapid urbanization and industrialization under military dictatorship. The rise of the Charismatic movement with independent networks happened in areas with steady urbanization.

In contrast, after the Chinese Cultural Revolution, the initial independent church movement was predominantly rural. However, urban churches planted during the period of strong urbanization tended to grow into larger congregations, whether in the house church movement or in church networks. The urban culture of Chinese Christian spirituality transformed expressions of their spirituality and religious conviction within their settings of rising education, economic, and even social standards.

For the Future . . .

The radical shift of global Christianity currently places the Asian church, especially Pentecostal-Charismatic Christianity, in a crucial position. Two-thirds of the world's Christians live on the three major southern continents: South America, Africa, and Asia. Asia, with the largest population in the world, is the least Christianized.[52]

Asian Pentecostalism has a unique opportunity to propel Asian—and consequently global—Christianity to an unprecedented and sustainable expansion. Whether or not Christianity grows beyond one-third of the world's population (for the first time in history), may depend on what happens in Asia in the next decades.[53] Judging from the growth trajectory of Asian Christianity (including Pentecostal varieties), the twenty-first century of world Christianity may well be centered in Asia.

About 50 percent of Asian Christians are Pentecostals. This form of Christianity holds the key to this historic possibility. Making this exciting prospect a reality comes with enormous challenges, as we have already observed from the incredible variety in theology and practice. One priority that Asian Pentecostal communities need to explore is their mission engagement. Most likely, Asia will remain

---

[52]Latin America is 92.5% Christian and Africa is 47.9% Christian, whereas a mere 8.5% of Asia is Christian, in Todd M. Johnson and Kenneth R. Ross, ed., *Atlas of Global Christianity* (Edinburgh: Edinburgh University Press, 2009), 57.

[53]This projection is based on an assumption that the rest of the world maintains their current level of Christians, particularly in the West. Any further growth will accelerate the global growth rate.

a religiously pluralistic continent.[54] If so, Pentecostals, while continuing their committed evangelistic activities, need to learn to live alongside other religions. They need to add "living peacefully in the same society" to their mission theology, further requiring them to develop a good theology of religions.

Serious reflection on contextualization is also required: The movement has already proven the "creativity of the Spirit" in extremely challenging social environments. However, a critical examination of historic Pentecostal groups reveals that not all have been admirable, as seen in the excesses of the prosperity gospel.

Equally challenging will be the construction of a Pentecostal identity and mission in free and affluent environments. Chinese Christianity is moving from an inclement environment to a relatively open and prosperous context. The future of Chinese Christianity will significantly depend on its response to the changing social context in the next decades. Ra's Prayer Mountain no longer attracts throngs of visitors, signaling the dire need to move one step ahead of social change. A similar challenge is that characteristic signs and wonders are no longer witnessed in more "established" Pentecostal circles.

On the other hand, Ha's impact on urban middle-class Christians demonstrates the possibility for Pentecostalism to exercise an extraordinary contextual flexibility. However, when the context overwhelms the theological construct, this flexibility and creativity can lead some communities into "more Pentecostal but less Christian" paths. Also, the Pentecostal formulation of a theological foundation for the church-state relationship is not uniform; it requires a careful negotiation between the Pentecostal reading of the Scriptures and the appropriation of contemporary contexts into theological dialogue.

All this requires theologically reflective minds that are connected to real-life settings. In the theologizing process, we will

---

[54]Daniel H. Bays, *A New History of Christianity in China* (Malden, MA: Wiley-Blackwell, 2012), 92-95, contested the American idea of Christian China at the turn of the twentieth century.

be well advised to remember that Pentecostal theologies naturally venture into edgy areas; thus, the job will be rather messy.[55]

Finally, if Asian Pentecostalism holds an important key to the future of global Christianity, its communities need to develop a global perspective in their local engagement. Is this too much to ask from such a diverse movement? The challenge is to expect the Spirit's empowerment, mixed with a good amount of human sweat and effort.

[55]Ibid., 207.

Chapter 2

Doing Theology in the Philippines: A Case Study of Pentecostal Christianity[1]

Doing theology inevitably involves at least three elements to make it meaningful to listeners in a specific context, be it special or temporal: revelation, context, and the theologizer-communicator. First, revelation in theologizing refers to primary sources: the Scripture and a specific theological tradition prompted by a particular socio-historical situation. Second, context is found in two major categories: cultural and contemporary. Third, a theologizer-communicator brings an individual's experiential involvement in both revelation and context, plus the method of presentation/communication of the fruit of the theological inquiry in a way that is understandable to and acceptable by the audience.[2]

In this reflection on Pentecostal Christianity in the Philippines, only two components will be discussed due to the limitation of space: the revelation and the context. For revelation, the focus is on the theological and spiritual tradition of this specific family of Christianity, particularly as witnessed in the last century. The context is the socio-cultural setting of the Philippines, which has interacted with the Charismatic theological and spiritual tradition, particularly in the second half of the twentieth century.

---

[1]First published in *AJPS* 8, no. 2 (2005), used by permission.

[2]Bays, *New History of Christianity in China,* 207.

Pentecostalism in the Philippines

The main thrust of Pentecostal Christianity to the Philippines was initiated by *balikbayans*, Filipino-Americans who repatriated from California and Hawaii in the 1920s and 30s, where they had experienced the baptism in the Spirit. Three of the four "classical" Pentecostal groups included in Joseph Suico's report owe their existence to such *balikbayan* missionaries.[3] Even before Pentecostal denominations were officially registered, these *balikbayan* missionaries conducted evangelism and teaching activities in their hometowns and provinces. When other missionaries arrived (primarily from the USA) "classical" Pentecostal denominations were organized: Filipino Assemblies of God of the First Born in 1943 in La Union, the Foursquare Church of Gospel in 1937 in Iloilo City, Church of God (Cleveland, TN) in 1952 in Ilocos Norte, and the Assemblies of God in 1953 in Pangasinan.

The 1980s brought another wave of spiritual awakening among Catholic believers. With encouragement from the Vatican II, Bible study groups and prayer groups proliferated. Often led by gifted lay leaders, the groups met in homes, offices, restaurants, and hotels. They were influenced by the Catholic renewal movement that started in North America in 1967 and later spread throughout the world through prayer and Bible study groups that prayed for healing and renewal. Local communities mushroomed. Some grew into national networks.[4] Many such groups eventually left the Catholic Church and formed their own "fellowships," such as the Jesus Is Lord Christian Fellowship by Eddie Villanueva in 1978 and the Bread of Life Ministry by Cesar "Butch" Conde in 1982. This wild growth of the groups and the exodus of Catholic members from their parish churches prompted the

---

[3]Wonsuk Ma, "Philippines," in *NIDPCM*, ed. Stanley M. Burgess and Eduard M. van der Maas (Grand Rapids: Zondervan, 2002), 201-207. Also, for a good survey, Joseph Suico, "Pentecostalism in the Philippines," in *Asian and Pentecostal: The Charismatic Face of Christianity in Asia*, ed. Allan Anderson and Edmond Tang (Oxford: Regnum Books, 2005), 350-56.

[4]For a study on Philippine Catholic renewal movement, see Lode Wostyn, "Catholic Charismatics in the Philippines," in *Asian and Pentecostal*, 363-83.

Archdiocesan Office of Manila to publish a booklet in 1983 titled *Guidelines of the Catholic Charismatic Renewal Movement.*[5] The intention was to prevent the Catholic "faithful" from becoming "born again," a popular term referring to Protestantism, while providing room and supervision for their "Charismatic" activities. One guideline allowed Charismatic Catholics to have their own gathering on weekdays and participate in their parish church on Sunday for mass. However, the rise of the powerful El Shaddai broke this guideline, as the group celebrated its Sunday worship among themselves all over the country and overseas.

According to 2020 statistics, Pentecostal-Charismatic believers totaled 38 million, close to 40% of the nation's 100 million Christians. Denominational (or Classical) Pentecostals accounted for 4.2% or 1.6 million, the smallest among the three categories. Independent Pentecostals or Neo-Charismatics numbered 9.7 million or 25.4%. The largest group, as expected, was Charismatic believers, with 26.7 million believers or 70.3% of the total Pentecostal-Charismatic Christians. This represented a startling proportion of 34.8% of the population of 109.7 million.[6] With an impressive annual growth rate of 7.19% between 1970 and 2020, it exceeded one prediction of growing to over 30 million by 2025.[7]

Goal and Purpose

Unique theological and spiritual traditions of Pentecostalism developed primarily in the twentieth century. Although a biblical basis may occasionally appear in this section, attention will be given primarily to the historical tradition of the movement. Under each theological uniqueness, the Philippine context will be briefly

[5]Archdiocesan Office for Research and Development, "Guidelines of the Catholic Charismatic Renewal Movement in the Archdiocese of Manila" (Manila, 1983).

[6]*ISEC*, 153.

[7]David B. Barrett, George T. Kurian, and Todd M. Johnson, ed., *World Christian Encyclopedia: A Comparative Survey of Churches and Religions in the Modern World, Vol. 1*, 2nd ed. (Oxford: Oxford University Press, 2001), 594.

discussed to justify the theological application useful to Philippine Pentecostal churches, believers, and leaders. Whenever possible, such theological potential will be explored in three categories: 1) fundamental issues as they apply to Pentecostals; 2) issues that have to do with the larger church communities in the country; and 3) issues related to society.

This segment assumes a reasonable familiarity of the reader with the socio-cultural and religious scene of the Philippines. Hence, no extensive discussion of the society is made, nor is any detailed discussion on Pentecostal history, theology, and spirituality provided, as the author assumes sufficient exposure of the audience to such information.[8]

This chapter is intended to help fellow Pentecostal-Charismatic believers in the Philippines become more aware of their theological potential inherited from the worldwide movement, encouraging and challenging them to engage in an intentional theological process. This will involve conscious awareness of the context where this theological tradition has been placed by God's providence and seeing the perspective of this unique theological tradition in the context of the larger Christian mandates. The latter task requires the movement to shed its sectarian and fundamentalist mindset and actively dialogue with other theological traditions. Thus, the exposition of its unique theological potential is not to minimize other Christian traditions and their unique theological contributions in any way. In contrast, the call is to view each tradition as a unique gift from the Lord to the Body of Christ and

---

[8]There are helpful publications on Philippine Pentecostal history. See, for example, Dave Johnson, *Led by the Spirit: The History of the American Assemblies of God Missionaries in the Philippines* (Pasig City, Philippines: ICI Ministries, 2009); Johnny Loye King, *Spirit and Schism: The History of Oneness Pentecostalism in the Philippines* (Kindle, 2020); Dynnice Rosanny D. Engcoy, *Pentecostal Pioneer: The Life of Legacy of Rudy Esperanza and the Early Years of the Assemblies of God in the Philippines* (Eugene, OR: Wipf & Stock, 2017). Also, see Lora Angeline Embudo Timenia, *Third Wave Pentecostalism in the Philippines: Understanding Toronto Blessing Revivalism's Signs and Wonders Theology in the Philippines* (Eugene, OR: Wipf & Stock, 2021) for a critical evaluation of Toronto Blessing revivalism in the Philippines.

to the dying world, that each can perform its unique tasks so that the entire Body will be edified. With this in view, several potential weaknesses in this theological system are also included in this discussion.

Theological Potential of Pentecostalism in the Philippine Context

Religion of Empowerment

The bedrock doctrine of Classical Pentecostalism is the "baptism in the Spirit," often witnessed by speaking in other tongues. This principal belief is anchored in Acts 2.[9] Among Charismatics, the same experience is identified differently, e.g., "fullness in the Spirit" with no doctrinal emphasis on speaking in tongues as "the initial physical evidence" of baptism in the Spirit. However, tongue-speaking still plays an important role, as described in the experiences and ministry of Dennis Bennett, which is commonly recognized as the beginning of the "Charismatic movement" in the early 1960s.[10] Regardless of the locus of tongues in the wider Pentecostal movement, what is universallyaccepted is the empowerment impetus of this theology. As in Acts 1 : 8, "But you will receive power when the Holy Spirit comes on you; and you will be my witnesses in Jerusalem, and

---

[9]For example, the "Fundamental Truth of the (US) Assemblies of God," http://ag.org/top/beliefs/truths.cfm#/ (accessed May 29, 2005), reads: "All believers are entitled to and should ardently expect and earnestly seek the promise of the Father, the baptism in the Holy Ghost and fire, according to the command of our Lord Jesus Christ. This was the normal experience of all in the early Christian Church. With it comes the enduement of power for life and service, the bestowment of the gifts and their uses in the work of the ministry," and "The baptism of believers in the Holy Ghost is witnessed by the initial physical sign of speaking with other tongues as the Spirit of God gives them utterance."

[10]See his popular accounts in Dennis Bennett, *Nine O'clock in the Morning* (Plainfield, NJ: Logos International, 1970), 79-80. On speaking in tongues as the focus of the new spiritual experience: "Joy, freedom, and spiritual understanding came as the new language poured from their lips," 80.

in all Judea and Samaria, and to the ends of the earth,"[11] the coming of the Spirit is understood as the empowerment of the Holy Spirit for witnessing.[12] Empowerment theology presumes the calling of believers for ministry regardless of gender, age, and training. Roger Stronstad, a Pentecostal scholar, aptly labeled this as the "prophethood of all believers," that is, every believer is called to proclaim to be an active witness, in comparison with the traditional notion of the "priesthood of all believers."[13] This theological breakthrough provided an incredible release of people in the pew for ministry, while mainline and Evangelical churches still consider "ministry" as done predominantly by properly trained clergy. The explosive expansion of the Pentecostal movement in the first century of its existence, the birth of mega-churches, and the emergence of Pentecostalism as a main missionary force find their theological rationale in the empowerment theology of Pentecostalism.

In the uniquely Pentecostal tradition, the making of theology is now primarily in the hands of the masses in the pews. This theologizing process has been shaped through two essential practices, among others. First, a spontaneous public utterance is given in the form of prophecy and messages in tongues, often with interpretation. Based on 1 Corinthians 14, practices promote an open invitation to everyone in the congregation to participate in worship and proclamation. As in the Azusa Street revival, spontaneous congregational worship called the "heavenly choir," often in tongues, is a common feature of Pentecostal worship. This has a similar effect on the participatory nature of Pentecostal worship and ethos.[14] Although presumably, the message is not

---

[11]Unless otherwise indicated, all scripture references are from the *New International Version* (NIV), Grand Rapids: Zondervan, 2011.

[12]The unique feature of Lukan pneumatology, particularly in contrast with Paul's, has been the subject of several critical Pentecostal treaties such as Roger Stronstad, *Charismatic Theology of St. Luke* (Peabody, MA: Hendrickson, 1984) and Robert P. Menzies, *Empowered for Witness: The Spirit in Luke-Acts* (London: T. & T. Clark, 2004).

[13]Stronstad, *The Prophethood of All Believers.*

[14]E.g., Larry Martin, *The Life and Ministry of William J. Seymour* (Joplin,

from a human source, this provides a conducive atmosphere for a participatory theologizing process.

Second, more directly than the first contributing element, are testimonies. Pentecostals most likely inherited the Holiness practice of public testimonies, particularly in the camp meetings. In most Pentecostal circles, except in the highly organized and prescriptive services often found in mega-churches, testimony time is an important part of the order of worship. With no prior arrangement, anyone is expected to share their testimony, often in the form of his or her recent encounter with God. Even in tribal churches in the Cordillera Mountain region of the Philippines, old and young members stand or come forward to the pulpit to share their experiences with God. Testimony time can last more than an hour. Occasionally, prayers are offered for specific needs that have been expressed in the testimonies. This tradition provides participation in theology-making. It gives the rest of the congregation space to reflect, evaluate, and if accepted as genuine and valid, to share the theological experiences of one member as a community possession. This makes Pentecostal theology a "people's theology." The uniqueness of this feature should be understood in the context of most Christian traditions, where theologizing has been left exclusively in the hands of theological and ecclesial elites. In addition to empowering individuals, the role of Pentecostal theology in strengthening the church in general has significant consequences in church growth, mission, and social upliftment.

Empowerment of all believers as per the Pentecostal tradition has several theological implications in the Philippine setting. Although church polity historically has produced varied church governance, few would deny that the formation of theology needs broad participation, particularly from real-life situations. However, trained clergy must provide guidance and a theological framework.

In the Philippines, as in many non-Western societies, social and historical factors have contributed to the existence of social classes. In "modern" times, egalitarianism with democratic

MO: Christian Life Books, 1999), 187.

idealism has strongly influenced Asian societies, although the long cultural tradition of social class systems persists, often in subtle forms. This cultural force and the long Roman Catholic influence have fostered clergy-oriented Christianity. Protestantism has not differed much from the Catholics. In such a setting, the "anti-cultural" pattern of lay leadership in Pentecostal churches and independent Charismatic fellowships has revolutionized religious norms in the Philippines. The Pentecostal tradition is known for mobilizing the laity—including women, youth, and sometimes children—in leadership.[15] In Philippine society, the general role of women has traditionally been strongly encouraged. The Pentecostal empowerment of all believers for ministry has further enhanced church leadership positions for women.

Successful lay founders of charismatic groups are another unique expression evident in Philippine Charismatic Christianity: Eddie Villanueva of the Jesus Is the Lord Church, "Butch" Conde of the Bread of Life Ministries, and, recently, Mario "Mike" Z. Velarde of the El Shaddai Catholic Charismatic group, to name just a few.

Despite this radical shift in church leadership, a broad participation of the laity in forming "our" theology remains a challenging ideal. Filipino Pentecostals need to articulate and foster this meaningful theological gift, given by the Spirit to the church.

In a broader sense, Pentecostals need to continue developing the theology of the empowerment of all believers for their own sake. This will also affect church traditions, including those in mainline Protestant and Catholic churches. Adding the "prophetic" call to the traditional "priestly" call for all believers is one of Pentecostalism's unique theological contributions to the

[15]Suico, "Pentecostalism in the Philippines," 350. In 2001, in Buguias, Benguet Province, I was delighted to see a nine-year-old girl leading a song service for a Sunday morning worship. For many decades, the cell system in Yoido Full Gospel Church has included children's cells. They are led by children in cell gatherings, worship, and other activities under the supervision of a clergy or teacher.

churches. In adopting the already advantageous cultural traditions of empowerment of its laity in missionary activities, Philippine Christianity can influence Asian churches, especially in traditional class or male-dominant societies.

Pentecostals can develop the theological potential of empowering the socially marginalized, which will contribute positively to a traditionally elite-dominant society. "People Power II" has been interpreted by some sectors as a hegemony war between the established socio-political elites and the powerless majority. This provides an interesting reflection to an outsider as it demonstrates the longing of the masses to be socially and politically empowered as positive and forceful movers of society. Here, Pentecostals can provide a creative role of empowerment from their theological traditions.

One crucial area to watch is the mushrooming of independent churches (mostly Pentecostal-Charismatic type) in the past decades. These are often led by people with little or no theological training. With little regulation for ordination, hundreds, if not thousands, of "ministers" were born during this period.

Schisms among churches have become a scandal of Pentecostal Christianity in many parts of the world. The downside of the democratization of ministry is an "entrepreneurial" and casual approach to ministry. Sometimes, some leaders' moral standards and lifestyles are questionable in a religious "free market" where anyone can set up a church or even a denomination. Thus, it is an ongoing challenge for Pentecostal-Charismatic Christianity to establish credibility in the Philippines.

Theology of Transformation

In a way, closely related to the empowerment emphasis of Pentecostal theology is the potential for transformation in various levels of human life. The "uninherited" and marginalized masses suddenly acquired a radically new worldview in their perception of self and everything around them.[16]

---

[16]A helpful study of Pentecostalism's potential for social transformation

In many testimonies, the chain of changes is attested to with a radical inner transformation, through conversion experiences, but far more often through the "baptism in the Holy Spirit." One typical description of this unique experience was given by C. H. Mason, a prominent leader of the Church of God in Christ, the largest Pentecostal denomination in North America:

> So there came a wave of glory into me, and all of my being was filled with the glory of the Lord. So, when I had gotten myself straight on my feet, there came a light which enveloped my entire being above the brightness of the sun. When I opened my mouth to say, "Glory," a flame touched my tongue then ran down to me. My language changed and no word could I speak in my own tongue. Oh, I was filled with the glory of my Lord. My soul was then satisfied.[17]

Even when it is not fully articulated, the Pentecostals assume that a genuine and unmistakable change begins with a person's inner being. This is an opposite approach to the liberation theology of Latin America, which experimented with a structured and community-based transformation. The general perception of net results from liberation theology has not been satisfactory despite much planning, financial support, studies, and effort.[18]

---

is found in Joseph R. Suico, "Institutional and Individualistic Dimensions of Transformational Development: The Case of Pentecostal Churches in the Philippines" (Ph.D. diss., University of Wales, 2003).

[17]E. W. Mason, *The Man; Charles Harrison Mason: Sermons of His Early Ministry* (1915–1929) and *A Biographical Sketch of His Life,* (n.d.), 15-19; quoted in Martin, *The Life and Ministry of William J. Seymour*, 215.

[18]For instance, a Latin American Mennonite's reflection is helpful: César Garcia, "Beyond Liberation and Prosperity Gospel: A Third Way," in *Good News to the Poor: Spirit-Empowered Approaches to Poverty*, edited by Wonsuk Ma and Opoku Onyinah (Tulsa: ORU Press, 2022), 141-155. Also, David Martin's sociological study of Latin American Pentecostalism can be understood in the context of liberation theology, David Martin, *Tongues of Fire: The Explosion of Protestantism in Latin America* (Oxford: Wiley-Blackwell, 1993).

On the other hand, Teen Challenge provides a good example on the Pentecostal side.[19] A core value is the inner transformation of individuals, and earlier, this radical transformation was sought through the experience of the baptism in the Spirit. This powerful experience radically changes one's values, priorities, life goals, attitude, habits, and entire life, often instantly, although there is a continuing process of molding. Its unusually successful drug rehabilitation program began in 1960 in New York[20] and attracted much attention from government agencies and private sectors. A 2005 report revealed a stunning success rate of 67-86% after seven years of participants' graduation from the Teen Challenge program. Furthermore, 72% continued their education to the college level, 75% were employed, 67% were regularly attending church while 57% were involved in ministry, and 92% maintained good to excellent health.[21]

This transformational potential of Pentecostalism is well-attested in the growth of churches. Although multiple factors contribute to the growth of a local church, each member contributes to its health and growth. Hong's study reveals that ten of the twelve megachurches in Korea are Pentecostal or Pentecostal-like in their ethos, worship, and message.[22] Harper makes a similar observation about Philippine churches, stating that Pentecostal churches would lead the growth of Christianity in the Philippines.[23] A study of

---

[19]See David R. Wilkerson with John and Elizabeth Sherrill, *The Cross and the Switchblade* (New York: B. Geis, 1968).

[20]Teen Challenge, "History," www.teenchallenge.com/index.cfm?info1D=7¢er1D=1194 (accessed February 21, 2005). One report reveals that "Teen Challenge claims . . . a 70% cure rate for the drug addicts graduating from their program . . . [while] most secular drug rehabilitation programs only experienced a cure rate of 1–15% of their graduates." See Teen Challenge, "National Institute on Drug Abuse Report," http://www.teenchallenge.com/index.cfm?studies1D=3/ (accessed February 21, 2005).

[21]Teen Challenge, "National Institute on Drug Abuse Report."

[22]Young-gi Hong, "The Backgrounds and Characteristics of the Charismatic Mega-churches in Korea," *AJPS* 3, no. 1 (2000): 99-118.

[23]George W. Harper, "Philippine Tongues of Fire? Latin American Pentecostalism and the Future of Filipino Christianity," *Journal of Asian Mission* 2, no. 2 (2000): 225–59.

several large churches in the country proves that growing churches are Pentecostal in orientation.[24]

The issue of growth may not be as critical in the Philippines as in many other Asian nations. It is important to note that Christianity is a minority in the sea of religions in Asia. The growth of churches is, in fact, a powerful demonstration that the Christian God is indeed true and powerful, rendering credibility to the Christian message. On the other hand, the Pentecostal contribution to the "renewal" of churches is unquestioned. The most critical "growth" of the church is influenced by Pentecostal Christianity. Its aggressive evangelism, church planting, lay mobilization, lively music, and celebratory Pentecostal worship bring a paradigm shift in individual and church life.

When it comes to social transformation through Pentecostal influence, many studies from and on Latin America illustrate another form of empowerment: the Pentecostals' potential for social "upward mobility."[25] This trend has also been noticed in Asia, as many Pentecostals have advanced in their socioeconomic status. In Korea, David Yonggi Cho's theology of blessing challenged many urban poor to believe in the "good God" who is concerned not only with their eternal life but also with their daily needs.[26]

Unlike Catholic and mainline social programs, the Pentecostal approach to individual, family, and social transformation has been remarkably effective. This "religion of the poor" (against the "religion for the poor," referring to the church's program for the underprivileged) has holistically empowered the marginalized masses. As a result, many Pentecostals in Latin America are now middle-class citizens. Popular Philippines televangelists, including Mike Velarde, preached the immanent aspect of God's presence

---

[24]Julie C. Ma, "Growing Churches in Manila," *Asia Journal of Theology* 11 (1997): 324-42.

[25]E.g., David Martin, *Tongues of Fire: The Explosion of Pentecostalism in Latin America* (Oxford: Blackwell, 1990).

[26]E.g., Wonsuk Ma, "Asian (Classical) Pentecostal Theology in Context," in *Asian and Pentecostal*, 64-75.

with instantaneous provision of physical and material needs and attracted large followings.

Undeniably, the emphasis on God's immediate provision has contributed significantly to church growth. But the relevance of the Christian message in the minds of the masses has also contributed to the "pop" version of Christianity. Sometimes, such groups are accused of being shamanistic, in the sense that God is exploited for the worshipper's personal gain.[27]

In the social context of the Philippines and Asia, a more serious social issue is moral transformation in and by Pentecostal Christianity. The Philippines, the only Christian nation in Asia, has failed to demonstrate the high moral standards generally expected among Christian nations. For example, the nation's 2023 corruption index is one of the lowest in Asia.[28] The latter warrants asking: why have political, government, and business leaders trained in Christian (in this case, primarily Catholic) universities become part of the social corruption and graft in the Philippines? If, in the last fifty years, Pentecostal and Charismatic Christianity has almost reached ten million (about one-seventh of the total population), what difference has that made to the moral standards of the society?[29] Highly publicized moral failures of some Western Pentecostal preachers likewise pose hard questions for Pentecostals.

In the 2004 and 2010 general elections, the Philippines experienced the political potential of Charismatic Christianity for the first time, on two fronts. First, a presidential candidate came

---

[27]For a slightly different reason, see Harvey Cox, *Fire from Heaven: The Rise of Pentecostal Spirituality and the Reshaping of Religion in the Twenty-First Century* (Reading, MA: Addison-Wesley, 1995), 218-19, 224-28, 240-41; also Walter J. Hollenweger, *Pentecostalism: Origins and Developments Worldwide* (Peabody, MA: Hendrickson, 1997), the entire section under "The Black Oral Root."

[28]Transparency International, "Corruption Perceptions Index 2023," https://www.transparency.org/en/cpi/2023/ (accessed December 5, 2024).

[29]For a helpful biblical basis for Pentecostal contribution to moral restoration, see Matthias Wenk, *Community-Forming Power: The Socio-Ethical Role of the Spirit in Luke-Acts* (Sheffield: Sheffield Academic Press, 2000).

from a large Charismatic congregation with the voting power of El Shaddai, perhaps an eight-million-strong Catholic Charismatic movement. Some suggested that Charismatic Christianity demonstrated its potential to replace one of the existing three "determinants for the presidential election in the Philippines." This might be Iglesia ni Cristo, or it might become a new determinant in this highly visible demonstration of political power.[30]

Whether consciously recognized or not, Pentecostal-Charismatic Christianity has expanded its influence on society. At this point, proper theological reflection is needed to provide guidelines that promote a just society, while sharing Christian witness.

Potential for Unity

The theological potential for Pentecostal religion to cross barriers of differences was initially validated in the incredible racial and ecclesial diversity of the participants of the Azusa Street revival (1906-09). Although severely scorned by white-dominant mass media and existing ecclesial establishments, the revival led by a humble African American Holiness preacher was a powerful demonstration of the Holy Spirit's potential to bring radically different people together in genuinely celebrating God's presence.

> Although the revival started among a few who were African American by race, Holiness by doctrine, and lower to middle in economic class, eventually men and women from all races, creeds and socioeconomic positions worshiped together in the unassuming little mission.[31]

[30]For the involvement and influence of Charismatic Christianity, see, for example, Evelyn Macairan, "2 Charismatic Leaders Set to Join 2010 Presidential Derby," *PhilStar Global* (Manila), August 21, 2009.

[31]Martin, *The Life and Ministry of William J. Seymour*, 194.

Christian unity, this "spontaneous ecumenicity"[32] among Spirit-filled believers, regardless of their ecclesial affiliation, has been demonstrated repeatedly. Robeck reminds Pentecostals of the powerful yet hidden potential for ecumenism found in the work of the Holy Spirit.[33] Kitano, employing a sociological analysis, determined that the socio-religious distance between Pentecostals and non-Charismatic Catholics is significantly far apart, giving little expectation that they would engage with each other. However, the socio-religious distance between Pentecostals and Charismatic Catholics is close, even though fundamental theological differences remain.[34] This study in Metro Manila in the 1980s proves that genuine ecumenism is possible, not through efforts to reduce theological differences but through a powerful encounter with the Holy Spirit. Also, the emergence of the Charismatic movement in the 1960s among mainline churches and the Roman Catholic Church powerfully demonstrated the interconfessional potential that Pentecostal spiritual experiences can easily be incorporated into existing theological systems.

Pentecostalism faces two challenges to fully recognize its ecumenical potential and make positive contributions to the larger church world. First, it is a historical reality that Pentecostals have caused church divisions due to their unique doctrinal positions, but also, more often than not, due to personality conflicts. For example, today, there are at least four groups in Korea using the name "Assemblies of God." The repeated divisions and attempts to unite them within the Korean Assemblies of God can often be

---

[32]Koichi Kitano, "Spontaneous Ecumenicity between Catholics and Protestants in the Charismatic Movement: A Case Study" (Ph.D. diss., Centro Escolar University, Philippines, 1981).

[33]E.g., Cecil M. Robeck, Jr., "Pentecostals and the Apostolic Faith: Implications for Ecumenism," *Pneuma: The Journal of the Society for Pentecostal Studies* 9, no. 1 (Spring 1987): 61-84; "Growing Opportunities for Pentecostal Ecumenical Engagement," *Pentecostal Education* 7, no. 2 (Fall 2022): 173-190.

[34]Koichi Kitano, "Socio-religious Distance between Charismatics and Other Religious Group Members: A Case Study of the Philippines in the 1980s," *Journal of Asian Mission* 5, no. 2 (2003): 231-42.

attributed to non-doctrinal issues, especially relational ones. The proliferation of Pentecostal denominations in early twentieth-century North America, especially in some areas, directly curtailed their theological potential. This is also true in the Philippines and other countries. In big cities and rural areas, the mushrooming of independent Pentecostal congregations is both concerning and encouraging.[35]

Second, Pentecostals need to live up to their theological mandates and distinctives. Such a commitment requires intentional action toward church unity. A recent new ecumenical initiative of creating the Global Christian Forum (GCF) and its warm invitation extended to the Pentecostals is an encouraging move.[36] The Asian Consultation of the GCF in Hong Kong (May 2004) included 150 Asian Christian leaders: Catholics, Pentecostals, and every possible group in between. As a result, an ecumenical academic conference took place in Baguio (January 2005) with Catholic, mainline (including Episcopalian, Methodist, Lutheran, United Church of Christ in the Philippines), Evangelicals, and Pentecostal representatives.

Another area of concern is multi-racial unity. Bartleman, an eyewitness and participant in the Azusa Street revival, reported its unheard-of interracial nature: "Divine love was wonderfully manifest in the meetings . . . The message was the love of God. It was a sort of 'first love' of the early church returned. . . . The 'color line' is washed away by the blood."[37]

---

[35]Proselytism is a frequent topic raised in ecumenical dialogues with Pentecostals, due to their aggressive evangelism and proliferation of small and large churches. In the 1990-1997 cycle of the Reformed-Pentecostal Dialogue, this very word is included in the title, "Evangelization, Proselytism, and Common Witness: The Report from the Fourth Phase of the International Dialogue 1990-1997 between the Roman Catholic Church and Some Classical Pentecostal Churches and Leaders," *AJPS* 2, no. 1 (1999): 105-151.

[36]"Taking Shape: Global Christian Forum," http://www.wcc-coe.org/wcc/news/press/00/25pre.html/ (accessed July 1, 2005).

[37]Frank Bartleman, *Azusa Street* (Plainfield, NJ: Logos International, 1980), 54.

Unity at the Azuza mission went beyond racial differences to transcend socio-economic differences as well. During an era when the majority of established churches represented clearly demarcated socio-economic lines, the "educated and illiterate, rich and poor, brown, black and white all worshiped together"[38] under the leadership of a "one-eyed, illiterate, Negro" preacher.[39] *The Apostolic Faith*, the official monthly publication of the Azusa mission, reported:

> One token of the Lord's coming is that He is melting all races and nations together, and they are filled with the power and glory of God. He is baptizing by one Spirit into one body and making up a people that will be ready to meet Him when He comes.[40]

This interracial fellowship was quickly met with a harsh reaction from local communities and media. The media was particularly strong in condemning the interracial nature of the mission. Captions such as "Disgraceful Intermingling of the Races" appeared regularly.[41] Harsh criticism came not only from the secular media but also, more disappointingly, from other Christian traditions. Unfortunately, this signaled the devastating development of the mission. Schisms were initiated by white Christian leaders from within as well as without. The long-awaited visit of Charles Parham, the mentor of William J. Seymour, in September 1906 ended with Parham's harsh condemnation of the interracial fellowship of the Azusa Street mission. He established his own racially exclusive (white), congregation not far from the mission.[42] Two white female leaders of the mission took the

---

[38]Martin, *The Life and Ministry of William J. Seymour*, 196.

[39]"Weird Babel of Tongues: New Sect of Fanatics Is Breaking Loose; Wild Scene Last Night on Azusa Street; Gurgle of Wordless Talk by a Sister," *Los Angeles Daily Times,* April 18, 1906, 1.

[40]"One Token. . .," *The Apostolic Faith* (Los Angeles, Feb.–Mar. 1907): 7.

[41]Martin, *The Life and Ministry of William J. Seymour*, 248.

[42]It was the Women's Temperance Christian Union building at Broadway and Temple Street, literally a few blocks away from the Azusa Street Mission.

mailing list of *The Apostolic Faith* to establish their own ministry in Oregon. This triggered the unrecoverable decline of the Azuza Street mission. Underwood attributes this racial division partly to the immense pressure consistently exerted by the secular press.[43]

What the Holy Spirit miraculously put together was miserably divided by humans.[44] Until the last decade of the twentieth century, most Pentecostal denominations in North America were exclusively either black or white. The so-called "Memphis Miracle" of 1994 was intended to resolve the exclusively white body of Pentecostal churches in North America. The "white" denominations joined the more inclusive (thus, black-controlled) Pentecostal-Charismatic Church of North America.

Samuel Huntington and many others argue that the post-Cold War era has seen increasing and intensifying conflicts along racial and religious lines. Somalia, former Yugoslavia, and East Timor are a few examples. The rise of radical religious fundamentalism and its clash among religious groups, predicted by Harvey Cox,[45] was horribly and powerfully displayed in the 9/11 incident.

In the Philippines, as elsewhere like Sudan, subtle or overt racial conflict and rivalry persists, and many cases also follow religious lines. The breakdown of Yugoslavia starting in 1991 into eight nations was along racial and religious lines. The same characterizes the independence of South Sudan and East Timor. In the Philippines, the ongoing religious conflict is between Islamic groups in Mindanao. This conflict is religious in nature, but one cannot ignore racial/ethnic components embedded in the issues.

Contextualization

Pentecostalism has a different worldview orientation from many traditional Christian groups. In the West, the spiritual world has been ignored for a long time. The influences of the Enlightenment in education resulted in a rationalistic Christian

---

[43]B. E. Underwood, "Memphis Miracle," *Legacy* 4 (Summer 1997): 3.
[44]Ibid., 3-6.
[45]Cox, *Fire from Heaven*, 302-04.

orientation. Anything that could be explained scientifically was removed from Christian thinking, including healing, miracles, prophecy, exorcism, etc. Within the West's increasing affluence and social welfare systems, rationalistic Christianity flourished; God was less needed in everyday life. The existence and role of angels and demons steadily diminished in this social and mental environment.

When such spiritually devoid Christianity is brought into a radically different world, existing religions assume a lively and active spiritual world and its close interference with human daily life. In such settings, rationalistic Christianity is handicapped in responding to daily needs. Inevitably, this has resulted in "split-level Christianity."[46] A Christian's loyalty and commitment become divided between their new Christian religion for sin, salvation, and the afterlife, and their old religion for daily and existential matters such as disease, omens, daily material needs, etc.

The Pentecostal worldview, with its restored spiritual world, worship, and power, brings the lost elements of Christianity into the forefront. The emotive or expressive element of worship (singing in particular) and the demonstration of spiritual power result in healing, miracles, exorcism, and prophetic words. Julie Ma argues convincingly that the worldviews of Pentecostalism and animism share many similarities with each other.[47] The demonstration of the tangible reality of God as Pentecostal ethos has a better potential for contextualization among animistically-oriented minds (and Asians, including Filipinos, are mostly animistically oriented). The stark contrast and substantial disparity between Western Christianity and animistic worldviews offer an ideal environment for contextualization.

---

[46]E.g., David S. Lim, "A Critique of Modernity in Protestant Missions in the Philippines," *Journal of Asian Mission* 2, no. 2 (2000): 156 n. 29.

[47]Julie C. Ma, *When the Spirit Meets the Spirits: Pentecostal Ministry among the Kankana-ey Tribe in the Philippines* (Frankfurt am Main: Peter Lang, 2000), 213-31.

The practical side to Pentecostalism's contextual potential is a response to poverty. Poverty is the number one challenge in Asia. The Pentecostal response to felt and daily needs has resulted in its explosive growth. For instance, the prevailing message of Mike Velarde of the El Shaddai Charismatic group is God's ability to meet people's daily needs and desires. This positive notion of God and Christianity has resulted in social and economic "upward mobility" in Latin America. Hearing many testimonies of God's miraculous material and physical blessings is not unusual.

At the same time, the emphasis on pragmatic and self-oriented religious expectations can easily create a form of "animistic" Christianity. David Yonggi Cho, the pastor of the world's largest single congregation in Korea, was accused of propagating shamanistic Christianity. There are instances of Pentecostal syncretism across Asia and the Philippines. In Africa, religious groups form that are "more Pentecostal but less Christian." For example, traditional "priests" and witchdoctors transition to Christianity and continue their "profession" as Christian prophets and healers. The adoption of traditional religious beliefs and practices into Pentecostalism requires a critical process of contextualization. A related danger is that Pentecostalism may become a "pop religion," where increasing elaborate music and worship resemble consumer-oriented entertainment industries.

The holistic worldview of Pentecostalism offers the possibility of culturally acceptable and viable Christianity for Filipinos and other Asians where "post-colonial" thinking is advocated.[48] Self-awareness of Asian Christians is a constant call from within and without. The goal is to obtain "theological independence" from

---

[48]See R. S. Sugirtharajah, *Asian Biblical Hermeneutics and Postcolonialism: Contesting the Interpretations* (Sheffield: Sheffield Academic Press, 1998). Also, the Association of Theological Education in Southeast Asia (ATESEA) began a project to re-evaluate and revise the so-called "Critical Asian Principles" in doing theology in Asia, at the center of which is the colonial history in Asia. In the theological arena, coming out of missionary-, thus, Western-led theologizing in Asia to relevant Asian theology by Asians has been a continuing call.

Western missionaries with Western-dominant theological agendas and processes.[49]

Summary

Historically, Pentecostals are activity-oriented with less emphasis on reflection and theological construction. This "intuitive Pentecostal theology," deduced from religious practices, needs to be articulated, especially in its socio-religious context. The raw material for theologizing is Pentecostal narratives such as testimonies, songs, sermons, and the like. Despite its danger of subjectivism, theology from ordinary people (or "theology from down to up") makes an important contribution to the theological process and the fruit of theologizing.

Pentecostal spiritual tradition can make a significant contribution to the theological process in the Philippines, so Philippine churches hold an important promise for the entirety of Asia and beyond. The growth of Pentecostal Christianity resulted in an increasing impact on the large church world and society, including the political arena. Also noted is the rapid growth of international mission movements. Filipinos are well-equipped for cross-cultural ministries due to their adaptability in language and culture, along with high educational standards. They have a constant supply of young ministerial candidates, minimal budgetary requirements, and other advantages. Their worldviews and religious experiences, including signs and wonders, play an important part in the future of missions, particularly on non-Western continents. Philippine Christians face the critical challenge to fully augment a holistic approach to their own society through moral transformation, whether they identify as Christians at large or Pentecostals.

---

[49]For example, Warren Newberry, "Contextualizing Indigenous Church Principles: An African Model," *AJPS* 8, no. 1 (2005): 110-14, proposed an additional component to the traditional "Three Self" indigenous church principle, "self-theologizing."

With the growing scholarly reflections among Filipinos, it is plausible for Filipino Pentecostals to increase their contributions to the future of the Asian Pentecostal movement through theological reflection. Coupled with the steady growth and missionary movement, Philippine Pentecostalism is poised to impact Philippine and Asian Christianity (including Roman Catholicism).

CHAPTER 3

Lord and Giver of Life: The Holy Spirit Among the Spirits in Asia[1]

Asia is the cradle of all the major religions of the world. Interaction among diverse religions is part of the daily life of its 4.62 billion people. All Asian cultures have deep religious roots, making it difficult to separate culture and religion. The Christian presence in the continent has a varied history. Some countries have had a Christian presence since the early centuries (e.g., Georgia and India), and others for only a few decades (Mongolia). Most are somewhere in between. Even though Christianity was born in Asia, many parts of the region view it as a "foreign" or "Western" religion. However, this "Western" face of Christianity has engaged with Asian religions and cultures to influence the theological shaping of the church.

The frontline of engagement is in the realm of the S/spirit(s). Here, Christianity and existing beliefs interact, adapt, challenge, and compromise with each other. This active engagement occurs everywhere: at family gatherings, markets, and schools. Grassroots spirituality and theology confront the established theological structures of Western missionaries, who have often fashioned Asian churches in the image of their historic churches. The gap is particularly wide between Western churches with a "sensitized"

---

[1]First published in *Christian Theology in Asia: Evangelical Perspectives* (Carlisle, UK: Langham Global Library, 2019), used by permission.

theology motivated by Enlightenment thinking and their counterpart churches in Asia.[2]

The resurgence of pneumatology in the global church in recent decades is warmly welcomed by churches in the southern continents (or "Global South"). Veli-Matti Kärkkäinen attributed this growing pneumatological interest in part to the birth and exponential growth of Pentecostal Christianity and the radical southward shift of the global Christian balance both in number and theologizing.[3]

The current state of pneumatology among Asian Evangelical churches affects the healthy development of pneumatology, both in theology and in praxis. A mapping exercise follows, with two categories that are useful in identifying the diverse expressions of belief in the Holy Spirit: 1) contextual range and 2) experiential range. It is necessary to integrate various sources, both ancient and contemporary, to imagine the future shaping of Asian pneumatology. The intended outcome is a construction of pneumatology that is deeply rooted in Scripture, faithful to Christian orthodoxy through each confessional tradition, and relevant to Asia's religious and socio-cultural context.

In undertaking this task, pure literary research is not viable. In addition to the scarcity of published material by Asians or on Evangelical pneumatology, discernment is called for to hear the voices that are authentic but hidden. This challenge is acute, particularly among "younger" churches, as their theologizing is grassroots in nature or a bottom-up process. Also, pneumatology, more than any branch of theology, is shaped and practiced in pastoral and mission settings. For this reason, resources for understanding it must include sermons, songs, and prayers,[4] which

---

[2]Hwa Yung, *Mangos or Bananas? The Quest for an Authentic Asian Christian Theology*, 2nd ed. (Oxford: Regnum, 2014), 2-3.

[3]Veli-Matti Kärkkäinen, *Pneumatology: The Holy Spirit in Ecumenical, International, and Contextual Perspective*, 2nd ed. (Grand Rapids: Baker Academic, 2018), 2-3.

[4]Simon Chan, *Grassroots Asian Theology: Thinking the Faith from the Ground Up* (Downers Grove: InterVarsity Press, 2014), 8.

can be read in frequent conversation with established theological documents.

Pneumatology in Asia Today: Two Continua

At the risk of overgeneralization, two continua represent the current state of pneumatology in Asia. Other conceptual categories can be fruitfully explored in delineating the varying shapes, emphases, and nuances of theological beliefs about the Holy Spirit. Nonetheless, these two are the most evident and useful categories for capturing diversity in Asia.

The Extent of the Spirit's Presence and Work

The first continuum relates to the extent to which the Holy Spirit is present and at work in creation. As an Asian Pentecostal, when I began an ecumenical theological dialogue with the Reformed tradition, one question repeatedly appeared in the annual week-long gatherings: "Is the Holy Spirit at work outside of the church?" This theological question probes if and how active the presence and work of the Holy Spirit is throughout God's creation. The answer reflects a complex theological understanding of creation, fall, pneumatology, religions, and mission.

Some theological questions explore the role of the Spirit of God in creation and his continuing care, as well as the effect of the fall on the Spirit's presence and work in creation. They also include the potential work of the Holy Spirit in cultures and religions as a part of God's creation and his overall missional plan for people of alternative faiths. The range of answers to this—from the pews—spans from an absolute "no" to an "of course, yes." Theological responses may be more nuanced. Given the multi-religious context of Asia, this is an important question, as most Christians in this region have, at some point, changed their religious affiliation and allegiance.

One may be tempted to place this inquiry in the conservative/progressive theological grid. Churches with conservative theological tendencies lean toward narrowly defining the presence and work of the Holy Spirit exclusively to the church and God's people. The churches rooted in more liberal or progressive theologies would be open to the presence and work of the Spirit in cultures and other religions as well. Although this may serve as a useful perspective, especially at the pew level, it fails to do justice to the complex process of theological formation that culminates in an answer.

In Asia, established Christianity's attitude toward culture had been greatly affected by the ways early missionaries demonstrated and taught their views and attitudes toward culture. Sixteenth-century Chinese Catholics came into contact with Matteo Ricci and his missionaries, who affirmed many elements and practices of Chinese culture and religion. They would have had a positive, open understanding of local culture. By contrast, Catholic missionaries who were active in nineteenth-century Chosun (Korea) strictly prohibited followers from participating in ancestor rites. They also encouraged Christian men to cut their customary long hair.

At one end of the continuum are churches that have totally severed the Christian experience from traditional religious and even cultural practices. Many churches in Korea are highly sensitive to any suggested link between Korean Christianity and Shamanism. Harvey Cox, in his widely acclaimed book on Pentecostalism, insisted that David Yonggi Cho had incorporated roles and concepts of old Shamanism in his theology. This was intended as an endorsing commendation, as Cox argued that Korean Pentecostalism had wisely adapted Shamanistic rituals for healing, exorcism, childbearing, and blessing.[5] However, the church immediately rejected Cox's praise, and the theologians of Yoido Full Gospel Church began to produce critical responses, adamantly refuting Cox's thesis. The Korean church invited Cox several times to experience Korean Pentecostalism and its practices and understand what it was. Although his appreciation for the vibrancy and openness of the church increased, it is not clear whether he withdrew his conclusion. Regardless of how one evaluates this dispute, it was a catalyst for deeper theological engagement on the role of the Holy Spirit in religion.

---

[5]Cox, *Fire from Heaven*, 219.

Nonetheless, the absolute denial of any linkage between Korean Pentecostal practices and the old religions in the land, despite practical and functional similarities, indicates an extremely narrow view of culture and traditional religions. Malaysian theologian Hwa Yung suggested that Cho assumed traditional religious functions in response to the needs of the people and religious expectations. Yet, according to him, this was only a case of functional substitution, denying any continuity between Shamanism and Korean Pentecostalism in substance.[6] The Holy Spirit's "pre-evangelistic" work before regeneration, especially on an individual level, is generally accepted as valid. However, the denial of any other activity in this realm implies that all non-Christian religions are outside the Spirit's present activity. This attitude is widely held among Evangelicals in Asia.

At the opposite end of the continuum is an inclusive attitude toward the presence and work of the Holy Spirit in cultures and religions. An extreme example may be the controversial ritual dance by a Korean woman theologian at the General Assembly of the WCC in 1991 in Canberra, Australia. Joined by Aborigines in the dance, she summoned the spirits of the victims of injustice and the spirit of the abused earth and rainforests. Finally, calling "the spirit of the Liberator, Jesus Christ," she declared that through these spirits, we could experience the Holy Spirit.[7] Even among the delegates of the general assembly of the largely liberal WCC, the pneumatology implied in her performance drew heated reactions and controversy. Among Asian Evangelicals, though there is still caution, a steady flow of reflections and suggestions has emerged, especially among academics, signaling an increasing openness to the role of the Holy Spirit in non-Christian religions. This trend may be part of the worldwide openness to, and re-evaluation of, the presence and work of the Holy Spirit in cultures. Such growing attention is a stark contrast to the extreme view taken by earlier

---

[6]Hwa, *Mangos or Bananas?* 166.

[7]See Peter Steinfels, "Beliefs," *New York Times*, March 16, 1991, https://www.nytimes.com/1991/03/16/us/beliefs-385491.html (accessed September 24, 2018).

Evangelical missionaries to consider indigenous cultures as "pagan" or even demonic.

The Nature of Christian Experience of the Holy Spirit

The second continuum relates to religious experience, which is extremely subjective and challenging (or impossible) to measure in intensity. Despite this subjectivity, such experiences occur with varying degrees of intensity and extent of personal impact. For example, medical professionals can verify some claims of supernatural healing, and declarations of "radical" heart transformation can be observed by a changed lifestyle. Furthermore, how a Christian community understands, believes, anticipates, and claims the person and work of the Holy Spirit differs markedly as one crosses denominational lines. At one end are churches claiming that their belief and experience of the Holy Spirit is marked by immediacy and supernatural gifts. On the other hand, those maintaining a cessationist stance contend that the use of supernatural gifts is no longer necessary or valid.

Churches focused on the immediacy of the Spirit's presence and work, particularly in healing and miracles, land on the "Charismatic" side of the spectrum. The most affirmative Christian groups today are Pentecostal and Charismatic churches and indigenous Christian communities. In studying the development of Chinese Christianity since the 1980s, Luke Wesley used the simple criterion that Charismatics are those Christians who believe that all of the gifts listed in 1 Cor 12:8-10, including prophecy, tongues, and healing, are available to the church today. According to the same categorization, "Pentecostals" add belief in the Spirit's baptism for empowered service. At the same time, "Classical Pentecostals" would further believe that speaking in tongues is the "accompanying sign of this baptism."[8]

Wesley concluded that four of the five major house church networks he studied fell into the Pentecostal/Charismatic category.[9]

---

[8]Wesley, *The Church in China*, 37.

[9]Ibid., 60.

Their commonalities in belief and practice were expressed in an unprecedented formal Statement of Faith adopted by four house church networks in November 1998, "On the Holy Spirit:"

> The Holy Spirit bestows upon believers all kinds of power and witnesses the powerful deeds of God with signs and wonders. . . . In Christ, God grants a diversity of gifts of the Holy Spirit to the church to manifest the glory of Christ. With faith and desire, Christians can experience the pouring down of the Holy Spirit on them and be filled with the Holy Spirit. We deny any doctrine that teaches the cessation of signs and wonders or the termination of the gifts of the Holy Spirit after the age of the apostles."[10]

In another study on Chinese Christianity, Chambon argues that healing rituals and engaged (dynamic and emotional) worship characterize Pentecostalism in China.[11] He points out that the popular reception of Pentecostal-type spirituality and worship is attributed to three factors: first, the propensity and ability of Chinese popular religion to incorporate elements of other religions; second, the enduring interest of Chinese religion in healing and good health; and third, the increasing openness of the Chinese society to Christianity.[12] However, according to Chambon, the same appeal has backfired, as the similarities in Pentecostal beliefs and practices to the traditional Chinese religions are a critical reason why some churches have been reluctant to embrace Pentecostalism. The visible effect of such spirituality is the growth of churches and dynamic and lively worship. Pentecostal members tend to be zealous and eager evangelists, often with testimonies of miracles and healing.

---

[10]China for Jesus, "Statement Faith of Chinese House Churches," 1998, http://www.chinaforjesus.com/StatementOfFaith.htm (accessed April 9, 2018).

[11]Michel Chambon, "Are Chinese Christians Pentecostal? A Catholic Reading of Pentecostal Influence on Chinese Christians," in *Global Chinese Pentecostal and Charismatic Christianity*, ed. Fenggang Yang, Joy K. C. Tong, and Allan H. Anderson (Leiden: E. J. Brill, 2017), 181.

[12]Chambon, "Are Chinese Christians Pentecostal?" 183.

At the other end of the continuum are churches that maintain that the primary work of the Holy Spirit is in the area of enlightenment. The Holy Spirit convicts people of their sinfulness, leads people to repentance, and enables them to experience redemption. For such believers, the focus of the Spirit's role, drawn primarily from Johannine and Pauline pneumatology, is providing believers with "staying power" or perseverance. In this camp, the supernatural manifestation of the Spirit is either ignored or even theologically denied. This partly explains the traditional neglect of the Holy Spirit among many theologians and church traditions. Although the Reformers' description of the Third Person as the "shy" member of the Trinity refers to his ministry pointing to the Father and the Son, limiting the Spirit's work to a behind-the-scenes, "quiet realm" is also a historical reality. Perhaps the most avid "cessationism" (of the supernatural gifts of the Holy Spirit today) may be the extreme dispensational stance, limiting the gifts to the apostolic era. According to this position, Scripture has replaced the supernatural manifestations that were the norm during the apostolic dispensation. Some are even hostile to those who advocate the supernatural gifts of the Holy Spirit being in operation today.

However, not all churches that are not open to the immediate and supernatural work of the Holy Spirit adhere to a strict cessationist theology. The long theological development in the West based on a rationalistic and cerebral approach has resulted in a "demythologized" attitude, downplaying, or even denying, the historicity of the records of supernatural events, especially in the Gospels and Acts. The "quiet" work of the Holy Spirit, however, is no less vital in the life of believers. In this sense, "shy" may not be the best expression for today's mind. The Spirit indeed points us to Christ and fills us with bold faith to proclaim him.[13]

The point is, however, that the "supernatural" camp also recognizes the illuminating and sustaining presence of the Holy

[13]Frederick Dale Bruner and William Horden, *The Holy Spirit: Shy Member of the Trinity* (Eugene, OR: Wipf & Stock, 2001).

Spirit, although they tend to give more weight to demonstrable and dramatic experiences over the "mundane" work of the Spirit.

Tomorrow's Pneumatology in Asia

Having briefly surveyed the Asian landscape of pneumatology in belief and practice, our attention can now be directed to future theological possibilities. The diversity found in Asian Christianity is increasing as new forms of the church are rising. Moreover, growing theological maturity is an encouraging sign as more theologians reassess the received forms of theologies and their suitability for Asian socio-cultural contexts. In Chinese Christianity, rapid social change has contributed to this complexity in recent decades. The diverse beliefs in the person and work of the Holy Spirit in this region are likely, at least in part, the result of the relative underdevelopment of pneumatology in church history and the rich and pervasive notion of the spirits in most Asian religions. The church in Asia is now on something of a quest to find paths forward in pneumatology that are first, faithful to the Scriptures; second, informed by Christian tradition (notwithstanding the unwarranted silence in some Western theological traditions); and third, capable of speaking to key cultural religions as well as social realities in Asia.

With these challenges in mind, I will list several areas of pneumatology and priorities that may facilitate the Asian church's theological exploration, both in thinking and action. This theological exploration cannot be purely intellectual. It must be informed and inspired by pastoral and missional realities in Asia, along with the historical development of the doctrine. Before turning to specific regional topics and their accompanying challenges, I will begin with a global task to which Asian theological communities are called to contribute.

Pneumatology "Under Construction"

In a sense, pneumatology is still in the making. When reading the ancient creeds, it is immediately apparent that Christology received the primary attention of the early church. The description of the person and work of the Son in the Nicene Creed (325 CE), for example, was proportionately elaborate. In contrast, the person of the Holy Spirit received only a mention: "And [we believe] in the Holy Spirit." The Nicene-Constantinopolitan Creed (381 CE) added the first descriptive elaboration: "And [we believe] in the Holy Ghost, the Lord and Giver of life, who proceeds from the Father, who with the Father and the Son together is worshipped and glorified, who spoke by prophets." At the same time, Christology was further expanded in the same creed. When Christology was fully explored, the church's attention was finally directed to pneumatology. This expansion affirmed the Holy Spirit as the "Giver of life" and as the third person of the Trinity, and the life-giving work of the Spirit is amply attested to in the Old Testament.

The logical step for the next development would have been the Holy Spirit's dynamic presence and empowering work found in the New Testament canon. However, the church was immediately caught up in the heated debate about the relational nature of the Holy Spirit in the Trinity. This debate divided the church into two theological factions, starting in the sixth century: the Eastern Church upholding the position that the Holy Spirit proceeded only from the Father, and the Western Church insisting on the double proceeding of the Holy Spirit from both the Father and the Son (a position known as the *filioque*, the Latin term meaning "and the Son").

This division marked the end of the era of genuinely ecumenical (worldwide) theological affirmation and pneumatology and, in the end, became the casualty of a divided church. The implications of this "underdeveloped" and divided nature of pneumatology may explain much of the fragmented beliefs that different church traditions hold today. The Asian church, therefore, is called to join in the global theological effort to explore pneumatology continually. This theological participation is a rare opportunity to develop a global and ecumenical pneumatology in the post-

Christendom setting. Moreover, the development of regional (or even local) pneumatologies should have a direct bearing on global concerns.

The Spirit in Creation, Culture, and Religions

The continuity and discontinuity between the Holy Spirit and spirits in traditional religions and beliefs is at the core of the debate around the question: "Does the Holy Spirit work in other religions?" Koo Dong Yun, along with other theologians, has pointed out the root of this debate in the identity of the Holy Spirit as the Spirit of God vs. the Spirit of Christ. In this view, the Spirit of God, as the creator and sustainer of life, is universally present in all his creation, even if that creation is corrupted and marred due to human fallenness. The Spirit of Christ, by contrast, is the redemptive Spirit present in the church, the body of Christ.[14] According to this argument, the Orthodox Church upholds the single proceeding of the Holy Spirit from the Father. Thus, it is sensitive to the presence of the Holy Spirit in nature, focusing on God's presence through the Spirit in creation and creation care. There is a clear division when it comes to the question of the Spirit's presence and work in other religions. Mainline Protestantism, often represented in the WCC, recently produced a new mission statement called "Together Towards Life." It acknowledges the Spirit's work in the religions, pointing to the Truth: "We believe that the Spirit of Life brings joy and fullness of life. God's Spirit, therefore, can be found in all cultures that affirm life. The Holy Spirit works in mysterious ways, and we do not fully understand the working of the Spirit in other faith traditions."[15]

In contrast, the prevailing Evangelical and Pentecostal attitude toward the religions stems from their narrow view of the extent of the Spirit's presence, often restricting his work to the believer's life.

---

[14]Koo Dong Yun, *The Holy Spirit and* Ch'i (Qi): *A Chiological Approach to Pneumatology* (Eugene, OR: Pickwick, 2012), 131.

[15]WCC, *Together Towards Life: New Affirmation on Mission and Evangelism* (Geneva: WCC, 2013), 34 no. 93.

Even the universal outpouring of the Spirit promised in Joel (2:28) is considered universal only upon believers. Of course, it is biblical to say the Holy Spirit is active outside of the church, at least insofar as he convicts sinners, causing them to become open to the saving work of Christ.

In Asia, the church must wrestle with traditional theological divisions within its confines and contextually rooted concerns. Prevailing animistic beliefs have deeply penetrated major religions in Asia, including the presence of spirits in animate and inanimate objects.

Considering this reality, how should Christians theologically differentiate between God's Spirit as the Creator and the animistic understanding of spirits' ubiquitous presence? An extreme form of Christian theology denies or ignores the immanent presence and work of the S/spirits altogether, limiting the Spirit's work to illumination and guidance among God's people. The other extreme, represented by some Pentecostals, is the belief in the widespread presence and work of the Spirit, angels, and evil spirits today. The similarities between the Pentecostal and tribal (that is, animistic) worldviews can pose a significant challenge of confusion and open up opportunities. Julie Ma, studying a tribal group in the northern Philippines, argues that the similarities in Pentecostal and tribal worldviews provide a ready audience for Pentecostal evangelism. At the same time, she contends that the supernatural manifestation of God's power in healing and miracles can prevent any confusion between the Holy Spirit and the spirits.[16]

Despite these hopeful signs, Christian theology of the S/spirits remains somewhat splintered. This challenge calls on the Asian church to overcome its historically bifurcated approach to the issue. Each church and theological tradition need to approach the claims of other traditions with openness, humility, and genuine inquiry. Such theological exchanges and conversations lead to mutual understanding, respect, and appreciation. They also help us to recognize the distinctiveness as well as the limitations of our traditions. A global cross-denominational dialogue, therefore, has

---

[16]Julie Ma, *When the Spirit Meets the Spirits*, 222-25.

a distinct role to play.[17] At the same time, a careful examination of the role of the Holy Spirit in creation, including diverse cultures (which bear the marks of God's common grace in spite of their corruption), is called for. An expanded pneumatology may enable Christians to engage their faith more actively with cultural and social issues, including creation care. A recent statement arising from a dialogue between Reformed and Pentecostal churches is quite balanced:

> We agree that the Holy Spirit is present and active . . . in human history and in various cultures. The work of the Spirit is broader than we think. Nevertheless, we believe that every culture . . . is in need of being reshaped by the Holy Spirit in accordance with the revelation in Jesus Christ as witnessed in Scripture.[18]

The Spirit and Life

The life-giving, sustaining, and restoring work of the Holy Spirit has been prominently featured from the ancient creeds to more recent days. As we have already noted, the Nicene-Constantinople Creed (381 CE) describes the Holy Spirit as "the Lord and Giver of life." Similarly, the third major document of the Lausanne Movement, the "Cape Town Commitment" (2010), affirms Christian work toward the flourishing of life as an integral part of Evangelical mission.[19] The recent publication

---

[17]For example, a recent Reformed-Pentecostal dialogue extensively dealt with the pneumatological foci of each tradition. See Statements 68-73 in "Word and Spirit, Church and World: The Final Report of the International Dialogue between Representatives of the World Alliance of Reformed Churches and Some Classical Pentecostal Churches and Leaders 1996-2000," *AJPS* 4, no. 1 (2001): 41-72.

[18]"Word and Spirit, Church and World," 49.

[19]Lausanne Movement, "The Cape Town Commitment," https//www.lausanne.org/content/ctc/ctcommitment/ (accessed September 23, 2018). The fifth section of the Confession of Faith is on the Holy Spirit, and its first paragraph (A) reads, "In the Old Testament we see the Spirit of God active in creation, in works of liberation and justice."

of the mission document of the WCC, *Together Towards Life*, is highly pneumatological. As the title suggests, it emphasizes that the work of the Holy Spirit in allowing life to flourish is at the core of Christian mission.

It is important not to dismiss the document as a "liberal" understanding of mission. This pneumatological feature is prominent in the Scriptures. Amid human suffering, for example, the full restoration of God's people would be ushered in by the coming of the Spirit (Isa 32:15). And the effect is the holistic and comprehensive flourishing of individual and communal life until the perfect state of *shalom* is achieved. This life-giving work of the Holy Spirit is emphasized in the New Testament through regeneration (e.g., John 3:5). Paul climaxes his description of the Spirit's life-giving work with the glorious resurrection of Jesus and our corrupt bodies which are subject to death (Rom 8:11). Evangelicals and Pentecostals were brought into the process of this document, and their voices have exerted substantial influence. Regardless of theological or ecclesial tradition, this is an excellent starting point for pneumatology.

This consensus on the Holy Spirit's work in life is expressed in various theological and missional emphases. For Pentecostals, the priority in mission has historically been evangelism. Yet their commitment to the well-being of life becomes evident upon further observation. Although frequently motivated by their evangelistic goal, they nonetheless responded quickly to human suffering.[20] The Orthodox focus has historically been on meditative spirituality and care for creation as the practical expressions of its pneumatology, which contends that "the Spirit is present everywhere and fills everything."[21] Various types of liberation theology anchor their

---

[20]See Ivan Satyavrata, *Pentecostals and the Poor: Reflections from the Indian Context* (Baguio, Philippines: APTS Press, 2017). Perhaps the best field-based study is Donald Miller and Tetsunao Yamamori, *Global Pentecostalism: The New Face of Christian Social Engagement* (Berkeley: University of California Press, 2007).

[21]Georges Khodr, "Christianity in the Pluralist World: The Economy of the Holy Spirit," in *Orthodox Perspectives on Mission*, ed. Petros Vassiliadis, *Regnum Edinburgh Centenary Series 17* (Oxford: Regnum, 2013), 120.

theological roots in the life-flourishing work of the Holy Spirit. The struggle for social justice for the oppressed has had a diversity of manifestations, including the Minjung movement among Korean Protestants and armed resistance by select Catholic clergy against the Marcos dictatorship in the Philippines. Evangelicals and Pentecostals, meanwhile, have generally tended to provide care for the needy but have stopped short of seeking complete social justice or structural changes.

Regardless of their response, churches often do not see their reaction to issues such as poverty and suffering from a pneumatological perspective. In truth, whenever Asian churches seek to mitigate the effects of poverty, assist the marginalized, and offer comfort for the suffering, the Holy Spirit's life-giving and life-flourishing work is introduced. For this reason, careful pneumatological exploration is a theological and missional priority.

Evangelization

Asia is the least evangelized continent in the world. Less than one in ten of the vast population of Asia is Christian, while the world average is around one-third (or 33.3 percent).[22] For global Christianity to continue its growth trend, the Asian church's engagement in evangelism is crucial. Pneumatology is at the center of any theological study about taking the call to witness the saving grace of Christ in Asia. There are at least two theological and two practical bases for the central role of the Holy Spirit in Christian witness.

The first theological basis is the nature of the Holy Spirit's work: to lead the world to the redemptive work of Christ. This includes convicting the world of its sin (John 16:8), birthing and forming

---

[22]The Pacific Research Center's Forum on Religion and Public Life indicates that only 7.0 percent of Asia Pacific were Christians in 2011. See The Pew Forum, "Global Christianity: A Report on the Size and Distribution of the World's Christian Population," December 19, 2011, http:/www.pewforum.org/2011/12/19/global-christianity-exec/.

the church (Acts 2:1-41), and sending God's people as witnesses (Matt 28:19-20). The growth of Christianity, therefore, is the work of the Holy Spirit. Asia, along with other parts of the world, is called to develop a theological and missiological understanding of the Holy Spirit.

The second theological basis is the Spirit's work of empowering believers to be effective witnesses (e.g., Acts 1:8). This dimension of pneumatology is the rediscovery of the modern Pentecostal movement. Beyond the Spirit's regenerative ministry, he equips, enables, and empowers believers. This missional gift assumes the divine calling and commissioning to spread the good news of Christ's redemption to the ends of the earth. Empowering results not only in the giving of various gifts, including the supernatural manifestation of God's power[23]—but also in the resolute commitment to fulfill God's call in the face of adversity (e.g., Isa 42:1-4; Acts 4:29-31). In addition to healing and miracles, the book of Acts records the empowering work of the Spirit in the circumstances of imprisonment, persecution, shipwreck, mobs, and trials. Stephen is second only to Paul in having the most references to the presence and work of the Holy Spirit in his life (Acts 6:5; 7:55).

As a practical basis for the central role of the Spirit in witness, revivals provide primary evidence. From the early church to present times, revivals have been the space in which the fresh work of the Holy Spirit is experienced. This results in repentance, radical encounters with God's presence, the experience of God's grace (especially through the supernatural work of the Spirit), renewed zeal for evangelism, and a resultant surge in the missionary spirit. For example, in East Malaysia in the 1970s, the Barrio Revival began among the youth, who quickly organized evangelistic teams to travel to nearby villages. As a result, the revival, along with stories of healing and miracles, quickly spread throughout

---

[23]Claudia Währisch-Oblau, a German Evangelical Lutheran, observes the validity of these in evangelism in her "Power Evangelism in a Protestant Context? Reflections after a Workshop in Samosir/Indonesia," *International Review of Mission* 107, no. 1 (June 2018): 142-158.

Borneo Island and beyond. This revival added thousands to local churches and gave birth to the vibrant indigenous church, Sidang Injil Borneo, the largest Protestant denomination in the country.[24]

A second practical basis for the Holy Spirit's centrality in evangelism is the supernatural work of the Spirit. The effect of supernatural healing or miracles in drawing people to the message of God's Kingdom is well attested in Jesus' ministry (in the Gospels) and the early church (in Acts). A large portion of Christian conversions in the house churches in China were motivated by experience or testimonies of healing (of themselves or a known person).[25] Miracles serve as a powerful draw for people to accept the Christian message. Indeed, Christianity, which claims to serve the supreme deity, is expected to offer a greater possibility of healing than other religions. The phenomenal growth of David Yonggi Cho's Yoido Full Gospel Church is attributed to experiences of divine healing and the spread of such stories.[26] For the church to fulfill the urgent task of evangelizing Asia, it is essential for it to recognize the role of the Holy Spirit in empowering believers and preparing the minds of unbelievers.

Issues Surrounding Supernatural and Spiritual Warfare

The deep cognition of the spirit world in Asia has been almost ignored by cerebral Western (Evangelical) Christianity as superstition or simple heathenism. Scholars argue that this dissonance has resulted in so-called split-level Christianity: many Christians seek ultimate spiritual answers to sin and eternal life

---

[24] Jin Huat Tan, *Planting an Indigenous Church: The Case of the Borneo Evangelical Mission* (Oxford: Regnum, 2011). Also, see the recent study on the revival by Michelle Chan and Hwa Yung, *Revival in Ba'kelalan: Discerning God's Purposes for Today* (Petaling Jaya, Malaysia: Canaan Land, 2023).

[25] Währisch-Oblau, "Church Growth in Anhui." Also, Fielder, "The Growth of the Protestant Church in Rural China," 49.

[26] Myung Soo Park, "Korean Pentecostal Spirituality as Manifested in the Testimonies of Members of Yoido Full Gospel Church," in *David Yonggi Cho: A Close Look at His Theology and Ministry*, ed. Wonsuk Ma, Hyeon-sung Bae, and William W. Menzies (Baguio, Philippines: APTS Press, 2004), 43-67.

from Christianity while seeking answers to immediate daily matters, such as sickness, misfortune, childbearing, and business success, from the traditional religions.[27]

Theologians and Christian workers from the Majority World first voiced the need for thorough theological work on the spirit world.[28] Even before the introduction of Pentecostalism, revivals in Africa, Asia, and Latin America included encounters with the spirit world and manifestations of power. The spread of Charismatic Christianity has brought together these two concerns in Christian theology and practice. Its theology has opened discussions on prayer practices for healing and exorcism. Scholars contend that this partly explains the success of Pentecostalism in many tribal communities in Asia.[29]

Every religion in Asia features supernatural manifestations. Islam regards dreams and visions as a prominent means of supernatural revelation. Its Sufi branches advocate more supernatural experiences, such as miracles and healing. Encountering evil power is an integral and practical part of religious life in Asia. Therefore, Asian Christianity has a unique opportunity, along with its African and Latin American counterparts, to develop a robust theology and practice of the supernatural work of the Holy Spirit. They already have parallels to Scripture in their theology and ministry. In the process, the power of the Holy Spirit over evil spirits is a primary theological and pastoral building block. Openness to the Holy Spirit in encounters with evil powers is widespread among Christians across denominational boundaries.

At the same time, Asian Christians are aware that this is tricky ground, where Christian theology and popular religiosity can easily overlap. The teachings of the Third Wave movement, a Charismatic expression of Evangelical Christianity from the

---

[27]Jaime Bulatao, *Split-Level Christianity: Christian Renewal of Filipino Values* (Manila: Ateneo de Manila University, 1966).

[28]For example, a consultation was organized by the Lausanne Movement on the issue: Scott Moreau, ed., *Deliver Us from Evil: An Uneasy Frontier in Christian Mission* (Monrovia, CA: World Vision International, 2002).

[29]See Julie Ma, *When the Spirit Meets the Spirits*.

1980s, influenced specific sectors of the Christian population in Asia. On the one hand, they helped Christians understand the reality of the spirit world and how to confront evil (spiritual) powers. Popular authors of the movement, such as Charles Kraft and C. Peter Wagner, spread awareness of the spiritual world and its reality through their writings.

On the other hand, some Third Wave teachings straddle the border between biblical and traditional Asian beliefs. Consider, for example, the idea of territorial spirits, which argues that each geographic area has a spirit in charge of it and that any Christian work should be preceded by the "binding of the strong man of the territory." The similarity between this view and the Asian animistic belief that the spirits animate objects and territories explains why it gained such an enthusiastic reception among some Christian sectors. Still, thin biblical support for this argument has posed a missiological and pastoral challenge. Identifying the "strong man" and its "stronghold(s)" led to the concept of spiritual mapping, which later led to the development of the practice of prayer walks and commanding prayers.[30]

Similarly, teaching on inter-generational curses and the related practice of inner healing has fascinated some Christians but has been the cause for serious doubt in many churches. Reports of prayer meetings to "cancel" the curse originating in an ancestor have at times been sensationalized in the Asian church. The so-called inner healing practice contains several controversial components, including the notion of an inner child, which has no biblical support whatsoever.[31]

Also, an age-old question has resurfaced in the process: "Can a believer be demon-possessed or demon-influenced?"[32] This short

---

[30]See Neil T. Anderson, *Victory over the Darkness: Realize the Power of Your Identity in Christ*, 2nd ed. (Bloomington: Bethany House, 2000).

[31]For a Pentecostal assessment of Third Wave teaching, see Wonsuk Ma, "A 'First Wave's Look at the Third Wave:' A Pentecostal Reflection on Charles Kraft's Power Encounter Terminology," *Pneuma* 19 (1997): 189-206.

[32]Helpful biblical studies on this question can be found in William K. Kay and Robin Parry, ed., *Exorcism and Deliverance: Multi-Disciplinary Studies* (Milton Keynes: Paternoster, 2011).

list of controversial and yet important theological and pastoral topics illustrates the urgent need for the continuing development of pneumatology and related subjects (such as angelology and demonology) within Asian contexts.[33]

A Way Forward

The above-discussed five themes serve only as a representation of the plethora of pneumatological issues that the Asian church faces in its missional engagements. The Evangelical church in Asia faces a critical choice: to stay away or engage. Although it is easy to make a quick vote for engagement, it will take much courage, for example, for persecuted believers to shed the defensive or survival approach to Christian life. In many parts of Asia, the contextual forces are overwhelming, and Christian (or theological) resources are inadequate. Indeed, a Western-imported theology would ultimately prove to be handicapped in properly responding to the Asian contextual issues. This challenging circumstance calls for a concerted effort to collaborate in theological construction.

The complexities of theology (specifically in pneumatology), contemporary issues, and abundant theological opportunities should compel Asian Evangelicals to explore several levels of collaboration. The first level of working together is across the church and theological traditions. Asian Evangelicals have long been served by the Asia Theological Association through its publications, including its two journals: *Journal of Asian Mission* and *Journal of Asian Evangelical Theology*. Its monographs and the Asia Bible Commentary Series can potentially engage with Asian pneumatological issues creatively.[34] In addition, select Evangelical institutions have been active in theological construction within the Asian context.[35]

---

[33]See Moreau, *Deliver Us from Evil*.

[34]See Asia Theological Association, "ATA Publications," http://www.ataasia.com/atapublications/ (accessed January 8, 2025).

[35]Asian Theological Seminary (Manila, Philippines) has explored contemporary issues in Asia in its annual theological forum, including one

The older mainline churches in Asia likewise operate various networks and publishing arms and have a longer history of cultural and social engagement. Journals such as the *Asian Journal of Theology* have extensively published reflections on such engagements.

Many topics, such as ancestor worship and spiritual realities, are common to Asian churches regardless of theological leanings. The spread of Pentecostal-like experiences across denominational divides demonstrates the supra-denominational character of such experiences.[36] Again, the widespread beliefs in and practices of healing among Chinese Christians are more evidence of the universal nature of the Spirit's operation.[37] For these reasons, working with other theological traditions like mainline churches may be equally important. There is much for Evangelicals to gain through such collaborations.

The second level of working together is inter-regional, especially the South-to-South, collaboration. There are important

---

particularly relevant to our discussion, focused on "Principalities and Powers" (see "ATS Theological Forum Books," https://www.ats.ph/ats-theological-forum-books/. APTS (Baguio, Philippines), a Pentecostal institution, has been at the forefront of Pentecostal theological publications through *AJPS* and monographs published by its APTS Press.

[36]It is notable that the relationship between Pentecostal theology and mainline trends is often the subject of dispute. For example, a Korean theologian from a liberation-theology-leaning Presbyterian church, Boo-Woong Yoo, has contended that *Minjung* theology, a Korean version of liberation theology, is essentially equivalent to Korean Pentecostal theology in *Korean Pentecostalism: Its History and Theology* (Frankfurt: Peter Lang, 1988). This equation was uncritically presented and even expanded by several key Western theologians, such as Walter Hollenweger. An otherwise authoritative voice about global Pentecostalism, Hollenweger wrongly pegs *Minjung* theology as the core of Korean Pentecostalism while at the same time giving hardly any attention to David Yonggi Cho, the founder and pastor of the most influential Pentecostal church in Korea. See Hollenweger, *Pentecostalism,* 99–105.

[37]See Yi Liu, "The 'Galilee of China:' Pentecostals without Pentecostalism" and Rachel Xiaohong Zhu, "The Catholic Charismatic Renewal in Mainland China," in *Global Chinese Pentecostal and Charismatic Christianity,* ed. Fenggang Yang, Joy K. C. Tong, and Allan H. Anderson (Leiden: E. J. Brill, 2017), 200-215 and 264-285, respectively.

reasons why such cooperation should be actively pursued. First, the southern continents, particularly Asia and Africa, share similar worldviews. They are closer to the Hebrew and Jewish worldviews than to the Western worldview shaped by Enlightenment rationalism. In this worldview, demythologization is not a rule when reading the Bible. Second, many common theological issues (from poverty to healing to ancestor veneration), born of their socio-cultural and religious contexts, are commonly shared. Common interests can bring diverse groups to the same theological ground.

Christianity is no longer a "Western or northern" religion. Close to two-thirds of the world's Christians now live in the South, while the churches in the North are constantly declining. The churches in the South are called to rise and take leadership in theology-making today. Inter-regional collaborations will bring together theological reflection undertaken in their unique contexts for mutual learning and enrichment. A steady stream of theological work from Africa, Asia, and Latin America should interact robustly with the strong Western theological traditions. Pneumatology would particularly benefit from such a global theological enterprise because its status as a doctrine is still "under construction." The Asian church is called to bring its experiences and reflections to contribute to and benefit from this global undertaking. After all, the Holy Spirit gives life to God's creation and the church of Christ, including the church in Asia!

CHAPTER 4

Two Tales of Emerging Ecclesiology in Asia[1]

The Christian presence on this continent is ancient. The church was founded in Asia. Yet, today, Christianity remains a foreign religion in many parts of Asia. This directly affects how Christians, as well as society, understand the community of followers of Christ that is called the "church," especially its nature and function.

Historic churches have shown encouraging efforts in reflecting on the engagement between the Christian gospel and socio-cultural contexts. The Roman Catholic Church has done impressive theological work, especially after Vatican II. The Federation of Asian Bishops' Conferences has been shaping a new participatory model of the church for decades, particularly paying close attention to a dialogue between the church hierarchy and women.[2] Equally active is the publication program of the Christian Conference of Asia (CCA), the regional arm of the WCC. Again, it

---

[1]First published in *The Church from Every Tribe and Tongue: Ecclesiology in the Majority World*, Majority World Theology Series, Volume 5 (Carlisle, UK: Langham Literature, 2018), used by permission.

[2]An extensive study is found in Thao Nguyen, "A New Way of Being Church for Mission: Asian Catholic Bishops and Asian Catholic Women in Dialogue: A Study of the Documents of the Federation of Asian Bishops' Conference (FABC)" (Ph.D. diss., Graduate Theological Union, Berkeley, 2013). For other Catholic resources, see Federation of Asian Bishops' Conferences, www.fabc.org/pub_p8.html/.

has consciously engaged with Asian contexts and issues.[3] Mainline Protestant churches seem to have been paying attention to this theologizing process. With their theological identities relatively well established, the natural next step will be to become relevant in the Asian setting. One CCA publication, although dated, is explicitly devoted to the diverse nature of the church and its life in several Asian countries, primarily in response to each church's historical, cultural, and social context.[4]

When it comes to the Evangelical and "Free Churches," including Pentecostal ones, studies of the nature and function of the church are relatively rare, especially ones that take Asian contexts into account. Only recently, some efforts began to appear among Evangelicals.[5] Theological reflection is even scarcer for indigenous churches with little or no affiliation with Western churches. Of course, these churches will have different theologizing processes from historic ones, which received their theology from Western mother churches. Unlike historic churches, free churches tend to be more autonomous, without a mother church or its accompanying well-developed theology. Moreover, even Asian churches with Western mother churches may exercise relative autonomy in their ecclesial structure and theology.

---

[3]CCA, "CCA Publications," www.cca.org.hk/home/publications (accessed October 10, 2016). Although dated, a fine example of a ten-year process of developing Asian theology with Asian resources is John C. England and Archie C. C. Lee, *Doing Theology with Asian Resources: Ten Years in the Formation of Living Theology in Asia* (Auckland: Programme for Theology and Cultures in Asia, 1993).

[4]Kwok Nai Wang, *The Local Church* (Hong Kong: CCA, 2005).

[5]In the Philippines, Asian Theological Seminary has held a successful annual theological conference dealing with theological and missional themes. Its proceedings have been published, serving as valuable resources: see "ATS Theological Forum Books," Asian Theological Seminary, http://www.ats.ph/ats-theological-forum-books/. Its first publication was E. Acoba, "A Locus for Doing Theology: Theological Stories at the Front Line of Grassroots Missions Engagement," *Doing Theology in the Philippines,* ed. John Suk (Mandaluyong City, Philippines: OMF, 2005), 24-36.

Two Case Studies

This chapter attempts to address the immense need in the new churches in Asia through two case studies. Two church groups in East Asia were selected to trace the development of their ecclesiologies. The first is a house church network in China called the Word of Life Church in Henan Province, a post-Cultural Revolution-era indigenous house church. The second is Yoido Full Gospel Church in Seoul, Korea, a Pentecostal congregation with a network of sister and daughter churches. Both are representative of the "newer" churches in Asia.

These two cases were chosen for several reasons. Both are highly influential churches, and both claim a large membership. The Word of Life Church was once estimated to have three million followers throughout China, while Yoido Church and its network formed the world's single largest congregation, with 750,000 members. The rise and growth of the Word of Life Church provide a model for and influence on house church movements in China. Its subsequent decline also reveals the structural vulnerability of rural house church networks, which rely heavily on their leader-founders.

Yoido Church and its founder, David Yonggi Cho, established a unique Korean interpretation of Pentecostal theology and spirituality. Its "full gospel" theology has had a far-reaching impact on Korean Christianity and beyond. Most importantly, however, my two choices were motivated by their active engagement with their contexts, their reading of the Scriptures, their adaptation or modification of any "received" theology (especially in the case of the full gospel theology), and the processes of their theology-shaping. This creativity has resulted in some controversies, yet their theologizing processes are noteworthy.

Approaching the Subjects

My focus is on the shaping of local theologies, preferably those perceived among members of the churches. How has each community been shaped, and how are its functions and operations understood? On the one hand, a community negotiates, interacts with, and sometimes reacts to its context. On the other hand, it reads and interprets the Bible, drawing from Christian traditions. This theology, often unarticulated, is lived out in church and daily life.

As I began observing these two churches, I realized that traditional theological categories would not be adequate for analyzing the living process of theologizing. This is primarily because the received theology and its categories are shaped and sustained in a Western Christendom setting. In such a religious context, the Western church exists predominantly to provide pastoral care to the parishioners. The "world" is perceived to be a Christian empire, to some degree. In contrast, the Asian church is constantly engaged with the world, which is sometimes hostile to Christianity. Therefore, the church's place and function are heavily shaped by its context and experience.

Several creative inquiries on contemporary ecclesiology are immensely helpful. The first is by Veli-Matti Kärkkäinen. Well-exposed to Asian realities through his missionary work, he characterizes each of the six major ecclesiological traditions with their theological foci. His exploration of several new and emerging churches and their ecclesiologies (for example, African Independent Churches) is particularly enlightening.[6] This chapter focuses on the "Free Church" category in Kärkkäinen's categories.[7]

The ecclesiological categories Gerald Bray has proposed through his historical study are equally refreshing. In his survey of the New Testament church and subsequent persecuted and imperial churches, Bray raises the question of what the church's fundamental tenets might be, in light of diverse traditions and forms.[8] If this question were posed to believers in the Global

---

[6]Veli-Matti Kärkkäinen, *An Introduction to Ecclesiology: Ecumenical, Historical and Global Perspectives* (Downers Grove: IVP Academic, 2002), 194-201.

[7]Ibid., 59-67.

[8]Gerald Bray, *The Church: A Theological and Historical Account* (Grand

South, whose population corresponds to two-thirds of the world's Christians, the responses would be challengingly different than answers from believers in the Global North.

Simon Chan's book on grassroots theology in Asia has a strong appeal in constructing ecclesiologies.[9] It is useful in the case of the Word of Life Church due to the scarcity of any "magisterial" theology. As Chan proposes, this study will assess each church in two categories: first, the stories of its members, often expressed in the church's testimonies, sermons, programs, and leaders; and second, ancient theological traditions, specifically the Nicene-Constantinopolitan Creed.

Several foci are worth particular attention: the theological formation of the founding leader of each church, the self-understanding of the nature of the church, and the perception of the mission of the church. Relying on empirical evidence is pertinent in observing the Word of Life Church, as I have had a few encounters with founder Peter Xu. For the Yoido Church, I have maintained a reasonable degree of contact with both the clergy and the laity.[10]

Peter Xu and the Word of Life Church

Peter Yongze Xu (1940-)

David Aikman categorizes Xu as one of the three "uncles" who served as the founders of three large house church networks in the post-Cultural Revolution era.[11] These founders were responsible for the miraculous resurrection of Chinese Christianity after the Communist takeover of this vast nation. Xu is also linked to today's Chinese Christianity through the previous or "Patriarch" generation. He grew up in a Christian family and was prayed

Rapids: Baker Academic, 2016), viii.

[9]Simon Chan, *Grassroots Asian Theology: Thinking the Faith from the Ground Up* (Downers Grove: InterVarsity, 2014).

[10]More published materials are also available for this case.

[11]Aikman, *Jesus in Beijing*, 73-74.

over by his Christian grandfather. It is recorded that he saw visions at the age of five.[12] His first house arrest occurred in 1967. During the Cultural Revolution, he was targeted for his "counter-revolutionary" offenses. In 1978, he emerged as a significant house church leader. His evangelistic teams spread beyond Henan Province to other parts of China. After his imprisonment in 1982, state persecution began. Many full-time evangelists were sent out for evangelism and church planting, and more than three thousand churches were established by 1988.

Xu was concerned about the widespread emphasis on healing and miracles among many house church networks. Perhaps in reaction to this, his ministry stressed genuine regeneration and discipleship. With increasing numbers of house churches and leaders joining Xu, the "Born-Again Movement" began and grew to become perhaps the country's most controversial house church network. The emphasis on a genuine experience of regeneration led this network to develop a heavy focus on evangelism.

Xu spent over two decades of ministry as a fugitive, hiding among the "floating population" during this turbulent time. He actively ministered to them as he kept discovering hidden believers, both active and inactive. It is not unreasonable to suppose that his theology and ministry practices were affected by this experience and shaped by his reflection. The ever-mobile nature of his life must have been particularly significant in understanding the nature and purpose of the church (that is, ecclesiology) within his particular historical and social setting. Two notable aspects of his ecclesiology are: first, how the nature of the church is understood; and second, the church's mission. These are "assumed" as their theology is practiced, especially without any articulate theology.

The Nature of the Church

First, the house churches often gathered secretly for worship, Bible study, prayer, and fellowship, the markers of the church. There was no visible building or an established organizational

[12]Ibid., 87.

structure. To a certain extent, the church was and is identified primarily as a community of believers, regardless of location. The first three items of their seven-point theology concern the purity of the church through genuine conversion. They are: first, salvation through the cross; second, the way of the cross; and third, discerning the adulteress (i.e., the Three-Self Patriotic Movement or TSPM).[13]

An important characteristic of the Word of Life Church, as with most other unregistered churches, has been shaped by three contextual realities. The first is that no identifiable Western "mother" church dictated the shape of the church. The second is the newness of its existence without a historical link, and the third is a social context that prohibits any open gathering of people for religious activities unless registered. In addition to these contextual factors, it is notable that reading the Book of Acts encouraged and reinforced this understanding of the church.

Second, its socio-political context kept this unregistered church illegal. Xu developed his profound ministry consciousness through his (Christian) reading during his vocational school years. Then, the authorities seriously questioned his Christian faith "for a nonstop period of forty days," . . . "forcing him to remain standing for seventeen hours."[14] Subsequently, during the Cultural Revolution, he was in self-exile to hide from the authorities and was mostly separated from his family. Throughout his life, he experienced several imprisonments and house arrests. Details of how he was treated are not readily available, but I have seen such a persecuted life. In light of all this, it is not surprising to find in the seven-point theology of the church a "theology of the cross." The second point reads: "Take the way of the cross to persevere in faith during suffering." Xin interprets such a period as a theologically formative process for becoming a "missionary."[15]

---

[13]Xin, *Inside China's House Church Network*, 80-81.

[14]Aikman, *Jesus in Beijing*, 87.

[15]For all seven points, see Xin, *Inside China's House Church Network*, 89-90.

Two female junior leaders from the Word of Life Church studied theology in the seminary where I served as the Academic Dean. Upon becoming Christians, they offered themselves to the service of the Lord, participating in different forms of training. They were sent to various parts of Henan Province for evangelism and church planting. Eventually, they were arrested by the authorities and sentenced to prison terms. They openly shared about the harsh treatment they had received during their incarceration, including utter humiliation before male prison guards as part of their punishment. They implied that most colleagues and leaders went through similar experiences. It was claimed that among ordinary believers, a widespread perception was formed that imprisonment was a mark of one's devotion, thus preferable, if not necessary, for a leadership appointment.

The world's hostility has reinforced the identity and mission of Christians and the church. As observed in some Christian sectors, Christianity is never viewed as a means to upward social mobility. Indeed, being Christian results in voluntary downward social mobility. At a seminary chapel session, one of the women leaders shared her prayer after she was physically exposed for humiliation: "Thank you, Lord, for considering me worthy of participating in your suffering." As Bray notes, persecution was a critical aspect of the early church, and some of the characteristics of this era are similar to the experiences of the Word of Life Church.[16]

The seven-point doctrine of the Word of Life Church includes a statement affirming that the official TSPM "embraces worldly authority."[17] The TSPM "registered" churches have lawful status and are visibly organized, but operate under government guidance. Therefore, a distinct mark of the true church (in the mind of most house church members) is suffering for refusing to submit to atheistic government policies.

---

[16]For example, the ascetic tendency and the decisive role of episcopacy (or leadership), the spread of the gospel, and an adverse social context largely resonate with the Word of Life Church. See Bray, *The Church*, 61-89.

[17]Xin, *Inside China's House Church Network*, 89.

Third, the Word of Life Church understands itself to be a community of the regenerated people of God. Following the Free Church model of ecclesiology, each member is expected to have repented of their sins, been forgiven by God, and become incorporated into the community of faith, which is the church.

Xu and the church have consistently stressed the necessity of discipleship, for which a genuine experience of regeneration is essential. Aikman contends this was a reaction to the increasing Pentecostal faith among the house church networks.[18] To foster such a lifestyle, the church encouraged its members to participate in spiritual retreats where repentance was emphasized and exhorted. Soon, it became common or even "normative for everyone to weep," often for a prolonged period, as evidence of genuine repentance.[19] Despite repeated denials by Xu and other leaders, many members and local-level leaders believe that weeping has a significant theological meaning.

The church became known as the Born-Again Movement or simply "the Weepers." By the mid-1990s, the security authorities and the TSPM labeled the church as a cult and Xu as a cultic leader. This controversy led various house church networks to come together to work out theological and personality differences and set criteria for orthodox Christianity. This was further developed in 1998 to create a unified front against government persecution by adopting a joint statement called "United Appeal of the Various Brands of the Chinese House Church."[20]

The strong emphasis on regeneration and Christian discipleship attracted many Christian groups, especially in the 1980s. A 1998 issue of *Christianity Today* rejected the claim of heresy and estimated that the church had reached about three million members.[21] Like most house church networks, Xu and his

---

[18]Aikman, *Jesus In Beijing*, 88.

[19]Ibid.

[20]For the full text, see Aikman, *Jesus in Beijing*, 293-294.

[21]Timothy C. Morgan. "A Tale of China's Two Churches," *Christianity Today* 42 (July 13, 1998): 30-39. Similarly, Bays, *A New History of Christianity in China*, 195.

church often pray for healing and God's miraculous intervention. The work of the Holy Spirit in evangelism is particularly stressed. However, they do not encourage other spiritual gifts that are common among Pentecostals, such as speaking in tongues or prophecy. Luke Wesley, a Pentecostal academic working in China, concludes that the group is Evangelical but not Pentecostal:

> The Word of Life Church represents an interesting mixture of conservative theology and experiential piety. They expect to see miracles, pray for healing, and look to the Holy Spirit for supernatural guidance and deliverance; but at the same time, they are generally quite closed to some manifestations of the gifts of the Spirit, such as prophecy and tongues. I would classify this group as non-Charismatic.[22]

The Mission of the Church

Based on the strong emphasis on genuine regeneration, the church has set evangelism as its foremost and primary mission. Xin points out that Xu deeply appreciated Christian leaders of previous eras. He recalls how Xu drew much inspiration from Charles Finney's books, which had been hand-copied during a difficult period.[23] In 1983, the church's most important theological process took place when the church's theological position was articulated in the seven points (or "Seven Principles"). They begin with "salvation through the cross" and end with "frontier evangelism." New life in Christ is the absolute foundation for Christian discipleship and mission. The description of the last point is worth quoting, as this is the only one with a specific action plan prescribed: "This is the Great Commission of Christ to the Church for the fulfillment of God's eternal salvation scheme. As Chinese Christians, we are burdened with the one hundred million souls that need salvation. To preach the gospel to all the people in

---

[22]Wesley, *The Church in China*, 48.

[23]Xin, *Inside China's House Church Network*, 88-89.

China, frontier evangelistic teams should be organized and sent to the unreached areas."[24]

In the same year, 1983, with the renewed government crackdown, the church's top seventeen itinerant evangelists, called "Messengers of the Gospel," scattered and hid. Circumstances effectively pushed them into full-time ministry. The authority's persecution and opposition were instrumental in creating the powerful evangelistic program of the church, called the "Gospel Band."[25]

The church intentionally created a massive training program to serve the entire process of Christian discipleship, from conversion to evangelism and church planting. Each congregation implemented various levels of training programs, often mobile in location. Completing and publishing the two-volume training manual in 1987 enhanced the development of the training programs. The "missiological cycle" illustrated the life of an evangelist of the church, from short-term training and theological education (called "Seminary of the Field") to leading members to join the Gospel Band. Eventually, teams of evangelists were sent to frontier regions to establish house churches.[26]

Within the given social context, the development of house churches drew many women. Thus, young women have had a prominent leadership role. Wesley described eight leaders of the Word of Life Church, seven of whom were women. Most, if not all, of the Chinese leaders the Philippines seminary trained were women. Xin, who participated in several congregations, estimates that about 70 percent of the church's members are women. He also believes that women comprise about the same proportion of the Messengers of the Gospel, the backbone of the church's leadership structure.[27] This is common with other house church networks, reflecting the social circumstances in which they exist. In several

---

[24]Ibid., 90.

[25]Ibid., 91; see 102-105 for details of the training, activities, and fruits of this program.

[26]Ibid., 99.

[27]Ibid., 105.

places, Xin stresses the critical leadership role of Xu Yongling, Peter's younger sister, especially when he was imprisoned. She may have served as a role model for women in leadership within the church.

However, the subsequent drastic decline of the Word of Life Church raises a serious question about this church's nature and shape, particularly about the leaders' role. Without strong leadership, the entire church network is in danger of disintegration. The following case demonstrates a more stable structure.

David Yonggi Cho and Yoido Full Gospel Church

An extensive study shows the development of this largest single congregation under Cho's leadership. Its sixty-year history highlights the development of its ecclesiology. Due to the decisive role of Cho in this process, his theological formation has been integral to the church's "full gospel" ecclesiology.

David Yonggi Cho (1936-2021) and the "Full Gospel"

The global development of this largest single congregation is traceable in three geographically oriented stages of David Yonggi Cho's life. First, he grew up in the turbulent changes of Korea, including Japanese colonialism (1910-45), independence (1945), and the Korean War (1950-53). The second season was the military dictatorship (1970s and 1980s). The third was the economic development of Korea (from the 1990s on). His conversion occurred in his youth as he was dying of tuberculosis. He was healed at the same time as his spiritual birth. This radically transformed his life and his attitude towards daily life in this post-war society.

His first tent church, Full Gospel Church, was established in 1958 on the outskirts of the war-torn capital city of Seoul. When ministering to the urban poor, Cho's "full gospel" was centered on the gifts of healing and miracles. His church always expected the sick to be present, and the ministry of healing was an integral part of almost all church gatherings. The tent church was looked down upon by the general population and nearby churches. Many objected to the makeshift state of the building and the internal makeup of the church. At the same time, the power of God attracted those who were marginalized and helpless. True to the Pentecostal tradition, this was a church *of* the poor, not one *for* the poor. Cho himself *was* sick and poor.

When Cho took his congregation to downtown Seodaemun in 1961, the venue had been secured by American missionaries as a Central Revival Hall. Cho regularly served as their interpreter. The main message was hope and healing. The new congregation represented a convergence between Cho's "full gospel" message and mainstream Pentecostal theology.

The church in this urban setting started a phenomenon that has characterized Korean Christianity until today: the megachurch movement. Cho's passion for church growth is understandable, as Christianity was still around 10 percent of the national population at the beginning of the 1960s. While continuing his message of God's power in healing and miracles, he presented a theological notion of a "good God."

The exponential growth of Cho's church began to attract the world's attention. In 1973, he moved the church to Yoido Island, the newly emerging financial center of the capital. During this era, his congregation reached the unprecedented size of 750,000 members.

Cho theologized his concept of "a good God" into a Five-fold Gospel and Three-fold Salvation. The Five-fold Gospel was an adaptation of the traditional Christological formula of the Assemblies of God: he added "Jesus the Blesser" to "Jesus the Savior, Baptizer, Healer, and the Coming King."[28] Based on 3 John 2, his Three-fold Salvation included spiritual, physical, and circumstantial (which includes material) salvation. His emphasis on God's blessing triggered a theological controversy. Many alleged that his ministry had shamanistic tendencies or advocated

---

[28]Wonsuk Ma, "David Yonggi Cho's Theology of Blessing: Basis, Legitimacy, and Limitations," *Evangelical Review of Theology* 35, no. 2 (April 2011): 140-41.

the prosperity gospel. As Cho's ministry expanded globally,[29] he became the most recognized Korean in the world. At the same time, the church increased its mission program. Before his formal retirement, Cho began to strengthen the church's ministry to the socially marginalized. His successor, Younghoon Lee, has taken the church's social responsibility even further.[30]

"Full Gospel" Faith as Lived Out

Why are people attracted to Yoido Full Gospel Church and its massive Jashil Choi Fasting and Prayer Mountain? Their expectations are a valuable window through which to deduce the popular perception of Yoido Full Gospel Church.

First, Yoido Church is a popular haven for those with nowhere else to turn. Almost every teaching opportunity, from Sunday sermons to cell group Bible studies, contains the message of God's power to solve life's problems. These often include physical and mental illness, family problems in marriage and parent-child relationships, financial difficulties, business issues, addiction to gambling and substance abuse, suicidal tendencies, and many more.

The church's unique character was defined from the beginning, and it has continued. Myung Soo Park's analysis of selected published testimonies in the *Shinang-gye* (World of Faith), the church's monthly magazine, points to this. He lists "the last hope for solving problems of life" as the "starting point of Pentecostal spirituality."[31]

---

[29]Myung Soo Park, "Globalization of the Korean Pentecostal Movement: The International Ministry of Dr. Yonggi Cho," in *Korean Church, God's Mission, Global Christianity*, ed. Wonsuk Ma and Kyo Seong Ahn (Oxford: Regnum, 2015), 228-41.

[30]See Younghoon Lee, "Yoido Full Gospel Church: A Case Study in Expanding Mission and Fellowship," in *Called to Unity for the Sake of Mission*, ed. John Gibaut and Knud Jorgensen (Oxford: Regnum, 2014), 275-84.

[31]Park, "Korean Pentecostal Spirituality," in *David Yonggi Cho: A Close Look at His Theology and Ministry*, 47.

Praying for healing and life's problems is a regular feature of all services in the church. To provide various spaces for people to come and experience God's power, the church developed many prayer programs in addition to the traditional daily dawn prayer and Wednesday evening prayer meetings. The church's Friday overnight prayer meeting spread to almost all the churches in Korea and was extended to all weekdays. It instituted a unique series of prayers, such as the Daniel Prayer (for twenty-one days) and the 40-Day Dawn Prayer. Members were encouraged to dedicate a designated time frame to pray for a specific need. Fasting prayer was uniquely promoted and encouraged by Choi, Cho's long-time ministry partner. The massive Jashil Choi Fasting and Prayer Mountain draws thousands of people from different churches in Korea and far beyond.

Second, every church gathering is a space and time where God's power and love are expected and experienced. Every part of the service is designed to help worshippers encounter God through the Holy Spirit. The lively and contemporary pre-worship music and prayer welcome worshippers who fill the auditorium, which has been emptied minutes prior by worshippers from the previous service. The post-sermon session of the ministry is extended. Typically, it begins with a time of corporate prayer when each member is encouraged to put their problems into the Lord's care based on the sermon just heard. The famous three shouts of "*Juyo!*" ("Lord!") at the beginning of this corporate prayer powerfully transform thousands of individuals into a spiritual community.[32] The auditorium-filling prayers and shouts are followed by a prayer led by the preacher. Each member is asked to lay their hand on the part of the body that is ailing or on the heart if there is a problem other than physical. The prayer is a mixture of petition to God and a command to the force(s) responsible for the problem. This is the real climax of the service when shouts of "Amen" and "Hallelujah"

---

[32]For its biblical reference, see Robert P. Menzies, "Simultaneous Prayer: A Pentecostal Perspective," in *The Holy Spirit, Spirituality and Leadership: Essays in Honour of Younghoon Lee*, ed. Wonsuk Ma and Robert P. Menzies (Oxford: Regnum Books, 2024), 89-103.

continue. This ministry session ends with the eruption of praise and thanksgiving.

This modern scene of Yoido Church's worship has historical roots in the beginning of the tent church. Cho repeatedly declared that Jesus is the answer to all human suffering,[33] which overwhelmed his life and the tent church. His church was regularly filled with more sick people than healthy ones. The former often included the pastor himself! His radical conversion experience is well documented. On his deathbed, with no hope of recovery from tuberculosis, he experienced spiritual rebirth and physical restoration. By design, the church is a sacred space for an encounter with God's reality, where his gracious power is shared.

Third, this type of spirituality engenders countless narratives of who God is and what God has done. In a typical Pentecostal worship service in the early years, and still today in many parts of the world, sharing testimonies is a significant part of worship. Usually, participants are not prearranged: Anyone can stand up or come forward to tell of their encounter with God.

The exchange of such life stories is practiced regularly. Although the sheer size of Yoido Church prohibits a formal service from providing sufficient space for sharing testimonies, sermons utilize such experiences as a powerful illustration of God's love and power. The most active place for sharing is the weekly cell group meetings, often held in a member's home. This is the unique and powerful process of grassroots theologizing. True to the Pentecostal theological process, members actively contribute to the construction of theology by sharing, appropriating, adjusting, or discerning. By articulating their experiences, they reflect on the teachings of the Bible and the church. This helps members to build confidence and content for evangelism. Theologically, this is

---

[33]In his own words: "Pastoring is preaching the gospel of Jesus Christ, leading them to salvation through faith in Jesus, and helping them to serve the Lord as God's people, and to love their neighbors." David Yonggi Cho, "An Interview: Pastoring with the Holy Spirit" [in Korean], in *Charis and Charisma: Church Growth of Yoido Full Gospel Church*, ed. Sung-boon Myung and Yong Hong (Seoul: Institute for Church Growth, 2003), 14.

an example of the "prophethood of all believers." Practically, this theological and spiritual orientation is responsible for the church's numerical growth.

Mission of the Church

Closely related to the above, Yoido Full Gospel Church has taken three areas as its unique mission. The first is spreading the full gospel faith. At its core is the message of a good God, who blesses, heals, and intervenes on his people's behalf. This was radically opposite to the prevailing other-worldly orientation of Korean Christianity.

Coupled with his healing and exorcism, Cho and his church were looked at suspiciously by the mainstream church in Korea. In fact, he was either included in the watch list of doctrinally "questionable" groups or condemned outright as a heretic. He and the church were cleared from the "heresy" list not long ago.[34]

His belief and practice were also linked to shamanism by two well-known Western scholars. Harvey Cox and Walter Hollenweger made this link a positive and successful attempt at connecting the Christian faith with the widespread indigenous religious tradition. In this way, they applauded that Cho had successfully made Christianity relevant to the Korean cultural and contemporary context. Hollenweger regarded him as a "Pentecostal Shaman *par excellence*."[35] Understandably, the church emphatically denied such allegations, and the church brought Cox to its pulpit several times so that he could have a firsthand experience. However, Cho is still viewed suspiciously by many.

---

[34]The Presbyterian Church of Korea (known as the Tonghap Group) formally classified Cho as a heretic in its 1983 General Assembly and withdrew this decision in 1994. See also Dongjun Seo, "Testing the Spirits? The Theological Controversy Surrounding David Yonggi Cho and the World's Largest Church, 1983-1994," *Studies in World Christianity* 31, no. 2 (2025): 151-170.

[35]Hollenweger, *Pentecostalism,* 100 n. 2; Also, Cox, *Fire from Heaven,* 100.

These controversies prove how Cho's full gospel faith and ethos radically challenged normatively practiced Christian beliefs and practices. In the end, he convinced the Korean church of his full gospel faith, which can be argued on at least two fronts. First, churches across all denominations adopted the worship and songs of his church and various prayer programs. They were particularly popular among pastors who saw people attracted to such worship and messages. Through this powerful influence, Cho's Pentecostal spirituality became a common feature of the Korean church.[36]

Second, the growth of his church served as a sure and visible proof of the validity and impact of his full gospel faith. At the height of the church growth movement (for example, at the School of World Mission of Fuller Theological Seminary), the Yoido Full Gospel Church was a favorite illustration. There was a practical side to this as well. His prayer mountain and overnight prayer sessions drew people regardless of their church's theological standing. "Sheep stealing" was a common charge against Yoido Church and its branch worship centers in various parts of the metropolis.

Cho and his church have been the best advocates of church growth. Cho began with his intense desire for his church to grow in numbers and influence. At least in the early years, this could have been a reaction to his dilapidated tent church, which symbolized the downcast status of his members. In the 1960s, the icon of a decent church was Youngnak Presbyterian Church. In several ways, it served as a symbol of Christian glory. Many founding members of the church were land and business owners in the northwestern part of North Korea who had fled the communist regime before the Korean War.[37] It is well known that in the early days of his tent church, Cho and his partner, Mrs. Jashil Choi (who later became his mother-in-law), were returning from a

---

[36]The Pentecostalization of Korean Presbyterianism was pointed out by a concerned theologian: Chang-sup Shin, "Assessing the Impact of Pentecostalism on the Korean Presbyterian Church in Light of Calvin's Theology," *Chongshin Theological Journal* 3, no. 1 (1998): 115-31.

[37]Sebastian C. H. Kim and Kirsteen Kim, *A History of Korean Christianity* (New York: Cambridge University Press, 2015), 173.

disappointing trip downtown after his lottery ticket did not win. As the bus passed a large cinema, which was close to the location of his future downtown church, he said later that he heard the Holy Spirit say, "Do you see the cinema? I will give you a church which is larger than that."[38]

In 1976, Cho organized Church Growth International (CGI) to systematically spread the experience and principles of Yoido Church's growth. Its board members have been senior pastors of megachurches throughout the world. The annual meetings bring many pastors from around the world to hear the experiences of leaders of large churches and cell group leaders of the church and to participate in church life.

Third, the church is widely known for actively mobilizing the laity for ministry, particularly women. Logically, this is a natural development: The church enabled its members to have life-changing encounters with God and provided spaces to share their stories with people. At the beginning of the exponential growth of his church, Cho organized the church according to the administrative districts of the capital. When he announced to the church that he would select and train lay women to lead the small groups ("cells" in church language), resistance was strong, both within and without the church, from both men and women! Soon, however, this empowered women and laity to undertake ministries.

Christianity in Korea has a long tradition of promoting the welfare and education of women. Early Protestant missionaries began many schools, some exclusively for girls and women. Pentecostalism took this Christian contribution to another level. The Korean Assemblies of God, with which the church is affiliated, was one of a few denominations to ordain women ministers.

The first women ministers were ordained in 1979.[39] This is highly significant given the male-privileged social culture in Korea.

---

[38]David Yonggi Cho, *Dr. David Yonggi Cho: Ministering Hope for 50 Years* (Alachua, FL: Bridge-Logos, 2008), 51.

[39]The denomination's bylaws were amended to allow women to be ordained in 1972. Publication Committee of the 60-Year History, *With the Holy*

Cho's cell group system took this further by radically sharing ministerial responsibilities with the laity (primarily women)! This essential, contextual, and practical expression of the Pentecostal theology promoted the democratization of ministry to every believer.

Free Church Ecclesiology in Asia: A Preliminary Picture

A close look at the two churches in East Asia raises many questions. These two may not be typical enough to represent Asia's incredible variety of "Free Church" types. For example, in India, a recently published study presents the transformation of "Every Home Crusade," a mission operation, into "Christ Groups" by adopting rural Indian culture.[40] The shape of their ecclesiology is quite different from the two cases above.

Notwithstanding this deficiency, this two-church comparison indicates a close interplay between the social context, church tradition that was transmitted or lack thereof, and the way the gospel is understood. The nature of the church in both networks is defined by their function within their given contexts, perhaps with little or no consciousness of ancient ecclesiological formulae. Because this study used "ground evidence" to understand the nature and function of the church widely understood in each circle, the present ecclesiological description has the advantage of a close connection to actual ecclesial realities in these communities.

Also noticeable in both cases is the decisive role of the leaders in theological shaping. In a Free Church setting, where each congregation exercises a sufficient degree of autonomy, the leader's role is substantial in determining the congregation's culture, ethos, life, and theology. In the case of Yoido Full Gospel Church, Cho "revised" the fourfold gospel of the (USA) Assemblies of God. His experience of healing substantially influenced the construction of

---

Spirit: A 60-Year History of the Korean Assemblies of God [in Korean] (Seoul: Assemblies of God Korea, 2013), 103, 108.

[40]Saheb John Borgall, *The Emergence of Christ Groups in India: The Case of Karnataka State* (Oxford: Regnum, 2016).

full gospel theology. For him, this is part of the recovery of the apostolic ministry as spiritual gifts are restored.

The leader's role is especially prominent in independent churches, as in the Word of Life Church. Xu's encounter with hidden Christians during the Cultural Revolution caused him to prioritize genuine repentance and regeneration as the most foundational aspect of the Christian faith. Although the "apostolic" part of the Nicene-Constantinopolitan Creed (381 CE) has been interpreted variously, Xu and Cho's strong leadership and authority are reminiscent of apostolic succession in ancient churches. As in some house church networks, Xu's family holds the church's leadership in Xu's physical absence. Theological controversies notwithstanding, it is disturbing that both churches in the case studies have been subject to moral, ethical, and legal charges.

Recognizing other Christian communities, the "one" and "Catholic" dimensions of the Nicene-Constantinopolitan Creed are least manifest. The "survival" experiences of both communities have affected their attitudes. The Word of Life Church was and still is unlawful and subject to various restrictions. Its negative attitude towards registered churches in China among house church networks was caused by and resulted in a narrow definition of the true church. As a Pentecostal congregation, Yoido Church also experienced marginalization among Korean churches. Only lately, partly due to its massive growth and influence, has the church been able to join the National Council of Churches. Today, its ecumenical participation and leadership are significant.

Social context plays a critical role in the formation of church life. An average member of the Word of Life Church does not consider the presence of a building, church structure, or even clergy essential to be considered a church. The church's lack of legal sanction or recognition forced it to develop the notion of a church as the gathering of God's people. On the other hand, Cho's Yoido Full Gospel Church exists in a social setting where religious activities and entities are legally provided for and protected. Nonetheless, it has struggled with allegations of unorthodoxy.

It is not unexpected that both groups were caught in theological controversies. This may indicate their theological and spiritual creativity, exploring what the church is and what it does beyond the usual boundaries. Their Free Church nature affords this uninhibited freedom. At the same time, it points to a need for a historical framework of Christian orthodoxy to safeguard doctrinal and practical integrity. This is where the church's ancient "Catholic" nature can be particularly relevant.

The definition of church and the process through which it is shaped directly affect its mission. The two churches have stark contrasts in their missions. Both communities uphold the "holy" nature of the church, set apart as God's people for his mission in the world. However, the ways they understand and try to fulfill it are radically different. The core of Cho's message is a blessing, while Xu's is the cross. Their growth is symbolized by a massive auditorium (Cho) or an extensive network of congregations (Xu). Their mission is spreading the message of blessing and church growth (Cho), or evangelism and church planting (Xu). Both invoke the work of the Holy Spirit: to baptize in the Spirit (Cho) or to bring continual cleansing (Xu).

In Asia, more models of the church are expected to emerge both in historic and Free Churches. Many historic churches remain theologically Evangelical while seeking to integrate cultural elements into church life. Free Churches will proliferate as they actively begin sending their missionaries to many parts of the continent and reproducing themselves. An example is the growing passion of the Chinese house churches for the Back-to-Jerusalem movement.[41]

Varying and rapidly changing social contexts, especially in areas hostile to Christianity, play a decisive role in shaping the church and its understanding of its nature and mission. With their leadership in the hands of a younger generation, the two communities face formidable challenges. The population of Korea and China is aging rapidly, and the rise of urban house churches in China significantly impacts how churches operate. The ways the *de facto* denominational function of the Word of Life responds to the

---

[41]A prominent urban house church leader published a textbook for this movement: Mingri Jin, *Back to Jerusalem with All Nations: A Biblical Foundation* (Oxford: Regnum, 2016).

trend of urban churches to form denomination-like organizations will decisively affect its ecclesiological orientation.[42]

Therefore, churches and mission communities worldwide must extend their theological hospitality to "watch each other's back" while encouraging creativity, a gift of the Holy Spirit. This hospitality, as long as it remains an offer rather than an imposition, will give birth to varying dynamic and creative ecclesiologies that are lived out, reflected, and articulated by the newer and the older churches in Asia.

---

[42]Brent Fulton, *China's Urban Christians: A Light that Cannot Be Hidden* (Eugene, OR: Wipf and Stock, 2015).

CHAPTER 5

Asian Megachurch Ecclesiologies in Conversation with *The Church: Towards a Common Vision*[1]

What is the understanding, life, and mission of the church as assumed, taught, and practiced by megachurches in Asia? Their ecclesiology, or ecclesiologies, will be placed in dialogue with *The Church: Towards a Common Vision (TCTCV)* of the WCC. The broad question is: Would Asian megachurches take *TCTCV* to reflect their ecclesiology? If the response is an acceptance with reservations or qualifications, what are the differences between the two ecclesiological traditions? And what components are absent from the document that adequately reflect megachurches?

The task comes with a few challenges. There is no such thing as the ecclesiology of Asian megachurches; rather, it will be ecclesiologies. The ecclesial roots of the top twelve churches in Korea are Presbyterian, Pentecostal, and Independent. They have different theological roots coupled with their efforts of theological adaptation to their unique contexts. Also, only two in the list are identified as historic (here, Presbyterian) churches. The others are either Pentecostal or Independent. Ecclesiological studies are

[1]First published in *Towards a Global Vision of the Church*, Volume I: *Explorations on Global Christianity and Ecclesiology*, Faith and Order Paper No. 234 (Geneva, Switzerland: WCC Publications, 2022), used by permission. Henceforth, *TCTCV.* The full text is available at https://www.oikoumene.org/sites/default/files/Document/The_Church_Towards_a_common_vision.pdf/ (accessed December 6, 2024).

only starting to appear, especially those taking Asian contexts into account.

This analysis begins with an introduction to the *TCTCV* document, followed by a brief profile of Asian megachurches. The main discussion is divided by the faith, life, and ministry of the megachurch. Each discussion will actively interact with the *TCTCV* document. The model for the study is Yoido Full Gospel Church in Seoul, Korea. The choice of this church stems from several reasons. First, Yoido Church is widely viewed as the mother of the megachurch movement in both its size and its ethos. Second, many megachurches adopted its characteristic features, such as the home cell group system and social service programs. And third, it represents the Pentecostal faith, which dominates the megachurch list.

The Church: Towards a Common Vision

The Church: Towards a Common Vision is a convergence document produced by the Commission on Faith and Order of the WCC. Following the process of the earlier convergence text, *Baptism, Eucharist and Ministry* (1982), the *TCTCV* process took two decades to provide its member churches with a text for an "agreement on ecclesiology."

The text process began in 1993 when the Commission on Faith and Order convened and delegated the task to representatives of member churches. The body represented a wide range of ecclesial traditions, including Orthodox, Protestant, Anglican, Evangelical, Pentecostal, and Roman Catholic Churches. Accepting each other was a critical step toward the "visible unity of the church," the vision of the WCC. The process subsequently involved robust interaction between the text team and member churches. Drafts were studied by member churches, who sent their critical responses. Through an interactive process, various meetings, and deliberations, the *TCTCV* text was produced in 2013 "to uncover a global, multilateral, and ecumenical vision of the nature, purpose, and mission of the Church."[2]

The document has four chapters: "God's Mission and the Unity of the Church;" "The Church of the Triune God;" "The Church: Growing in Communion;" and "The Church: In and for the World." The document emphasizes the church's unity—all chapter titles include the term or its related expressions: "unity;" Trinity; and "communion." This forty-six-page text also reveals what the WCC constituent churches understand mission to be through its subheadings: for example, "The importance of unity;" "the church as sign and servant of God's design for the world;" "God's plan for creation: the kingdom;" and "the church in society."

The text is intended for study and learning by local churches. Recognizing that most Evangelical and Pentecostal churches were not members of the WCC, it organized a structured interaction between the text and Evangelical, Pentecostal, Charismatic, and Independent churches, especially from the Global South.[3]

Megachurches in Asia

The megachurch phenomenon is relatively recent, according to the Global Megachurch list, starting in the 1970s.[4] The threshold to be counted a megachurch varies depending on the social context. Hartford Institute for Religion Research considers over 4000 weekly attendees as a megachurch in North America. In contrast, in Africa and Asia, 10,000 weekly attendees is counted as a megachurch. Also, there are context-specific attributes. For example, in Singapore, internationalism is prominent.[5] Besides this

---

[2]*TCTCV*, viii.

[3]Cecil M. Robeck, Jr., Sotiris Boukis, and Ani Ghazaryan Drissi, eds., *Towards a Global Vision of the Church*, Volume I: *Explorations on Global Christianity and Ecclesiology*, Faith and Order Paper no. 234 (Geneva, Switzerland: WCC Publications, 2022). See "Introduction," vii–xxv.

[4]Warren Bird, "World Megachurches," Leadership Network, last modified 2024, https://exponential.org/world/.

[5]Terence Chong, "Megachurches in Singapore: The Faith of an Emergent Middle Class," *Pacific Affairs* 88, no. 2 (June 2015): 215-35.

variable, the general characteristics of a megachurch defined by the Hartford Institute for Religious Research represent megachurches well:

- a charismatic, authoritative senior minister
- an active seven-day-a-week congregational community
- a multitude of diverse social and outreach ministries
- an intentional small group system or other structures of intimacy and accountability
- innovative and often contemporary worship format
- a complex differentiated organization structure[6]

Warren Bird lists twelve churches in Asia with a weekly attendance of 40,000 or more. The top three (also in the six-digit figures) are Yoido Full Gospel Church (Seoul, Korea), with 480,000 members; Calvary Temple Church (Hyderabad, India), with 225,000 members; and Bethany Church of God (Surabaya, Indonesia), with 140,000 members.[7] Of the dozen largest churches in Asia, four are in South Korea, four in India, three in the Philippines, and one in Indonesia. Although half are Pentecostal (in this case, Assemblies of God and Gereja Bethany), the Hartford research concludes that most, if not all, embrace Pentecostal-Charismatic traits in their beliefs and practices. Theological traditions include Baptist, Methodist, Lutheran, Mennonite, and several "house" churches of China, but Pentecostalism remains the most represented tradition. Thus, diversity is constant in the social context, church traditions, and experiences of these churches.

Yoido Full Gospel Church and *TCTCV*

The following headings do not follow *TCTCV*'s but reflect the essential aspects of the Church, faith, sacraments, and ministry

---

[6]Hartford Institute for Religion Research, "Megachurches," https://hirr.hartfordinternational.edu/research/megachurch-research/ (accessed January 8, 2025).

[7]Bird, "World Megachurches."

(§37-57). In this discussion, "sacraments" represent the life of the Church, including its worship, koinonia, and discipleship.

Faith

Regardless of denominational affiliations, most megachurches in Asia exhibit aspects of Pentecostal-Charismatic beliefs. Often called the "apostolic faith," at its heart is the dynamic and immanent work of the Holy Spirit, the third person of the Godhead. Asian megachurches uncovered the early church's dynamic experiences of the Holy Spirit, which were historically underdeveloped, theologically buried under competing priorities, and almost forgotten in church life (in the eyes of Pentecostal-Charismatics). To be precise, the "Charismatic" aspect of the Spirit's work is restored by modern Spirit-empowered Christianity, often manifested by supernatural gifts.

The work of the Holy Spirit is particularly crucial in the Asian religious psyche, as almost all religions provide divine solutions to pressing needs such as healing, protection, and prosperity. Pentecostals would question whether all the references to the supernatural work by Jesus and the Church (such as *TCTCV §48)* are only lip service, as they are not practices in Christian life and work. Among various churches, some deny the current dynamic or supernatural work of the Holy Spirit in Christian life.

In this context, the birth story of Yoido Church is radical, full of testimonies of healing, exorcism, miraculous provision, and radical transformations, all through the power of the Holy Spirit.[8] *TCTCV* repeatedly uses the term "power" in conjunction with the Holy Spirit, especially in the context of the Church's mission (such as *TCTCV* §2, 3). However, the expectation of the Spirit's work in Christian life and mission among megachurches is more "real" than confessing the liturgy.

Related to the above is the role of experience in the Christian life. Among megachurches, terminology varies about the initial

---

[8]Cho, *Cho: Ministering Hope for 50 Years*, 32-36, for the initial miraculous healing of a woman which led to a rapid growth of his tent church.

crisis experience, from the baptism of the Holy Spirit to the fullness of the Spirit.[9] Messages from the pulpits and media outlets of Asian megachurches consistently stress the Spirit's radical coming upon believers. Testimonies abound to its formative and transformative effect on one's daily and religious life, often accompanied by speaking in tongues or healing. Pentecostal-Charismatic believers associate this with the "empowerment" for witnessing, based on Acts 1:8. Aside from its missionary impact, the Spirit empowers individuals to become better people, family members, workers, and citizens, as sociological studies attest.[10] Many Pentecostals would consider that *TCTCV*'s treatment of the experience of the Holy Spirit lacks the tangibility of the experience. They also believe it fails to adequately reflect the Pentecostal understanding of the Spirit baptism as an experience separate from regeneration (see *TCTCV* §41).

The prominence of the Holy Spirit among the Charismatically oriented megachurches in Asia brings more than vitality to Christian life. Amos Yong argues that their pneumatological perspective results in "new insight on established doctrines and formulations."[11] This significant theological contribution is propagated in mass fashion by Asian megachurches. One such insight is the goodness of God. Against the backdrop of the traditional religions of Asia, Cho preached that God heals, blesses, and saves. This attracted criticism from fellow Christians that his theology is shamanistic: blessing-seeking and self-serving.

---

[9]This is called "the crown jewel of Pentecostal distinctives" by Frank D. Macchia, *Baptized in the Holy Spirit: A Global Pentecostal Theology* (Grand Rapids: Zondervan, 2006), 20.

[10]For Latin American Pentecostalism, for example, see Martin, *Tongues of Fire*.

[11]Amos Yong, "I Believe in the Holy Spirit: From the Ends of the Earth to the Ends of Time," in *The Spirit over the Earth: Pneumatology in the Majority World*, ed. Gene L Green, Stephen T. Pardue, and K. K. Yeo (Carlisle: Langham Global Library, 2016), 24.

Church Life

The sheer size of a megachurch in the religiously plural Asian cities speaks volumes about the reality of the Christian faith. The Church, as the sign of God's Kingdom (*TCTCV* §25), takes on a new level of meaning. Indeed, the church, including the building, gains a sacramental value (*TCTCV* §27). For example, the Eternal Life ministry of Pakistan claims a weekly attendance of 10,000 in Lahore. Anwar Fazal, the founder, holds a large healing gathering each Wednesday, where thousands attend in this Muslim-majority nation.[12]

The impact of a church's size on society is also demonstrated by Yoido Church's history. In the early 1970s, five Sunday services with thousands of worshippers at each gathering paralyzed road traffic in front of the church. Trapped in a bus on the way to this church, passengers wondered what had frozen the traffic. None failed to notice the powerful impact. Everyone wondered what was taking place inside the building. Although critiques of megachurches argue that one hundred smaller churches have more impact than one megachurch, large-sized churches exercise a unique influence, both positive and sometimes negative.

Worship that encourages and expects divine encounters is another hallmark of megachurches. Yoido Church's Sunday worship maintains the traditional order, including the recitation of the Apostles' Creed. The contents, however, are lively singing (including the pre-worship session), a sermon punctuated by testimonies of healing and miracles, a prayer for healing, and the proclamation of God's work (through the word of knowledge). Thus, worship prepares the congregation to experience and encounter this good and powerful God. Pentecostals define this experience as the "apostolic" faith, while *TCTCV* uses the term with different emphases (cf. §24).

The inbreaking of God through the Holy Spirit into human life is the crux of the Pentecostal experience. Pentecostal worshippers

---

[12]Eternal Life Ministries of Pakistan, "About Us," http://elmpakistan.org/about-us (accessed January 8, 2025).

are convinced they can live in the future now, as God's people are to live "the present in the light of the activity of the Holy Spirit" (*TCTCV* §33). This activity of the Holy Spirit is a present reality as much as a future expectation.

Pentecostals have developed their own liturgical traditions.[13] Because of the underlying perception of a good God and a strong conviction based on experiences of the power of God, typical Pentecostal worship is celebratory. Sharing testimonies reinforces one's faith while encouraging others to be open to the work of the Holy Spirit. There are many spaces at Yoido Church where people can freely share their experiences with God. Some of them are the weekly home cell meetings, informal prayer meetings, social media, the weekly church newspaper, and monthly magazines. Interaction between the congregation and the worship leader, including the preacher, is extremely lively, involving the whole person: body, emotion, and spirit. Shouts of "amen" and "hallelujah" fill the entire worship. Singing is accompanied by clapping of hands, movements of the body, and dancing. The congregation may roar unison prayers with raised hands.

To Pentecostals and Asian megachurches, the apostolic nature of the church is not centered on the authority of episcopacy (such as §46) but on the restored faith of the early church. While the founder and senior pastor of a megachurch holds and exercises enormous authority (either in reality or by perception), the basis of this authority is often born from his sacrificial commitment to and "success" in ministry.

When it comes to the sacraments, Pentecostal churches celebrate the Eucharist with two streams of meaning: in remembrance of Christ's death and to experience God's benevolent presence, especially in healing. In a Pentecostal life, communion with God and one another takes place in worship, prayer, and

---

[13]Five roots of identity with resulting traditions are described in Hollenweger, *Pentecostalism,* including the black oral root (as embodied by William Seymour), the Catholic root, critical root, evangelical root, and ecumenical root. This paragraph spotlights several from the black oral root, 117-141.

small groups (often including meals). Indeed, worship (or *yebae* in Korean), which traditionally requires the Eucharist, is not sharply distinguished from prayer meetings. To Korean Pentecostals, the center of worship is God's Word and encounter with God. For baptism, Pentecostals take the words of John the Baptist literally: "I baptize you with water for repentance. But . . . one who is more powerful than I . . . will baptize you with the Holy Spirit and fire" (Matt 3:11). Thus, the baptism of the Holy Spirit is not an option: ". . . all believers . . . should ardently expect and earnestly seek . . . the baptism in the Holy Spirit."[14] There is only a vague suggestion to this effect in *TCTCV*: "Some churches see the gift of the Holy Spirit as given in a special way through chrismation or confirmation" (§41).

Ministry

The unique doctrine of the baptism of the Holy Spirit advocates empowerment for witnessing—that is, calling, equipping, and commissioning every believer to be a witness. This doctrine shapes "the prophethood of all believers." This radical democratization of ministry challenges the historically established exclusive claim of ministry by clergy. *TCTCV* also includes this belief: "The whole people of God is called to be prophetic people, bearing witness to God's word" (§19). The accomplishment of Pentecostal Christianity is the realization of this idea.

The most iconic expression of this underlying theology is the implementation of the cell group system by Yoido Church. Initially, in 1964, lay leaders were mobilized to radically expand pastoral resources to manage the exponential growth.[15] Mobilizing lay leaders to do pastoral care exemplified the "prophethood of all believers." As previously noted, in the male-dominant Korean

---

[14]See "7. The Baptism in the Holy Spirit," at Assemblies of God, "16 Fundamental Truths," https://ag.org/Beliefs/Statement-of-Fundamental-Truths#7 (accessed January 6, 2025).

[15]Cho, *Dr. David Yonggi Cho*, 83-96, provides details of the conceptualization and development of the home cell group system.

culture, authorizing a female lay leader to minister to a small group that included male members was a positive transformative challenge to the culture.

As a Pentecostal congregation, Yoido Church prepares its members to be zealous witnesses to Christ's saving grace. Equipped with testimonies of God's work of grace and power, their lives bear witness to God's specific intervention in human life. They are eager to share their stories, and neighbors are regularly invited to home cell meetings to hear them. In this religiously pluralistic society, the "otherness" of the gospel is critical, and Yoido Church members are best equipped for evangelization.

The *TCTCV* commitment to evangelism (in line with §59) is also manifested in Yoido Church's cross-cultural ministry. With the steady increase of international members and cross-cultural families, the church formed various language-oriented congregations within the international ministry department. It commissioned many cross-cultural missionaries. Before he died in 2021, Cho regularly conducted mass international gatherings for evangelism, healing, and church growth seminars.

For decades, Yoido Church has paid considerable attention to caring for those who struggle in life (in line with *TCTCV* §58). They have a long list of social service ministries, including church-initiated non-governmental organizations. One example is their program to support children's heart surgeries, which began in 1984. By 2008, more than 4,000 had received life-saving surgeries.[16] To finance the program, members collected recyclable material; this is perhaps the first sight one would encounter upon entering the church complex.

A vital aspect is the work of reconciliation, particularly between the two divided Koreas. Cho successfully negotiated with the two Korean governments to establish the Cho Yonggi Cardiac Hospital in Pyongyang, North Korea, as an extension of the church's care for young heart patients. This project was hailed as a symbol of

[16] "심장병 수술 4000명 돌파 감사예배" [Thanksgiving Service Celebrating 4000 Beneficiaries of the Children's Heart Surgery Program], *The Full Gospel Family Newspaper*, April 18, 2008.

national reconciliation led by Pentecostal Christians in the South. Unfortunately, the project was halted in 2010 as the relationship between the two Koreas soured. The project is close to completion, claiming that the final phase of the project requires only six months. Despite various efforts, Cho died with this life long vision uncompleted. Yoido Church, like many Korean Christians, views national reconciliation as the priority to interreligious issues, for which *TCTCV* dedicates much space (§60, 62).

Church Unity

Megachurches are part of Christ's universal church, offering unique gifts. At the same time, they need other gifts offered by the rest of the body. The most significant gift is their size and influence. Cho's decision to have his church and denomination (the Korean Assemblies of God) become part of the National Council of Churches in 1996 was only possible because of this special gift. He persisted against considerable pressure from their American counterpart. Younghoon Lee, Yoido Church's senior pastor, led a Pentecostal prayer and preached a Pentecostal sermon at the 10th Assembly of the World Council of Churches (in Busan, Korea) in 2013, continuing Cho's commitment to church unity.

This reflection imaginatively brought members of Yoido Church to read *TCTCV* to find out if they could affirm the document as speaking for them. The overall verdict was negative. As expected, the voice of Asian megachurches is not found in *TCTCV*. Even the points that Yoido Church would agree with in the document came not from the church's input to *TCTCV* and the process of the document, but from commonly held beliefs. Nevertheless, despite these reflections, the document contains elements that can benefit Pentecostal churches in Asia. Thus, this chapter welcomes the opportunity for interaction with the *TCTCV*.

Chapter 6

Asian Pentecostalism as a Growth Engine for Global Christianity: Potentials and Challenges[1]

The unique role of Pentecostalism has grown in significance over the past decades of research. Focused research on global Christianity and the role of Yoido Full Gospel Church shows how it has empowered churches toward numerical growth.[2] However, it is important to zoom out to the whole region of East and Southeast Asia to probe the global role of its Christianity.

Baselines and Observations

Based on the latest statistical studies of global Christianity, the following baselines set a foundation for discussion. The first baseline is the growth trajectory of Islam, poised to become the prime missionary competitor to Christianity. According to the third edition of the *World Christian Encyclopedia,* Islam is outgrowing Christianity. In 2020, Islam accounted for 24.3% of the world population, while Christianity claimed 32.3%. By 2050, Islam is predicted to constitute 28.7% of the world's population,

---

[1]First published in *The Holy Spirit, Spirituality and Leadership: Essays in Honour of Younghoon Lee* (Oxford: Regnum Books, 2024), used by permission.

[2]Wonsuk Ma, "The Future Growth of Global Christianity and Yoido Full Gospel Church: Its Potential Role in the New Context," *Great Commission Research Journal* 10, no. 1 (Fall 2018): 8-29.

with Christianity at 35.0%. However, Islam's annual growth rate is particularly alarming as it grew at 1.88% each year in the twentieth century, while Christianity grew at a rate of 1.28%. The growth gap in the 2000-2020 period widened with Islam's at 1.93% growth versus Christianity's at 1.19% growth.[3]

The second baseline is another fast-growing segment: atheists and agnostics (or "nones"). In the global picture, this category ranks fourth (11.3% in 2020) after Christianity, Islam, and Hinduism. The nones are particularly challenging for the West (or the Global North), where much of the "conversions" are suspected to occur from Christianity. Although its global picture is complex, this religious category is relevant to the Asian region.[4]

The third baseline is the significant growth of Pentecostal-Charismatic Christianity since the last century. Further elaborated below, two sets of numbers illustrate this point. It grew from 0.1% of the world's population in 1910 to 8.3% in 2020, and it is expected to reach 10.3% by 2050. Its annual growth rate has been the highest among Christian families. In the twentieth century, it recorded 6.3%, while the Christian average was 1.28%.[5] Thus, Pentecostal-Charismatic churches grew more than five times faster than all the other churches.

The last observation is the steady growth of global Christianity toward one-third of the world's population (as seen in the graph).[6] However, its recent population shift is staggering. Todd Johnson creatively identifies the center of the gravity of global Christianity in each century.[7] The most glaring shift is the southward move of global Christianity. In 1900, 82.4% of world Christians were found in the Global North and only 17.6% in the South.[8] In 2020, the North claimed only 33.1% and the South 66.9% of the world's Christians. This gap is expected to grow further. As the centers of

---

[3] *WCE*, 3rd ed., 6.

[4] Ibid.

[5] Ibid.

[6] ©Wonsuk Ma, 2016, used by permission.

[7] Johnson and Ross, *Atlas of Global Christianity*, 53.

[8] *WCE*, 3rd ed., 4.

gravity have made a three-quarter circle, the accelerated speed of changes is unmistakable, further widening the North-South gap.[9]

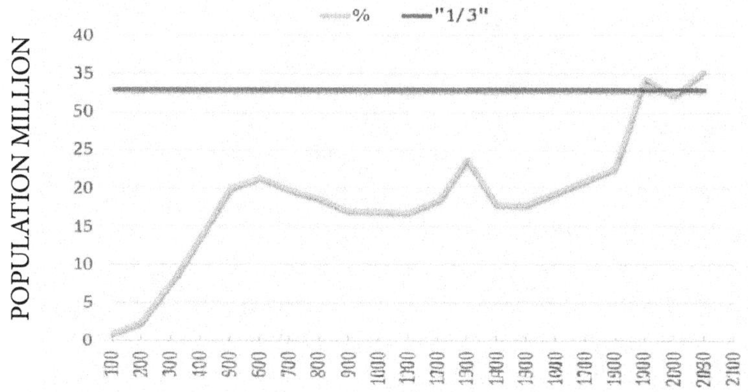

The Crucial Role of Christianity in the East and Southeast

Christianity in the East and Southeast is crucial to the continuing growth of global Christianity. At its center is Pentecostalism. To establish this premise, it is important to engage with Islam and the nones, the two religious groups that pose the most severe challenge to the continuing growth of global Christianity.

Four questions help to define the significance of this region. First, concerning Islam, what possibilities can be drawn from historical lessons, anchored by Andrew Walls' theory of the Christian movement? Second, how is Christianity's "growth room" visible in the region's two other southern continents? Third, how does the trajectory of Pentecostalism's growth compare to other Christian traditions and continents? Finally, what issues does Asian Christianity face in fulfilling this historical potential?

---

[9]Wonsuk Ma, "Global Christianity: Where Are We and How Did We Get Here?" *Pentecostal Education* 6, no. 1 (Spring 2021): 37-38.

Christianity and Islam

Islam has spread since the seventh century to become the second-largest world religion. It claims close to one-third of the world's population: 24.3% in 2020 and 28.7% in 2050.[10] Its recent growth rate threatens to unseat Christianity as the front-runner in the global religious scene.

Islam made an impact on global Christianity as it caused the first two significant setbacks to Christian growth. The first was that its birth stopped the trajectory of Christian growth. It took more than five centuries before Christianity recovered from this devastating impact. During this period, most of the ancient Christian centers in the Middle East and North Africa became Muslim territories. The second setback occurred during the rise and expansion of the Ottoman Empire from the fourteenth century. It practically canceled the recovered Christian growth for another three centuries. Thus, Islam's rise and expansion have significant implications for global Christianity.

Serial vs. Progressive Move

Comparing the life cycle of Christianity and Islam, the prominent mission historian Andrew Walls proposed a rather disturbing observation in 2005.[11] Initially published in a Swedish mission journal, a summary also appeared in *Atlas of Global Christianity*.[12] He concluded that Christianity advances serially, based on his historical analysis of the first millennium of Christian history and the twentieth-century shifts in global Christianity. A Christian center with strength, such as Northern Africa in the early Christian centuries, eventually withered while the margins

---

[10]*WCE*, 3rd ed., 6.

[11]Andrew F. Walls, "Mission History as the Substructure of Mission Theology," *Swedish Missiological Themes* 93, no. 3 (2005): 367-78.

[12]Andrew F. Walls, "Christianity across Twenty Centuries," in *Atlas of Global Christianity*, 48-49.

began to blossom.[13] This serial move can be likened to a life cycle: starting with birth, advancing to growth, maturity, and reproduction, and then aging and even death. The receding center, however, reproduces itself in new territories before the Christian center runs through the life cycle. In contrast, according to Walls, Islam advances progressively: once a Muslim territory, it remains Muslim permanently. At the outset, Christianity appears to lack resilience as compared to Islam. Indeed, since the seventh century, most of church history has seen the repeated pattern of Islam taking over Christian territories. Christianity was pushed to new areas in order to establish a Christian presence. Walls' generalization is disturbingly plausible despite minute exceptions, as he provided ample cases from early to recent times.

Are there exceptions to this historical "rule?" The first is in Africa. Three prominent religious blocs in Sub-Saharan Africa are traditional African religions, Islam, and Christianity (in the order of existence). As illustrated by the Pew graph,[14] in 1900, more than three-quarters of Africans belonged to Traditional African Religions (76%), followed by Islam (14%) and then Christianity (9%). As Christianity grew exponentially in the twentieth century (to 57% of the Sub-Saharan population), Islam continued its steady growth (20%) but lagged behind Christianity. The most notable change was the shrinking of Traditional African Religions (to 13%). Its loss (by 63%) was divided among Christianity (by 48% addition) and Islam (15%)—the exact number! Although transfer conversion between Christianity and Islam may have occurred, the majority of the gains by these two were the believers of the Traditional African Religions. Today, only a tiny population is left in the Indigenous religions, which is expected to be reduced to 5.4% by 2050 for the entire African continent.

[13]Walls, "Mission History," 368.

[14]Pew Research Center, "Tolerance and Tension: Islam and Christianity in Sub-Saharan Africa" (Washington, DC: Pew Research Center, 2010), https://www.pewresearch.org/religion/2010/04/15/executive-summary-islam-and-christianity-in-sub-saharan-africa/ (accessed December 2, 2022).

The most relevant fact is that Christianity took deep root in Africa and outgrew Islam, whose presence predated the Christian faith. Equally significant is the faster growth rate of Christianity than that of Islam. For the entire African continent, the annual growth rate of Christianity in the past century was 3.75%, vs. Islam's 2.32%. The pattern continued for the first two decades of the current century: 2.82% for Christianity vs. 2.45% for Islam.[15]

The second exception is in Central Asia, currently one of the most challenging Islamic heartlands for Christian witness. This region of the five "stans"—Kazakhstan, Uzbekistan, Turkmenistan, Kyrgyzstan, and Tajikistan—claimed only 8% of its population was Christian in 2015. However, the real challenge is its growth or decline rate: Christianity lost one-third of its share of the population in less than half a century. Thus, it is hard to imagine that this barren region was saturated with Christians, not just once but twice! This is illustrated in a beautifully crafted video, "The Spread of the Gospel," by GospelMap.com.[16]

Beginning in the third century, Christianity expanded eastward through the Silk Road. By the sixth century, the region was fully Christianized. This Christian era lasted for more than eight centuries through the rise and fall of the Mongols. But the Christian presence had disappeared by the mid-fifteenth century, even before Islam occupied the "-stan" lands. After four centuries of total absence, Christianity was reintroduced at the turn of the nineteenth century. Then, the region was overwhelmed by Communist dominance, a devastating blow (for a second time) to the Christian faith.

These two cases provide several valuable observations, challenging Walls' observation. First, while the first period of Christian presence in Central Asia ran its life cycle (serial move), Christianity was reintroduced many centuries later. This is a serial move in a complete cycle. Second, Christianity is not always

[15] *WCE*, 3rd ed., 8.

[16] Western Conservatory, "The Spread of the Gospel," December 6, 2014, https://vimeo.com/113801439?embedded=true&source=video_title&owner=2978961.

on the run while Islam chases after it. In Africa, Islam predated Christianity for eleven centuries (except in Northern Africa), but today Christianity is the dominant religion. Third, Christianity can outgrow Islam. Africa has brilliantly demonstrated this possibility, as discussed above with specific numbers.

However, it is imperative to remember that an organized religion poses more challenges for the missional front than unorganized or Indigenous religions. Also, the rise and fall of a religion in a given time is complex. An empire could support or suppress Christianity. It took an imperial force (Russia) to impose Christianity over Central Asia for the second time.

The Nones, Awaiting Mission

Several other groups deserve closer attention. These include the influence of the nones and other religious groups for the continuing growth of Christianity in the region.

Different Nones

Both in North America and Latin America, the nones (combining atheists and agnostics) is the fastest growing "religion." In the first two decades of this century, it recorded a 3.37% annual growth rate in North America and 1.93% in Latin America. In Europe, the nones remain the second-largest religious group. It recorded the fastest annual growth rate of 4.29% among all continents in the past century. Its sudden drop in the growth rate to -0.05% in 2000–2020 requires further study.

In East and Southeast Asia, the nones claim to be the largest religious group. In 1970, the combination of agnostics and atheists reached 41.1% (and 26.4% in 2020)! Gino Zurlo contends that many of the nones are due to the state's control of religious affairs, such as Communism.[17] Understandably, the most substantial number of

[17]Gina A. Zurlo, "A Demographic Profile of Christianity in East and Southeast Asia," in *Christianity in East and Southeast Asia*, ed. Kenneth R. Ross, Francis D. Alvarez SJ, and Todd M. Johnson (Edinburgh: Edinburgh

nones are found in China (453 million out of 503 million agnostics in the region in 2020). The nones in this region are quite different than elsewhere. The growth of Chinese Christianity may provide an encouraging mission implication. While Christianity grew at an annual rate of 1.42% between 2000 and 2020, the highest among all the categories, nones recorded a mere 0.17% increase.

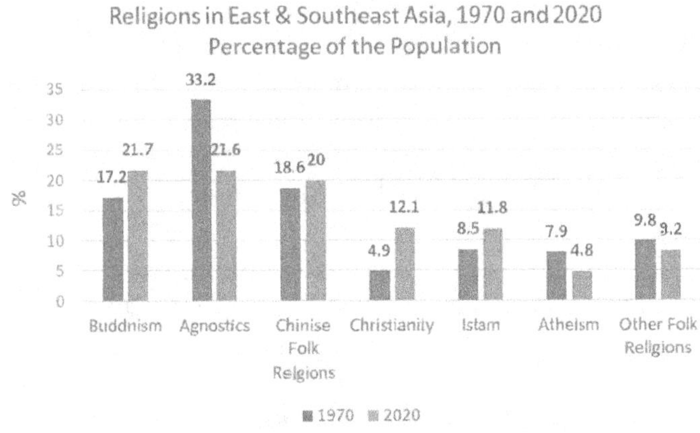

Different States of Islam

To understand the presence of Islam, which is different from other religions in the rest of Asia, a historical overview will be helpful. Islam had steadily and consistently advanced eastward from the Middle East to South Asia (including modern-day Afghanistan, Pakistan, and India). It followed the coastal states, such as today's Malaysia, Brunei, and Indonesia. As expected, it reached Mindanao, the southern island of the Philippines, and was going north through the Philippine archipelago.

In March 1521, Ferdinand Magellan and his crew landed on a Visayan island in the middle of the Philippines. The Spanish priests "Christianized" the islanders, and the nation became a Spanish colony. It has remained the only Christian nation in Asia except for East Timor (which gained full independence from Indonesian

University Press, 2020), 5. The graph is by the author.

occupation in 2002.) This Christianization by an imperial presence blocked the northward advance of Islam. Without this obstruction, Islam's spread throughout the coasts in East Africa and Southeast Asia would have continued to the coastal areas of China, Taiwan, Korea, and Japan.

Therefore, the region has a relatively weak presence of Islam. Islam in 2020 claimed 11.8% of the region's 2.33 billion population, the fifth largest after Buddhism, agnostics, Chinese Folk-Religions, and Christianity (12.1%).[18] For the whole of Asia, Islam topped the list (27.4%), followed by Hinduism, Buddhism, Chinese Folk-Religions, and Christianity (8.2%).[19] It lagged significantly behind Christianity in its growth trajectory.

In addition to the historical aspect, Islam in the region tends to be less fundamental than in West Asia. The result is often a legal provision for various religions to coexist. For instance, Indonesia, the largest Muslim country in the world, constitutionally allows Protestantism and Catholicism among the six recognized religions. Christianity is ranked as the second-largest religious group, with 12.2%.[20] Christianity is visible in large churches. The 2023 list of global megachurches includes three Indonesian churches among the top 35: Gereja Bethany (with 140,000 members), Gereja Bethel Indonesia (30,000), and Mawar Sharon Church (30,000).[21] This is a significant achievement, as almost all others are from countries with full or relative religious liberty. On the contrary, the share of Islam remains constant in this century: 79.1% of the population in 2000, 79.5% in 2020, and 79.0% projected in 2050.[22]

Although other Muslim-majority countries claim to provide protective measures for other religious groups in the rest of Asia, many Christians feel threatened if they practice their faith. Many Muslims in this region incorporate their folk religious elements.

---

[18]Zurlo, "A Demographic Profile of Christianity in East and Southeast Asia," 3.

[19]*WCE*, 3rd ed., 10.

[20]Ibid., 394.

[21]Bird, "World Megachurches."

[22]*WCE*, 3rd ed., 394.

This may explain why all three Indonesian megachurches are Pentecostal and Charismatic, where supernatural experiences, including healings, are preached and experienced.

Folk Religions

In East and Southeast Asia, Chinese Folk Religion and other Folk Religions accounted for 28.4% of the total population in 1970. In fifty years, it slightly decreased to 20.2% by 2020. Thus, much of the Christian gain in recent decades may have come from the nones. While this remains a primary mission target, folk religionists may also be the low-hanging mission fruit. The African experience provides critical insight.

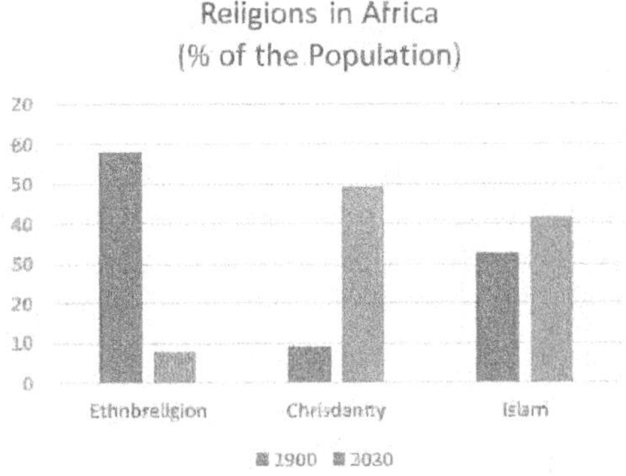

As seen in the chart,[23] explosive Christian growth in Africa was due to the mission success among ethno-religions or African Indigenous religions. In 1900, this category dominated with 57.9% of the population, followed by Islam (32.5%) and Christianity (with a meager 8.9%). By 2020, African Indigenous religion had shrunk to 7.9%, while Islam and Christianity grew significantly.[24] While the Indigenous religion lost by 50%, Christianity gained by 40.4% and Islam by 9.0%.

---

[23]©Wonsuk Ma, 2023, used by permission.
[24]*WCE*, 3rd ed., 8.

The gain of the latter two (and missionary) religions corresponds to the loss of the former. In the same way, Christianity in East and Southeast Asia is standing before a massive harvest field, where 46.6% (the combination of the nones and Folk Religions in 2020) of the population are considered "soft" missionary targets!

Growth Potential

Decades ago, I published a study with an audacious claim that the only limit for Asian Pentecostalism is the sky.[25] After almost two decades, my argument stands for Asian Christianity in general and Pentecostalism in particular. East and Southeast Asia held about half (2.33 billion) of the continent's population (4.62 billion in 2020). An ongoing investigation of the religious scene of the region supports the growth potential of Christianity from several angles.

Growth Room Factor

How can Asian Christianity be a "growth engine" for global Christianity? It claimed only 8.2% in 2020 and is projected to reach 10.2% by 2050. This is only about a quarter of the world's average (32.3% in 2020).

However, a comparison with two other Southern continents is worth considering. Latin America has maxed out its growth, with 95.2% of the population claiming to be Christian in 1900. Once one has reached the "sky," the only move is to stay up or come down. Unfortunately, Latin American Christianity has steadily lost its share in the population: 92.1% in 2020, with a projection of 90.2% in 2050. Its annual growth rate of 1.16% between 2000 and 2020 is below the population growth of 1.18%. Christianity is shrinking because there is no more room to grow! Even the phenomenal growth of Independents (2.38%), Protestants (1.80%), Evangelicals (1.71%), Unaffiliated (1.49%), and Pentecostal/

---

[25]Wonsuk Ma, "Asian Pentecostalism: A Religion Whose Only Limit Is the Sky," *Journal of Beliefs and Values* 25, no. 2 (August 2004): 191-204.

Charismatics (1.43%) cannot offset the substantial and steady loss of Catholics (0.72%).[26] Most "growth" takes place through transfers between Christian traditions. When Christianity is saturated, the best scenario is the rise of a missionary movement, as seen in the Western church. For this reason, the world is delighted with the growing missionary presence from this Christian continent. But this will not serve as the leading force of growth for global Christianity.

What about African Christianity? The Christian expansion in this region in the twentieth century was the marvel of Christian mission, transforming the whole continent into becoming Christian. In 1900, only 8.9% of Africans were Christian, but it grew to 49.3% in 2020. With 41.5% Muslims, less than 10% of Africa remains for missionary expansion by the two competing religions.

Proselytizing Muslims is an option. This is harder to accomplish and often bloody. The Christian growth rate topped at 2.82%, with Islam at 2.45% between 2000 and 2020. Christianity is expected to reach 52.4% of Africa, while Islam slightly shrinks to 41.0% by 2025. Again, there is small growth room in the continent.[27]

Like Latin America, we expect African churches to mobilize for mission. As African Christian migrants spread throughout the world, their dynamic spirituality impacts the churches of the host nations. Nonetheless, Christianity in homeland Africa has dwindling room for growth unless Muslim conversions increase. The two cases of Latin America and Africa show that Asia is the continent with the most growth potential.

Christian Growth

Also notable is the Christian annual growth rate of 3.1% in East and Southeast Asia between 2000-2020. This is the highest rate in the various regions of Asia. In 2000, 11.9% (62.2 million) of the East/Southeast Asian population was Christian, which grew

[26] *WCE*, 3rd ed., 14.
[27] Ibid., 32.

to 12.2% (281.9 million) in 2020. It is estimated to reach 13.3% by 2050.

In the rest of Asia (South Asia, Central Asia, and West Asia), fewer than 4% claimed to be Christian in 2020. Thus, East and Southeast Asian Christianity was more than three times larger than in the rest of Asia. Their annual Christian growth rate (3.1% between 1970 and 2020) in the region was two times higher than that of the whole of Asia (1.52% between 2000 and 2020). These two statistical sets prove that Christianity in East and Southeast Asia leads the Christian growth in Asia and beyond.

Chinese Christianity grew significantly, though the exact numbers are difficult to secure. The *World Christian Encyclopedia* reports that Christianity multiplied from 6.2% (or 80 million) in 2000 to 7.4% (or 106 million) in 2020 and is expected to continue its growth to 14.7% (or 200 million) by 2050.[28] After Chinese folk religions (predicted as 28.2% in 2050) and Buddhism (19.5%), Christianity is the third-largest organized religion! Its annual growth rate between 2000 and 2020 was the highest at 1.42%, compared with Buddhism (1.3%). The pressure and restrictions of the authorities over Christianity, especially the unregistered churches, have increased in recent years. However, its crucial role in Asian Christianity cannot be ignored, both in its numbers and dynamism.

Missionary Movement

Three of the top ten missionary-sending countries are in this region, according to the *World Christian Encyclopedia* (which includes the Catholic Church). South Korea was ranked third with 35,000 missionaries in 2020, the Philippines ranked fourth with 25,000, and China ranked sixth with 15,000. The combined number of missionaries from these three countries was 75,000. The total number of missionaries from the region is estimated at 80,000. To place this number in context, the total number of missionaries from the whole of Asia in 2020 was 91,200. About

[28]Ibid., 195.

88% of Asian missionaries came from this region. Also, this region ranks as the second-largest missionary-sending area after North America.

The missionary ratio to the Christian population is also encouraging. In 2020, East and Southeast Asia sent 283.8 cross-cultural missionaries per million Christians. This compares with 240.8 for the whole of Asia, 143 for Europe, 134 for Latin America, and 103 for Africa. The missionary commitment of the region is the highest among the Global South and second only to North America (563). For reference, the world average was 168 per million.[29]

Two snapshots illustrate the rising missionary zeal and commitment of the churches in this region. The first is the large "creative" group of mission workers who defy the traditional definition of a missionary. Mission watchers understand migration as part of God's missional move. Many studies argue that Christian immigrants to Western nations impact the declining host churches with zeal and commitment. Christian migrant workers in the Middle East have radically changed the Christian landscape of hard-to-reach places.[30]

The second is the surprising missionary movement of Chinese churches, primarily house churches. Its missionary impetus has been popularly expressed in the Back-to-Jerusalem movement. Initially spread among rural house churches, the idea received a significant boost as urban house churches inherited and developed it. One of its leaders published a biblical argument for the movement,[31] while the urban churches organized annual Mission China 2030 conferences between 2015 and 2018.[32] Increasing

---

[29]The ratios are calculated using the statistics found in *WCE*, 3rd ed., 5 and 32.

[30]Heartwarming stories are found in Miriam Adeney and Sadiri Joy Tira, *Wealth, Women & God: How to Flourish Spiritually and Economically in Tough Places* (Pasadena, CA: William Carey Library, 2016).

[31]For an insider's rationale, see Jin, *Back to Jerusalem.*

[32]David Ro, "Mainland China (House Churches)," in *Christianity in East and Southeast Asia*, 71-73; David L. Ro, "A Study of an Emerging Missions Movement in Urban China: From the Perspective of Four Beijing Pastors"

government restrictions prevented the urban house churches and their mission programs from developing fully. Yet the commitment to the Back-to-Jerusalem missionary vision has persisted.

The church in this region has always faced challenges, especially from dominant religions. It has the most significant potential to lead the growth of global Christianity. But weren't all these growth potentials, except the mission development, present in the past? If so, why is the Christian presence in Asia less than a quarter of the world's rate? Even if East and Southeast Asian churches have performed better than the rest of Asia, isn't it about a third of the world's rate? If the church remains in the same context, why would it be different in the future? Pentecostal Christianity offers a new and positive component to respond to these profound questions.

Asian Pentecostalism

As with all other church traditions, Pentecostalism, in its wide variety, comes with its unique promises and challenges. The best gifts it may bring are, first, its rapid growth in its brief history and its spread among and renewal impact on different church traditions,[33] and second, a unique missional pneumatology that fuels its growth.

Growth

In the global picture, Pentecostalism (644.3 million in 2020) in its three subsets of Classical Pentecostals, Charismatics, and Neo-Charismatics has become the second largest Christian family after Catholicism (1,239.9 million). It is expected to grow to 1,031.5 million by 2050, or to one in every ten people globally (10.3%). Its annual growth rates were staggering between 1900 and 2000

(Oxford and London, Oxford Centre for Mission Studies/Middlesex University, 2023).

[33]For a useful overview, see Wonsuk Ma, "Pentecostalism: A New but Big Kid in the Global Christian Block," *Pentecostal Education* 7, no. 1 (Spring 2022): 73-91.

at 6.30%, compared with overall Christian growth (1.28%) and general population growth (1.34%). In the first two decades of this century, it recorded the highest growth rate (1.89%) among Christian groups (an average of 1.19% per annum). Pentecostalism was followed by Evangelicals (1.80%) and Independents (1.61%). For comparison, the world population increased annually by 1.20% during the period. Any group with a lower rate was in decline. This includes Catholics (at 0.96%) and Orthodox (0.63%), lowering the net Christian annual growth rate to 1.19%, slightly below the population growth in 2000-2020.

These statistics raise a question that is relevant to Pentecostal Christianity. Why did its splendid growth not stop the steady decline of global Christianity? Did it expand primarily through the proselytization of Christians from other groups? In Christianized regions such as Latin America, Pentecostal growth is largely driven by conversions and transfers. However, in Asia, this question requires thoughtful consideration.

How does Pentecostalism fare in East and Southeast Asia? Between 1970 and 2020, Pentecostals/Charismatics grew from 4.6 million to 90.9 million, almost twenty times! This growth translates from 0.4% of its population in 1970 to 3.9% in 2020.[34] As illustrated in the graph, Pentecostal/Charismatics is the fastest-growing group among Christian traditions and all religions.[35]

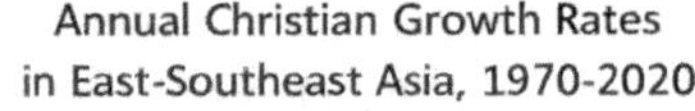

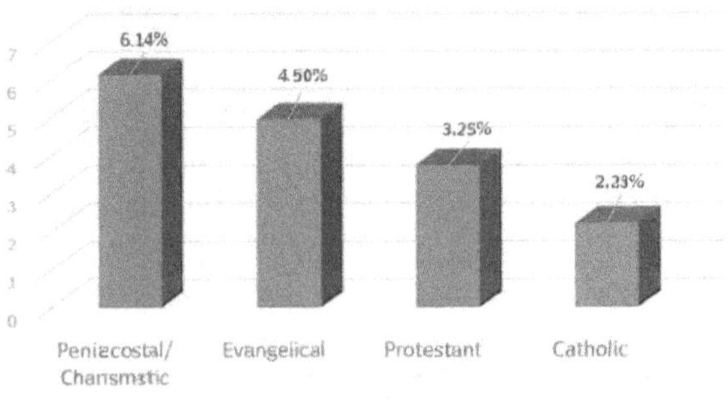

[34]Julie Ma, "Pentecostals and Charismatics," in *Christianity in East and Southeast Asia*, 336-338.

[35]©Wonsuk Ma, 2025, used by permission.

After checking the numbers, let's revisit two places in the region: Indonesia and China. In Indonesia, the annual growth rate of Pentecostals/Charismatics between 2000 and 2020 was 2.31%, almost two times faster than Islam (1.3%) and the population (1.27%). All Christian traditions grew faster than the population (except Catholics, at par) and Islam (again, except Catholics). Thus, the proportion of Pentecostal/Charismatic believers in the population grew impressively from 1.9% in 1970 to 3.3% in 2000 and 4.0% in 2020. It is expected to reach 6.2% by 2050. The growth is more pronounced when looking at the actual numbers: from 2.2 million in 1970 to 11 million in 2020. Following this growth trend, Evangelicals also grew quickly (at 2.28% in 2000-2020), as did Independents (1.75%) and Protestants (1.68%).[36] All the megachurches mentioned earlier are Pentecostal and Charismatic in nature.

The growth of Chinese Christianity from the third quarter of the previous century has triggered various studies. *Global Chinese Pentecostal and Charismatic Christianity*[37] provides helpful reflections, casting an encouraging future. Among Christian blocs, Independents led (4.4% of the population in 2020), although their 2000-2020 annual growth was only 0.83%. Pentecostal/Charismatics were the next largest (2.6%) with a yearly growth rate of 0.68%. Surprisingly, the third highest growth rate was recorded by historic Protestants at 2.4%, the fourth largest body after Evangelicals.

Categorizing Chinese Christians is complex. Most house churches prefer Protestant to Independent or Pentecostal/Charismatic for several reasons. David Ro observes theological fault lines between rural and urban house churches. According to him, rural house churches widely embraced Charismatic and

---

[36] *WCE*, 3rd ed., 394. Also, Sulistyowati Irianto, "Indonesia," in *Christianity in East and Southeast Asia*, 201.

[37] Yang et al., *Global Chinese Pentecostal and Charismatic Christianity*. Equally useful was Fulton, *China's Urban Christians*.

Holiness beliefs, so their practices are widespread among rural house churches.[38]

The demarcation between Pentecostal/Charismatics and Independents is complex, with much overlap.[39] One may argue that the majority of African Independent or Initiated churches are believed to practice a Pentecostal-Charismatic ethos. Independents are the second largest group in this region, with 103 million in 2020. It grew as the second fastest (4.3% per year) after Pentecostal/Charismatics. The largest Independents are Chinese house churches, some of which are classified as Pentecostal-Charismatic. (Some scholars argue that more Independents should be counted among Pentecostal-Charismatics.)[40]

Two Theological and Spiritual Dynamics[41]

Pentecostal pneumatology is missional in its nature. Although every Christian tradition affirms the person and work of the Holy Spirit, Pentecostalism has distinguished itself through its dynamic pneumatic beliefs and practices. Two distinctives deserve attention: the Spirit's empowerment and the "prophethood of all believers," based on the belief in the baptism in the Holy Spirit.

First, divine empowerment through the Spirit of God is a long-established tradition. Spirit empowerment assumes a divine call and God's commissioning for a specific task. Christ's promise of the Holy Spirit, thus, continues this pattern: "But you will receive power when the Holy Spirit comes on you; and you will be my witnesses in Jerusalem, and in all Judea and Samaria, and to the ends of the earth" (Acts 1:8). The key is "receiving (divine) power" (or "empowerment") through the Holy Spirit. The task is

---

[38]David Ro, "Mainland China (House Churches)," in *Christianity in East and Southeast Asia*, 67.

[39]E.g., Zurlo, "A Demographic Profile of Christianity in East and Southeast Asia," 14.

[40]Wesley, *The Church in China.*

[41]This is a summary of Wonsuk Ma, "Pentecostal Theological Formation: Serving the Future of Global Christianity and the Movement (sec 1)," *Pentecostal Education* 7, no. 2 (Fall 2022): 261-273.

to become Christ's witnesses to the ends of the earth. The Book of Acts can be called the Acts of the Holy Spirit, as his empowered witnesses scattered everywhere.

Spirit empowerment is the central dynamic causing the dramatic growth of Pentecostal and Charismatic Christianity. Spirit-empowered witnessing has several common elements. The early believers boldly proclaimed the lordship of Christ, as seen in Stephen's public proclamation in Acts 7. Their ministries were frequently accompanied by signs and wonders through the power of the Holy Spirit, such as healing and breaking prison doors. The newborn church met every day, breaking bread, praising the Lord, and sharing their possessions with the needy. As a result, the "Lord added to their number daily those who were being saved" (Acts 2:44-47). And this Spirit-empowered ministry is patterned after Jesus' ministry: ". . . how God anointed Jesus of Nazareth with the Holy Spirit and power, and how he went around doing good and healing all who were under the power of the devil because God was with him" (Acts 10:38). This is replicated in modern-day Pentecostal Christianity.

Second, this highly focused experience of empowerment was radically "democratized." The exclusive presence of God's Spirit upon a small number of selected individuals applied to all 120 on the day of Pentecost. Speaking to the puzzled audience in Jerusalem from many parts of the known world, Peter rightly chose the Joel 2 passage to explain the coming of the Holy Spirit:

> These people are not drunk, as you suppose. It's only nine in the morning! No, this is what was spoken by the prophet Joel:
>
> "In the last days, God says,
> I will pour out my Spirit on all people.
> Your sons and daughters will prophesy,
> your young men will see visions,
> your old men will dream dreams.
> Even on my servants, both men and women,
> I will pour out my Spirit in those days,
> and they will prophesy." (Acts 2:15-18)

The cataloging of diverse community members, including the marginalized, creates the clear impression that everyone (or "all people") is included. The advent of the Holy Spirit on the day of Pentecost fulfilled this promise of radical democratization. The Book of Acts demonstrates the witnessing of the good news by Spirit-empowered "everyone." Acts 11 records that "some" who fled persecution in Jerusalem reached various parts of the region, "spreading the word" initially among Jews (v. 19) but eventually to the Greeks (v. 20). They were the church planters in Syrian Antioch. Acts 19 reports that Paul's ministry in Ephesus began with the coming of the Holy Spirit (v. 6). While he and his companions continued their daily teaching in Tyrannus' lecture hall (v. 9) accompanied by "extraordinary miracles" (v. 11), within two years, "all the Jews and Greeks who lived in the province of Asia heard the word of the Lord" (v. 10). The new converts in Ephesus scattered to different parts of Asia as democratized Spirit-empowered witnesses.

To borrow from the law of physics, the more concentrated the power, the more power you can produce. The same rule reverses the strength of energy as the focus is spread. Pentecostal logic defies this scientific rule: the infinite amount of energy in the source will maintain the same power strength even if the scope is indefinitely expanded.

Equally encouraging is the missionary movement among churches in the region. As noted, the three top ten missionary countries are in the region of East and Southeast Asia: South Korea, the Philippines, and China. Also in Asia, though outside this region, India is ranked eighth. As the fastest growing segment of Christianity, Pentecostal/Charismatic (along with Independents) churches hold the key to the future expansion of the world's Christianity!

Summary

It may seem an audacious claim that Pentecostal Christianity in East and Southeast Asia is poised to play a pivotal role in the growth of Asian and global Christianity. The basis for this thesis is the region's Christian engagement with two prime religious competitors, Islam and nones, its growth potential and performance, and the unique possibility of Pentecostalism. As the stage is divinely set, human agency will determine the outcome of the growth potential.

Asian Christianity has failed for two millennia by achieving only a quarter of the world's Christian strength, but it is worth considering a question. What new elements would make it possible for the current and future Asian church to grow to the world's average and to lead the future growth of global Christianity?

This audacious proposition is a good possibility because of at least two new elements. The first is the emergence of new atheists in the region, with the largest group found in China. Since the middle of the twentieth century, the socialist state "converted" many religionists into state-initiated a-religionism. This socialist program reached its climax in the Cultural Revolution, denouncing the old Chinese way of life. A national campaign ran in a deeply opposing direction against the rich religious minds of the Chinese. When the destructive revolutionary decade ended in 1976, many were brought to various faiths, especially Christianity. Rural churches began to mushroom, primarily as house churches (literally and politically). The nones in the region comprised 26.4 percent of the population in 2020. Unlike their Western counterparts, who are primarily post-Christan, the region's nones seek genuine faith.

The second is Pentecostalism. This new and vibrant movement of Christianity has brought a new ability for Christianity to address both eternal hope and answers to daily struggles. It appeals to younger generations as well as the deeply religious Asian population. Pentecostalism, thus, has the best possibility of reaching out to folk religionists, the largest religious block in the region (54.6 percent). This versatility of Pentecostalism explains its fastest growth record among all religious groups.

Are these two new elements sufficient to warrant the exponential growth of Christianity in East and Southeast Asia? May fellow Pentecostals commit to the Lord's desire and become Spirit-empowered witnesses while trusting in the presence and power of the Holy Spirit! As Korean Pentecostals sang regularly,

Yes, I can do it,
It will be done.
Let's do it!
Nothing is Impossible to Those who Believe.
Even though I don't have enough,
I am not strong
The Lord will help you.
Don't doubt, don't be afraid. Miracles are coming!
In the Spirit and faith,
I can do it, and let's do it!

Chapter 7

Asian Pentecostalism: Serving All Pentecostal Waves[1]

At the emergence of the Third Wave movement in the 1980s, I critically interacted with Charles Kraft's lower-level power counter, questioning several assumptions, methodologies, and implied theologies.[2] At the end of my engagement, I voiced a clear need for First Wave (or Classical Pentecostals) to undertake a robust conversation with Third Wavers (now part of the Neo-Charismatic category).

Now, a half-century onward, the global landscape of Pentecostal/Charismatic Christianity has radically evolved. The need for exchanges, mutual learning, and mutual strengthening between all waves is even more urgent and essential. In looking toward the future, it is vital to map today's global Pentecostal families, the characterization of each family in the world, the Pentecostal scenery in East and Southeast Asia, and the role of the Classical Pentecostal church and academia to serve all the "waves" in the world.

---

[1]First published in *AJPS* 28, no. 1 (Feb. 2025), used by permission.

[2]Wonsuk Ma, "A 'First Waver' Looks at the 'Third Wave,'" 189-206.

Global Pentecostal Families/Waves

In this century, Todd Johnson and Gina Zurlo emerged as the dominant team for Christian statistics, beginning with Johnson's role in the second edition of the *World Christian Encyclopedia*[3] and the *Atlas of Global Christianity*.[4] The Johnson-Zurlo duo became responsible for the third edition of the *World Christian Encyclopedia* and the ongoing companion series to the *Atlas*. Many derivative titles come from their reference books, one of which is *Introducing Spirit-Empowered Christianity (ISEC)*.

In identifying Pentecostal believers, besides one theological definition by Kwabena Asamoah-Gyadu, the book uses a descriptive profile called "Family Resemblances." These include the baptism of the Spirit, glossolalia, and the validity of (especially supernatural) gifts of the Spirit.[5] Various terms have been attempted in referring to the diversity of Spirit-Christianity: "Pentecostal-Charismatic Christianity," "P/pentecostalism," "renewal movement," "full gospel," or "Spirit-empowered movement." I use Pentecostal(ism) as an umbrella term, sometimes interchangeably with "Pentecostal/Charismatics."

Three Families

The book has introduced three blocks or types of Pentecostal/Charismatic Christianity: Classical Pentecostals, Charismatics, and Neo-Charismatics (or Independent Charismatics). However, it is not always easy to determine who belongs to which group and for what reason. There are at least two reasons for this difficulty: 1) defining Pentecostalism itself has been long debated with no reasonable consensus, and 2) the entire movement is constantly evolving in new socio-cultural contexts with new ecclesial forms and theologies. The following is the generally agreed-upon

[3] *WCE*, 3rd ed.
[4] Johnson and Ross, *Atlas of Global Christianity*.
[5] *ISEC*, 14-30.

categorization, which was also adopted by the Johnson-Zurlo team. The figures are also from *ISEC*.[6]

The first type, Classical Pentecostals, is easiest to define. These believers belong to Pentecostal denominations. Most trace historically to the Azusa Street Mission (1906-1909), although some groups may predate it. As they are organized in denominations, they are structurally identifiable. They also share theological resemblances, such as the baptism in the Holy Spirit with speaking in tongues as its common evidence. Among the three types, this is the smallest (only 19.2% of global Pentecostals in 2020).

The second type, Charismatics, refers to those who accept and practice key tenets of Pentecostalism, such as fullness in the Spirit (instead of "baptism in the Spirit" as the first type calls it), and the validity of supernatural gifts such as healing and speaking in tongues. These believers remain in their existing churches. The origin of Charismatics is commonly attributed to the 1960s when Dennis Bennett, an Episcopal priest in California, publicly announced his experience with the Holy Spirit.[7] This is the second largest group though it is difficult to trace their numbers and practices. The largest part of this group is Catholic Charismatics (195.5 million in 2020), followed by Protestant Charismatics (68 million). Between 2020 and 2050, its annual growth rate is projected to be 1.28%, the lowest among the three (cf. 1.68% for Classical Pentecostals).

The third type is called either Neo-Charismatics (by the *New International Dictionary of Pentecostal-Charismatic Movements*) or Independent Charismatics (by Johnson and Zurlo). "Renewal" is another popular term referring to the pneumatic experiences of this group. By far, this category is the largest (projected at 42.1% of global Pentecostals in 2050). It is growing fastest (1.83% between 2020 and 2050). This group believes in and experiences the immediate and supernatural work of the Holy Spirit but does not identify with either type discussed above. As a "catch-all" category,

[6]The following table was constructed from the data in *ISEC*, 35–36.
[7]Bennett, *Nine O'Clock In The Morning.*

this type is extremely challenging to identify: who are they, and why are they counted in this category? Third Wave leaders once claimed that their movement represented this third category, which was proven to be presumptuous. Scholars frequently include the African Independent/Initiated churches and some Chinese house church networks in this broad yet ambiguous category.[8] Such a categorization offers its own challenge in distinguishing between this third category and "Independents" as a major Christian tradition.

Global Pentecostal Families						
	1900	Annual growth rate % 1900-2020	2020	Annual growth rate % 2020-2050	2050
Classical Pentecostals	20,000	7.75	123,700.000	1.68	203,700,000
Charismatics	12,000	8.70	268,300,000	1.28	393,200,000
Neo-Charismatics	949,400	4.76	252,300,000	1.83	434,600,000
Total	981,400	5.55	644,300,000	1.58	1,031,500,000

As previously noted, global Pentecostal Christianity is the main growth engine for global Christianity. Johnson and Zurlo projected that between 2020 and 2050, the world population would grow at 0.76% annually while global Christianity expanded at 1.03%. However, they expected global Pentecostalism to grow at 1.58%.[9]

[8]For a discussion on the Pentecostal nature of several Chinese house church networks, see Wesley, *The Church in China*. More recently, Yang, et al., *Global Chinese Pentecostal and Charismatic Christianity*.

[9]*ISEC*, 34. The table is by the author.

Two Global Networks

Today, there are two world networks for the Pentecostal world. The Pentecostal World Fellowship (PWF) was organized in Switzerland in May 1947. David du Plessis, at the helm of the fledgling Fellowship from 1948, led four triennial gatherings. Its mission statement is "To unite and mobilize the global Spirit-filled family in completing the Great Commission of Jesus Christ."[10] Its objectives emphasize fellowship and partnership among member churches, promoting world evangelization.[11] The PWF is a structured organization among Pentecostal denominations or Classical Pentecostals. This exclusive nature has historical roots: the founding of the Fellowship predated the Charismatic movement, although Neo-Charismatic churches both predate and postdate the PWF. It is assumed that at some point the Fellowship decided to serve the Pentecostal denominations. It currently has three Commissions: the Christian Unity Commission, the Education Commission (served by the independent World Alliance for Pentecostal Theological Education or WAPTE), and the World Mission Commission.[12] WAPTE's biennial journal, *Pentecostal Education*, serves as a voice of the Fellowship.

The PWF has held triennial conferences since its establishment. At its 2019 meeting in Calgary, William Wilson, President of Oral Roberts University and Chair of Empowered21, was elected Chair of the PWF. He was re-elected for a three-year term in the 2022 conference in Seoul.

---

[10]PWF, "Our Mission Statement," https://www.pwfellowship.org/about-us (accessed December 26, 2022).

[11]For the historical overview of the Fellowship, see William M. Wilson, "The Pentecostal World Fellowship: Its Past, Present, and Future," *Pentecostal Education* 7, no. 2 (Fall 2022): 153-164.

[12]The 2022 Conference edition of *Pentecostal Education* 7:2 (Fall 2022) includes a historical overview of each commission followed by a featured study. Until recently, there was the fourth commission, Pentecostal Commission on Religious Liberty, which has been combined into the World Mission Commission. For the full text, see https://wapte.org/wp-content/uploads/2022/09/Pentecostal-Education-7-2-Fall-2022-v2.pdf/.

The list of host nations reflects its heavy Euro-North American centrism in the early years. In later gatherings, the number of host countries in the Global South has increased.[13] Until the birth of Empowered21 in 2010, the PWF was the authoritative voice for global Pentecostal churches. It has exhibited stability and continuity as a membership organization. Throughout its history, the office address changed according to the elected chairperson. Thus, in recent years, the "headquarters" was in Kuala Lumpur, where Prince Guneratnam served as Chair (2010-2019). Then it moved to Tulsa, Oklahoma, USA (2019 to present), where Wilson operates as the President of Oral Roberts University.

An ongoing effort is to bring the scattered records to one place for posterity. All three commissions of the PWF agreed to deposit their records with the Center for Spirit-Empowered Research of Oral Roberts University. However, it has proven challenging to trace old documents of the central committee from its inception, digitize them, and collect them in one place. When the collection is complete, researchers will be significantly able to access official records of the Fellowship.

Whereas the PWF limits its membership to the Classical Pentecostal denominations (or Type 1), Empowered21 has an organic or relational structure. It traces its historical roots to the 2006 centenary celebration of the Azusa Street Mission. Its organizer, William Wilson, made the gathering international and inter-waval, going beyond the Classical Pentecostals. After this successful celebration in Los Angeles, California, he was left with the first database of who's who in global Pentecostal-Charismatic Christianity.

After a series of discernment processes (with the awareness that the PWF had been serving the Classical Pentecostal constituencies), Wilson launched the Empowered21 network in 2009 as an inclusive global network. It embraced all three families of Pentecostal Christianity. Through an extensive survey among the world's leaders of Pentecostal and Charismatic Christianity,

[13]See the list of the Pentecostal World Conferences in Wilson, "The Pentecostal World Fellowship," 156.

"Spirit-empowered" was selected as the umbrella term for the full spectrum of pneumatic Christianity.

A series of international preparatory meetings laid the groundwork for a 2015 Jerusalem gathering in the Pentecost week.[14] Its Global Council, the highest decision-making body, includes Pentecostal denominational leaders, megachurch pastors, independent ministry executives, evangelists, prophets, mission leaders, scholars, and younger leaders.[15] It currently has five specialty groups: Global Evangelist Alliance, NextGen Network, Global Prayer Alliance, Women's Alliance, and the Global Network of Spirit-Empowered Scholars, which organizes the annual Scholars Consultations.

Empowered21 holds annual regional meetings, with a global conference every five years (so far). The first was in Jerusalem in 2015; the second, planned for 2020 in Jerusalem, was moved online due to COVID-19. Despite its relational nature, the programs of Empowered21 are intentional through its active and engaging annual Global Council meetings.

The Scholars Consultation has met around a specific theme each year, culminating in a substantial scholarly book published each year. Before 2017, the publisher was Charisma House, but from 2018, it has been released by ORU Press.[16]

The Evangelist Alliance and NextGen also meets annually. Its 2023 gathering in Amsterdam launched the EveryONE campaign with a bold plan:

---

[14]Vinson Synan and Billy Wilson, *As the Waters Cover the Sea: The Story of Empowered21 and the Movement it Serves* (Tulsa: Empowered Books, 2021) includes Synan's introductory section (55-67) and Wilson's reflection on his journey from the centenary celebration of the Azusa Street Mission in 2006, the organization of Empowered21, and its vision for the two-thousand-year anniversary of the church's birth (75-148).

[15]Empowered21, "About Us," https://empowered21.com/about/global-leaders/ (accessed December 27, 2024).

[16]For details, see Wonsuk Ma, "Global Network of Spirit-Empowered Scholars: The Academic Working Group of the Empowered21," *Pentecostal Education* 9, no. 2 (Fall 2024): 243-261.

> In 2033, the world will celebrate the 2000-year anniversary of Christ's crucifixion, resurrection, and the birth of the Church on the Day of Pentecost. We believe the decade leading up to 2033 will be a defining decade, a decade in which it is possible for every person on earth to hear the gospel. Amsterdam2023 is the starting point for this decade of unprecedented evangelism.[17]

The "Vision of 2033" is the foundational commitment of Empowered21. It was first articulated at the 2013 Global Council meeting in Honolulu.[18] The 2023 meeting was sharply focused on this vision. Providentially, Wilson leads both the PWF and Empowered21, fully representing the world's Spirit-empowered or Pentecostal-Charismatic Christianity in many ecumenical platforms. This fast-growing segment of world Christianity now has a credible voice.

How well will each network strengthen the other? In the 2022 Seoul PWF triennial conference, Empowered21 maintained a service posture. Its Scholars Consultation was jointly organized by Empowered21, WAPTE of PWF, and the host church, although much of planning and managing rested on Empowered21's shoulders.

An Inventory Exercise of Gifts and Un-gifts of Each Wave

This section is the crux of this chapter. What is the identity of each Pentecostal-Charismatic family/wave and how can its unique gifts strengthen the other waves? Each family has weak (or "un-gifted") areas or gaps that can be filled by gifts from other waves. For each wave, it is important to consider: 1) gifts coming out of the mode of its organization; 2) the way it is represented in and recognized by the broader church world; 3) the general social

---

[17]Empowered21, "Amsterdam2023," https://amsterdam2023.com (accessed December 27, 2022).

[18]Synan and Wilson, *As the Waters Cover the Sea*, 83-85.

status of the adherents; and 4) areas of "un-gifts" (or weakness) in which other Pentecostal families may be of assistance.

Classical Pentecostals

Classical Pentecostals have the most organized operation as they are Pentecostal denominations. They bring strengths and gifts due to their intentional development. Mission comes first, as all the Pentecostal denominations subscribe to the belief in Spirit baptism and its missional purpose (based on Acts 1:8). The 2021 report of the USA Assemblies of God lists 5,224 mission workers out of its 2.9 million membership. This means every mission worker is sent by 561 members.[19] This is compared with North American statistics: 135,000 mission workers out of 267.9 million believers. That is, 1,984 members send out one mission worker.[20]

The distinguished mission operations of Pentecostal denominations can also be examined from other aspects, including finance. The 2022 report of the USA Assemblies of God World Mission included a total of $232.7 million given toward mission, with an average of $81.80 given per member per year.[21] As Pentecostals have expanded their understanding of mission and activities from evangelism to social service and public theology[22] and numerical growth, their voice is being heard by other churches and society. Although other statistics are not available, this giving must outperform the Christian average on the continent.

---

[19]Assemblies of God, "Statistics," https://ag.org/About/Statistics (accessed December 28, 2022).

[20]*WCE*, 3rd ed., 32.

[21]Assemblies of God World Missions, "Vital Stats" (2022 Issue 1), https://www.agwm.org/cms-data/file/vital-stats.pdf (accessed December 28, 2022). One should be reminded that other regional pictures may not closely correspond with the North American illustration.

[22]For the evolution of Pentecostal mission thinking, see Wonsuk Ma and Julie C. Ma, "Missiology: Evangelization, Holistic Ministry, and Social Justice," in *Routledge Handbook of Pentecostal Theology*, ed. Wolfgang Vondey (London: Routledge, 2020), 279-89.

Another strength of the structured nature of Classical Pentecostals is theological development. Pentecostal denominations have theological educational institutions that train the workers of their denominations and other churches. Some function as research centers, with faculty members acting as researchers. An increasing number of these institutions offer both academic and professional postgraduate programs. Denominations and theological institutions have developed publishing outlets. Initially, these served local churches of the denominations, but now they also disseminate theological studies to the broader Christian world. With financial resources, their theological identity is well established.

This growing institutional and theological strength led to the establishment of academic societies. The Society for Pentecostal Studies (SPS, with its journal *Pneuma*) was established in 1970 by three Classical Pentecostal scholars: William W. Menzies, H. Vinson Synan, and Horace Ward to advance Pentecostal scholarship. It also draws academics from Charismatic and Neo-Charismatic camps. SPS illustrates the convening power of Classical Pentecostalism to bring other "waves" together.

The organized structure of Classical Pentecostals offers a presence and voice among other churches. The sustained desire for the Secretaries of Christian World Communions was to have a representative of the world's Pentecostal churches. This invitation was fulfilled in 2021 at the Pentecostal World Conference by formally approving the creation of the Christian Unity Commission.[23] Despite the unofficial nature of the body for many decades until the formation of the CUC, it has exerted a significant influence on the ecumenical movement, international politics, and social issues.

Similarly, the Pentecostal World Fellowship is included on the Central Committee of the WCC. The GCF also offers a growing alternative space of church unity. From its inception, Pentecostals have been considered a "pillar" of world Christianity, thus, of the

[23]Cecil M. Robeck, "Growing Opportunities for Pentecostal Ecumenical Engagement," *Pentecostal Education* 7, no. 2 (Fall 2022): 180.

Forum. Such representation brings Pentecostal voices to various discussions and processes.

In a century, Classical Pentecostals evolved from their "poor" identity in social, economic, and even ecclesiastical status, to a recognizable, reputable, and invited position. This identity of "poor" has played a vital role in Pentecostal identity. The movement began as a marginal religious phenomenon among the socially and economically "disinherited." The participants of the Azusa Street Mission were primarily "colored," less educated, and poor, drawn from the lower social strata.[24]

The presence of "whites" in this beginning phase disgusted local media. Pentecostals were branded as religious fanatics. A local newspaper chose the headline of its report as "Weird Babel of Tongues: New Sect of Fanatics is Breaking Loose."[25] Participants were no longer welcomed by their churches due to their Pentecostal beliefs and experiences. This was a rich soil wherein to nurture and develop an explosive religious movement.

Since then, Pentecostal churches throughout the world have attracted the marginalized and deprived masses to the message of Christ's imminent return, spiritual empowerment, physical healing, miracles, and blessing. Unsurprisingly, the belief in and experience of the baptism in the Holy Spirit was the central tenet of Pentecostalism. The crux of it is "empowerment:" the "poor" are now "fired up" and revolutionizing their lives and the Christian faith.[26]

Pentecostalism's premillennial eschatological urgency further fueled its missionary zeal for the Spirit-empowered "poor." A century onward, the movement has spread like wildfire and "moved on" from its "poor" status, physically, economically, and socially.

---

[24]A window to the daily scene of the Mission is provided by Frank Bartleman, *Azusa Street* (South Plainfield, NJ: Bridge Publishing, 1980).

[25]*Los Angeles Daily Times*, April 18, 1906.

[26]For example, Wonsuk Ma, "'When the Poor Are Fired Up:' The Role of Pneumatology in Pentecostal-Charismatic Mission," *Transformation* 24, no. 1 (2007): 28-34.

Its presence is sought by the associations that once ignored and distanced themselves from these irreputable "fanatics."

These strengths have now become their weaknesses. The organizational structure (or "institutionalization") of the Assemblies of God, which once supported its spiritual vitality, is now "running" the organization. When asked how the Pentecostal denomination maintains a high level of mission operation in the face of eroded Pentecostal spirituality and waning premillennial urgency, a highly respected denominational leader and scholar reservedly responded in private, "The organization!"

A generation ago, the prominent Pentecostal sociologist Margaret Poloma issued a clear warning.[27] The steady decrease in baptism in the Spirit among Classical Pentecostal believers indicates the erosion of Pentecostal distinctives. Church attendance in the Assemblies of God has steadily declined from 1.9 million in 2011 to 1.7 million in 2021, a 10.5 percent loss in a decade.[28] The aging of ministers is another worrying indicator: the Assemblies of God 2021 status report lists the average age of its 37,557 credentialed ministers at 56, but 61 for ordained ministers.[29] This aging trend has been consistent over the years.[30]

There are signs of cultural and doctrinal rigidity, and of slowly moving away from the Assembly of God's original nature of a "fellowship." Several independent ministries/churches with global influence, such as Hillsong in Sydney and Bethel Church in California, were once Classical Pentecostal congregations.

One encouraging demographic change is the increase of multi-ethnic components within the Assemblies of God. These grew

---

[27]Margaret M. Poloma, *The Assemblies of God at the Crossroads: Charisma and Institutional Dilemmas* (Knoxville: University of Tennessee Press, 1989).

[28](USA) Assemblies of God, "Reports: Major worship Service Attendance by District Network, 2011-2021," https://ag.org/About/Statistics (accessed December 30, 2022).

[29](USA) Assemblies of God, "Reports: Ministers by Age 2021," https://ag.org/About/Statistics (accessed December 30, 2022).

[30](USA) Assemblies of God, "2023 Summary Statistical Report," https://ag.org/About/Statistics (accessed March 8, 2025).

from less than 30% in 2001 to 44.3% in 2021.[31] Perhaps this is the redemption of the denomination's infamous founding ideology, which divided American Pentecostalism along racial lines by creating a white Pentecostal group (away from the celebrated multi-ethnic nature of the Azusa Street Mission).[32]

The extensive use of the US Assemblies of God data is an unmistakable illustration of the organizational resource of Classical Pentecostalism. Pentecostal denominations in other parts of the world may not have such detailed data. It is even harder to obtain meaningful data from the two other Pentecostal families.

The challenges identified in this denomination are not limited to the Western Pentecostal denominations. Many Classical Pentecostal churches, both in the Global North and South, have aging memberships. The younger generation is slowly declining. Spiritual vitality is eroding with various signs of institutionalization. For example, the Korean Pentecostal church struggles with these issues and is desperately searching for answers.

Charismatics

The Pentecostal family of Charismatics is found mainly in historic Catholic and Protestant churches. Johnson-Zurlo provides the following figures:[33]

---

[31](USA) Assemblies of God, "Reports: Adherents by Race 2001 through 2021," https://ag.org/About/Statistics (accessed December 30, 2022).

[32]Sociologically speaking, the most astonishing accomplishment of the Azusa Street Mission was brilliantly captured in the saying, "the 'color line' was washed away in the blood." In Frank Bartleman, *How Pentecost Came to Los Angeles: The Story Behind the Azusa Street Revival*, ed. Cecil M. Robeck, Jr. (Originally published in 1925; Springfield, MO: Gospel Publishing House, 2017), 54.

[33]*ISEC*, 40. The table is by the author.

	1900	AGR%* 1900-2020	2020	AGR%* 2020-2050	2050
Catholic Charismatics	10,000	8.58	195,475,000	0.93	257,800,000
Protestant Charismatics	2,000	9.08	68,000,000	2.16	128,919,000
Orthodox Charismatics	0	9.40	4,813,000	0.99	6,464,000
Global Total	**12,000**	**8.70**	**268,288,000**	**1.28**	**393,183,000**

**Annual Growth Rate Percent*

Statistically, Charismatics grew fastest between 1900 and 2020, compared with 7.55% for Classical Pentecostals and 4.76% for Neo-Charismatics. However, for 2020-2050, Charismatics are expected to grow slowest (at 1.28%) among the three families (at 1.68% for Classical Pentecostals and 1.83% for Neo-Charismatics).

The table reveals that the largest group in the Charismatic family is Catholic Charismatics. They represented almost 73% of the global Charismatic believers in 2020. The overview of Catholic Charismatics by Johnson and Zurlo in the Americas is also helpful. They are frequently organized in covenant communities, such as The Word of God Community (Ann Arbor, Michigan, USA) and the El Shaddai DWXI Prayer Partners Fellowship International in the Philippines.

Francis MacNutt's Spirit-filled missionary itinerary illustrates the pattern of their growth and expansion through Latin America. After his experience with the Holy Spirit, this Dominican American priest journeyed through Bolivia, Peru, and Mexico. Teaching about and advocating the fullness of the Spirit in prayer meetings and conferences, Catholics who had this spiritual experience began to influence their parish churches. Various communities were established while "Pentecostalizing" existing prayer groups, communities, and parish churches.

The Philippines witnessed a similar surge of Charismatic prayer groups in the early 1980s. The resulting communities, including the large El Shaddai group, claim eight million adherents worldwide.[34]

Other prayer groups developed into Protestant fellowships and networks. With its growth and prominence advocated by Cardinal Leon Joseph Suenens (1904-1996), the Catholic Charismatic Renewal (CCR) has been recognized since the papacy of John Paul II. Today, the Vatican-based CHARIS International serves the worldwide Catholic Charismatic communities and believers. Pope Francis celebrated the CCR's 50th anniversary in June 2017.[35]

The organization of Protestant Charismatics is an entirely different matter. Charismatic Anglicans in Great Britain are identified by local churches, such as the Holy Trinity Brompton in London and St. Aldates of Oxford. Considering the parish nature of local congregations, the Charismatic identity of local congregations happens more in cities than in rural communities.

Charismatic churches and ministers created *New Wine* with a clear Charismatic identity: "A Spirit-empowered movement . . . to equip the local Church to release confident, Spirit-filled followers of Jesus."[36] Its annual conference gathers, builds relationships, and strengthens the Spirit-empowered churches. Although it is an "Evangelical" entity, *New Wine* has promoted and strengthened Charismatic segments of the Anglican Church.

There may not be similar structural support in Anglican or Episcopal Charismatics in other parts of the world. Similarly, most Protestant Charismatics are scattered (or even "hidden") in existing congregations with no structural support. Johnson and Zurlo sampled a wide range of churches with substantial Charismatic presence: Evangelical Church of Makane Yesus of Ethiopia, Evangelical Free Church of Finland, Wabag Lutheran Church of Papua New Guinea, Korean Presbyterian Church

---

[34]For Mike Velarde's theological controversy, see Wiegele, *Investing in Miracles*.

[35]Jeannie Ewing, "Golden Jubilee Year for Catholic Charismatic Renewal," *Today's Catholic,* December 11, 2017, https://todayscatholic.org/golden-jubilee-year-catholic-charismatic-renewal.

[36]New Wine, "About Us," https://www.new-wine.org/about/ (accessed January 1, 2023).

(Tonghap), Salvation of Army India, United Church of Zambia, and Ethiopian Orthodox Church.[37]

The unique strength is the interface of Pentecostal theology and spirituality with those of their "mother churches." The ultimate purpose of the modern Pentecostal outpouring was to renew the whole church. Charismatics have demonstrated that the vitality of the Holy Spirit can renew and revitalize any theological system. Many believe that Charismatic renewals have revitalized various Catholic congregations and slowed their ongoing decline.

The creative engagement between Pentecostal pneumatology and historic theological traditions has challenged rather narrow definitions of Pentecostal theology. A sermon on "Ethical Fashion" by Charlie Cleverly (a Charismatic Anglican preacher) admonished parishioners to count the human cost of cheap clothes.[38] This sermon was delivered in the wake of a fire in a garment factory in Bangladesh, which killed many female workers. Similarly, Andrew Lord (a Charismatic Anglican missiologist) published a study on charismatic missiology. He combined Anglican theological resources with the dynamic work of the Holy Spirit. This creative interaction and interface resulted in a holistic missiology by incorporating justice and public responsibility into the Pentecostal mission framework.[39] The Alpha course (from English Anglican Charismatics) is a widely used tool for evangelism with the Spirit baptism at the climax. Many more examples can be added from other ecclesial traditions.

The social status of Charismatics generally reflects the middle class in the population of mainline Christianity. Unlike the "poor" identity of Classical Pentecostals, Charismatic believers exhibit higher educational, social, and economic status with more influence on their society. They meet in hotels, restaurants,

---

[37]*ISEC*, 86-107.

[38]By Charlie Cleverly at St. Aldates Church in Oxford, UK (date unknown, but the sermon was delivered after the 2012 garment factory fire in Bangladesh, which killed at least 112 workers).

[39]Andrew Lord, *Spirit-Shaped Mission: A Holistic Charismatic Missiology* (Bletchley, UK: Paternoster, 2005).

or large homes. Their eschatology also tends to move away from premillennial urgency.

Several sociologists have suggested that the Pentecostal faith's explosive energy comes from individuals' deprived states. As Classical Pentecostals struggle to maintain Pentecostal fervor and ethos in economically developed settings, the flourishing of Pentecostal spirituality in a non-deprivation environment may hold the key to sustained spirituality in good and bad times.

On the other hand, the "mother church" theology and ecclesial hierarchy can limit the work of the Holy Spirit. For example, guidelines for Catholic prayer and healing meetings in the Philippines resulted in the formation of various fellowships by prayer groups, with resulting independence from the Catholic Church.[40] Critical theological tension is another possibility if the "mother" theology has no room to accommodate the immediate and supernatural work of the Holy Spirit. An example may be dispensational theology, which promotes the cessationist understanding of supernatural gifts today.

One area of vulnerability among Charismatics is their lack of organizational structure. As a result, their presence is not properly represented. Their voices are not heard within their churches or among fellow Pentecostal-Charismatics. Due to the lack of structured support, much of Charismatic growth results from the leadership of charismatic champions.

During its heyday in the 1970s, leaders of the Charismatic movement created an interdenominational service arm: the North American Renewal Service Committee. Organized by Vinson Synan, large interdenominational Charismatic conferences were held in New Orleans (1986 and 1987), San Antonio (1988), Indianapolis (1990), Orlando (1995), and St. Louis (2000).[41]

---

[40]Archdiocesan Office for Research and Development, "Guidelines of the Catholic Charismatic Renewal Movement in the Archdiocese of Manila."

[41]For archival collection, see Digital Showcase, "North American Renewal Service Committee," https://digitalshowcase.oru.edu/narsc/ (accessed January 3, 2023). See also the personal accounts of Vinson Synan, *Where He Leads Me: The Vinson Synan Story* (Franklin Springs, GA: LifeSprings Resources, 2019), 157-182.

This ambitious ecumenical corporation waned as the champions disappeared from the stage, one after another. The movement's relative instability is reflected in its projected slow growth, a 1.27% annual growth rate between 2020 and 2050, lower than Classical Pentecostals (1.68%) and Neo-Charismatics (1.83%).

Also noticeable is the stagnant "growth" of Charismatic believers. Catholic Charismatics are a good example. In the twentieth century, it grew at an annual rate of 8.58%. This is compared to the Catholic Church's growth of 1.36% per annum. Charismatics grew over six times faster than their mother church. However, almost all the "conversion" occurred within the Catholic Church. While it renewed the church with spiritual vibrancy, direct evangelism might have been negligible. This argument is supported by the stagnation of Catholic Charismatics in the current century. Between 2000 and 2020, they recorded only a 0.93% annual growth rate, even lower than the Catholic Church (0.96%).[42] This limitation is inherent in the nature of the Charismatic movement: its primary theological focus has been on the "renewal" of existing churches, unlike Classical Pentecostals who have been eager in evangelism.

This again shows the urgency and validity of inter-waval exchanges and engagements. One viable space for such interactions is academic networks and gatherings. For example, SPS first welcomed Catholic Charismatic and non-Classical Pentecostal scholars for fellowship and interactions.

Neo-Charismatics

Neo-Charismatics is the most challenging and scattered group among the three families. The sampling of Johnson and Zurlo illustrates this complexity: Apostolic, Charismatic (former Type 2), Deliverance, Full Gospel, Hidden Christian, "Believers in Christ," media believers, non-traditional, house, cell, Oneness, Pentecostal (former Type 1), Word of Faith, Zion,

[42]See the table above on page 146.

and Others (non-Charismatic networks).[43] Preferring the term "Independent Charismatics," Johnson and Zurlo argue that "while the classification and chronology of the first two types are rather straightforward, thousands of churches and movements that "resemble" the first two types do not fit their definitions. These constitute a third type and often predate the first two types."[44]

This family is by far the largest (about 42.1%) and fastest growing (1.83% annual growth rate) among the three types (using the 2050 projection). For comparison, the whole Pentecostal-Charismatics group is expected to grow at 1.57% and global Christianity at 1.03% per annum, as seen on page 146.

Due to their extremely diverse nature, a few samples are used to map the landscape. First is the Third Wave. Purported to be the third evolution of Pentecostal renewal after the two "waves," some scholars use this term to represent Neo-Charismatics. It started in the early 1980s with the "Church Growth and Miracles" course offered by Peter Wagner and John Wimber at Fuller Theological Seminary. This also marked the Pentecostalization of Evangelical churches. Signs and wonders characterize the Third Wave, with close attention to the theories and practices of power encounters.[45] Some early advocates later created the New Apostolic Movement. Today, many churches, networks, and ministries are loosely connected with this movement.

Second is the International House of Prayer (IHOPKC) in Kansas City, Missouri, USA. It was founded by Mike Bickle in 1999 to become a center of intercessory prayer and worship on a full 24/7 schedule. Perhaps taking a cue from the power-encounter teaching of the Third Wave, the goal became to prepare thousands of full-time intercessory missionaries for the Lord's return. Prominent on its website were the ministry's main emphases: "Prayer Room," "Prophetic History," "Works of Justice," and "Global Bridegroom

---

[43] *ISEC*, 39-40.

[44] Ibid., 107.

[45] E.g., C. Peter Wagner, *Signs and Wonders Today: The Story of Fuller Theological Seminary's Remarkable Course on Spiritual Power*, expanded ed. (Alamonte Springs, FL: Creation House, 1987).

Fast."[46] IHOPKC set the tone for many independent charismatics until its recent downfall regarding systemic sexual abuse. Fortunately, other organized ministries, including Youth With a Mission (YWAM) and The Call, led by Lou Engle, have maintained their similar outreaches to Neo-Charismatics, especially young adults oriented towards missions, prayer, and worship.

Third is the Universal Church of the Kingdom of God in Brazil, founded by Edir Macedo in 1977. Operating throughout Brazil and more than one hundred countries, it claims about 8 million members worldwide. In 2000, I attended the mid-week meeting of a local church in Sao Paulo. The service lasted the whole day, with singing, prayers, testimonies, preaching, and an extended session for healing exorcism. The message was about God's power and blessing. The entire rear wall was full of crutches and wheelchairs, signs of healing. The church is in the middle of a large market, and most attendees are from lower social sectors. Macedo's prosperity gospel is well-known, including his personal net worth of $1,000,000,000 in 2015.[47] With its substantial influence, the church influences politics by endorsing candidates.

Fourth is the Redeemed Christian Church of God, Nigeria, which is part of the African Initiated or Independent Churches. Founded by Olufemi Akindayomi in 1947 and succeeded by Enoch Adoboye, the church is known for its contemporary and lively worship, spiritual warfare, and prosperity message. The Redeemed Church has campaigned against Islamic influence and violence from the north, responding to the nation's delicate religious tension between Christianity and Islam. Its membership in its home country was 1.6 million in 2015, with another half a million globally.[48]

As in the sampled communities, most Neo-Charismatics are organized either as free-standing congregations or networked churches, including multi-site churches (often large or mega in

---

[46]International House of Prayer Kansas City, "About the International House of Prayer," https://ihopkc.org/about/ihopkc (accessed January 8, 2025).

[47]*ISEC*, 134.

[48]Ibid., 142-43.

size). Single independent churches tend to have charismatically gifted and strong leaders who attract followers. For example, Life.Church, founded and led by Craig Groeschel in 2006, is listed as the largest church in the United States with a reported weekly attendance of 85,000 in 2018.[49] This multi-site church is in several states (43 in the January 2023 count).[50] Its service, member demography, music, message, and ethos are modern, younger-generation friendly, celebratory, and uplifting. There is hardly any Pentecostal teaching, e.g., healing, praying in tongues, or prophecy, but Groeschel's illustrations and his own testimonies do not exclude God's supernatural intervention. The most "Charismatic" element of the church may be music: dynamic, celebratory, and participatory. The church exercises extreme generosity in freely releasing its ministry resources.[51] Perhaps the most significant contribution is the *YouVersion Bible*. Launched in 2008 by Life.Church, this Bible app offers the Bible in more than 1,900 languages. It has been installed on 545 million devices, with 5.5 billion app openings in 2022.[52] This free tool is offered to anyone, thanks to the church's substantial investment.

In this same category are many African denominations and networks under the umbrella of the Organization of African Instituted Churches (AICs). The organization's website claims about 60 million members over "tens of thousands of AICs denominations across Sub-Saharan Africa and the African Diaspora."[53] Each denomination has its unique history, leader's vision, and theology, so one church's structure, theology, and

---

[49]Hartford Institute for Religious Research, "Megachurch Database," http://hirr.hartsem.edu/megachurch/database.html (accessed January 6, 2025).

[50]Life.Church, "Locations," https://www.life.church/locations/ (accessed January 6, 2023).

[51]Life.Church, "What Is Open Network?" https://open.life.church/ (accessed January 6, 2023).

[52]YouVersion, "YouVersion reports Verse of the Year and Ukrainian movement," https://www.youversion.com/press/youversion-reports-verse-of-the-year-and-ukrainian-movement/ (accessed January 3, 2023).

[53]Organization of African Instituted Churches, "About Us," https://www.oaic.org/about-us/ (accessed January 6, 2023).

ethos are much different from another. Some are criticized for the indigenous spirituality incorporated into the church's theology and life. Others are known for extreme prosperity preaching and the flamboyant lifestyle of the leaders.[54]

Despite this challenging diversity, AICs are organized by congregations, networks, and denominations, unlike Charismatics. Because of this structured nature, some denominations are members of various global church networks, including the World Council of Churches. The Organization of AICs enhances the presence of member churches. The Organization is also a member of the All-African Conference of Churches.

However, such may not be true for other Neo-Charismatic churches and networks. For example, several house church networks in China are categorized as Neo-Charismatics, yet their data is hard to obtain. The sheer diversity of theology and organizational structures allows maximum autonomy for each entity to explore creative spirituality and engagement with their contexts. This may explain the move of Classical and Charismatic groups into this category, such as Bethel Church of California, with their theological slant towards the New Apostolic movement and its celebrated music.

The family of Neo-Charismatics tends to intersect with local communities, addressing their challenges. Most of their strength may also turn to weaknesses (or un-gifts). In this regard, prosperity preaching may have arisen from their concern over widespread poverty in their communities. Such preaching has become a theological and social challenge as some preachers boast of their wealth and private jets.

If all three Pentecostal families would combine their resources and reflections, they could more easily distinguish the biblical teaching of God's blessing from biblically questionable teachings.[55]

---

[54]For a useful snapshot, see J. Kwabena Asamoah-Gyadu, *African Charismatics: Current Developments Within Independent Indigenous Pentecostalism in Ghana*, Studies of Religion in Africa 27 (Leiden: Brill, 2004).

[55]For a reflective essay, see Wonsuk Ma, "Blessing in Pentecostal

Implications for Pentecostals in East and Southeast Asia

Statistics shed light on the number of Pentecostal-Charismatic believers worldwide. In 1970, about 4.6 million people were identified as Pentecostal-Charismatics among 1,277 million in East and Southeast Asia (0.36% of the population). In 2020, the Pentecostal-Charismatic believers grew to almost one hundred million followers, representing 0.43% of the population in the religion. They occupied a sizeable (more than one-third) proportion of the total Christian population. Equally noteworthy is their annual growth rate, especially in East Asia (7.94%), which is the second highest (after West Asia, which has a much smaller population).[56]

East & Southeast Asia, 2020 (in million)					
	Population	Christians	Pentecostal-Charismatics	% of Christians	Annual Growth Rate 1970-2020
East Asia	1,663.6	128.8	47.4	37	7.94%
Southeast Asia	669.0	153.1	52.5	34	5.51%
Total	**2,332.6**	**281.9**	**99.9**	**35.4**	

In conclusion, Pentecostal-Charismatics share many values, assumptions, and practices. There are apparent differences, including their social context. These distinctions open new space for fruitful engagement and gift-sharing among the waves. The First Wave is better positioned to reach out to the other waves and offer its organizational, institutional, and theological resources. At the same time, its institutionalizing trend and waning dynamic demand new vitality and energy from the other waves.

In 2024, I attended an annual leadership conference near Rome with approximately 200 Italian lay Catholic Charismatic leaders. The speakers were diverse: Catholic academics from

Theology and Mission," in *Pentecostal Mission and Global Christianity*, ed. Wonsuk Ma, Veli-Matti Kärkkäinen, and J. K. Asamoah-Gyadu (Oxford: Regnum Books, 2014), 272-91.

[56]*ISEC*, 158. The table is by the author.

England, Poland, Belarus, Argentina, and Brazil, in addition to Italian leaders. As the only non-Catholic presenter, I shared my informal observations. This included the stagnation of Catholic Charismatics in this century, offering the renewal focus as a primary reason.

I compared Brazilian Catholics (148.5 million adherents) and Pentecostal churches (in this case, the Assemblies of God with 21.0 million). The Assemblies of God has more local churches (160,978) than the Catholics (11,716). The results are staggering. Each Catholic church serves 12,675 members, while the Assemblies of God serves 130.5 people on average.[57] The other side of the same coin is the saturated presence of Pentecostal churches, sometimes a makeshift structure in small villages and storefronts. In contrast, a Catholic church is found only in cities and large towns with massive buildings. This difference comes from different theological foci of Spirit-filled and empowered life: renewal (from the life-giving work of the Holy Spirit) for Catholics and Spirit-empowerment for witness (from the charismatic gifting of the Holy Spirit) for Pentecostals. The latter expands to "the prophethood of all believers," with an endless supply of people called to serve. I admonished conference attendees to examine the Pentecostal understanding of the Holy Spirit.

This illustration and several suggestions above indicate that Pentecostal churches and institutions may offer unique gifts to other Spirit-empowered families. One area of benefit occurs when those with developed theological education and scholarly engagement serve groups with limited resources. Classical Pentecostals with highly developed institutional and theological assets and theological schools can proactively open their doors to smaller Pentecostal churches and Charismatic communities. They can also enhance independent and neo-Charismatic churches.

---

[57]The statistics are from *WCE*, 3rd ed., 138-42. It is well recognized that the Catholic Church has defined a "church" much more strictly than Protestant churches. For example, chapels, monasteries, and convents are not counted as local churches, while they regularly hold worship services open to the public.

With formal and informal agreements, a Pentecostal Bible college or seminary can offer common courses for future leaders of other communities. Unique courses, such as history, doctrine, etc., are taught by leaders serving as adjunct or associate faculty members. The explosion of online course delivery enhances such collaborations.

A joint colloquium or seminar on a common subject can also afford an opportunity for fellowship and mutual learning. The annual William Menzies Lectureship of the Asia Pacific Theological Seminary (APTS) in the Philippines has encouraged active interaction among Pentecostal theologians. Following its success, other Pentecostal schools began similar programs. The Pentecostal Leadership Conference, hosted by the Pentecostal Research Center of the Bible College of Malaysia, is one of the newest. Both programs extend their invitation to various Pentecostal-Charismatic constituencies.

For a more intentional mutual exchange, the Asian Pentecostal Society has the potential to bring Charismatic and Neo-Pentecostal academics to a common place for interaction and sharing. The history of the Society for Pentecostal Studies shows that an academic society is ecumenical in nature. Thus, the leadership must be ecumenically minded in broadly extending invitations to Pentecostal-Charismatic academics.

The Asia Pacific Theological Association (APTA) is another promising instrument. Established in 1990 among Assemblies of God Bible schools and seminaries in the Asia-Pacific region, the Association has expanded to other Pentecostal denominational schools.[58] It provides accreditation, teaching certification services, and theological resources for member schools. Its Theological Commission has organized conferences on national Pentecostal

---

[58]For its history, see Denise A. Austin and John F. Carter, "Asia Pacific Theological Association: Three Decades of Contribution toward Pentecostal Research and Ministry Training," *International Bulletin of Mission Research* 46, no. 4 (Oct 2022): 505-15.

histories, collecting and editing these for a valuable resource book.[59]

In its three-decade history, the Association has brilliantly achieved national representation and cooperation among theological educators and institutional leaders in the region. APTA has generously included non-member schools in its meetings from the beginning, taking advantage of opportunities to foster interactions and exchanges while enhancing the Association's visibility.[60] In the next decades, APTA can offer the same generosity to Charismatic and Neo-Charismatic institutions, including church-based training programs.[61] Every time the Association and its Commissions meet in different cities of the region, the leaders can carefully identify and invite Pentecostal-Charismatic theological institutions in the area.

This regional association also provided leadership in establishing WAPTE,[62] the global body serving various regional Pentecostal theological associations. WAPTE serves as the Education Commission of the Pentecostal World Fellowship.[63]

Academic periodicals afford similar opportunities for sharing studies and interacting with others. The launch of the *Asian Journal of Pentecostal Studies* in 1998 by APTS signaled the birth of Asian Pentecostal scholarship and its desire to dialogue with fellow Pentecostals and Evangelicals actively. For example, its "Speaking

---

[59]Denise A. Austin, Jacqueline Grey, and Paul W. Lewis, ed., *Asia Pacific Pentecostalism* (Leiden: Brill, 2019).

[60]Austin and Carter, "Asia Pacific Theological Association," 507.

[61]This extended vision is already present in the Association's Constitution and By Laws: "This association is a cooperative effort among these [Assemblies of God Bible schools] and other Pentecostal/Charismatic schools in the region," https://apta-schools.org/wp-content/uploads/2013/06/APTA-Constitution-and-By-Laws-2011-Edition.pdf (accessed June 12, 2024).

[62]John F. Carter, et al., "Advancing the Vision for Pentecostal Theological Education Worldwide: The Origins and Development of the World Alliance for Pentecostal Theological Education," *Pentecostal Education* 7, no. 2 (Fall 2022): 241-60.

[63]For the regional and ecclesial networks of Pentecostal education, see the entire issue of *Pentecostal Education* 9, no. 1 (Spring 2024) under the theme, "Movements and Associations for Pentecostal Theological Education."

Tongues" issue in 2000 included Evangelical scholars interacting with Pentecostals. The same seminary created the *Journal of Asian Mission* and later gifted it to the Asia Graduate School of Theology, the consortium of Evangelical schools under the Asia Theological Association.

There are other potential opportunities and spaces to promote an inter-waval engagement, fellowship, and cooperation. History teaches us that no church or denomination is so perfect as not to need others' gifts. Everyone is called to generously offer gifts to others to edify the whole Body of Christ while exercising humility in receiving others' gifts to strengthen themselves. Thus, Classical Pentecostals in Asia who know their gifts can share them with other Pentecostal-Charismatic communities.

CHAPTER 8

Asian Pentecostals Together with Global Churches

The previous two chapters affirm that Pentecostalism exists within the larger Christian or ecumenical context. Pentecostalism finds meaning only in relation to other churches. Its role in leading the whole of Christianity in sustained growth depends on two parts: encouraging its own growth to continue and serving other churches so that they also grow.

Pentecostal engagement with other churches is at the forefront when looking at the three Pentecostal families, particularly Charismatics. An increasing number of independent Charismatic churches began within the historic churches. Yet the most significant number of Charismatics remain in their "mother" churches. They are the Pentecostal "missionaries" to the historic churches to renew them by the power of the Holy Spirit.

A rich history of Pentecostal leaders actively brought the Pentecostal message to the ecumenical platforms, often against strong opposition from their Pentecostal denominations. Both Pentecostals and the ecumenical world have changed over the decades. Pentecostals are now sought by global, regional, national, and local ecumenical organizations.

There is a growing leadership call for Pentecostal-Charismatics to "lead" and reform the ecumenical landscapes! There are two underlying assumptions for this. First, the modern-day outpouring of the Holy Spirit was and still is to renew the whole church through the power of the Holy Spirit. With this premise for the whole movement, the place of Pentecostal denominations (Classical Pentecostals) and their call to broader Christianity is understood in a new light. Second, Pentecostal-Charismatic churches and believers have unique gifts that advance church unity and cooperation.[1] The biggest contribution of the movement toward churches is growth itself. Efforts to bring churches together become meaningful when more believers (or "warm bodies") join our churches.

What about the future? There are many helpful studies on the development of Pentecostal ecumenical engagements. A brief overview of the maturing of Pentecostals showcases their constructive role in the churches and argues for attitude changes among the churches toward Pentecostalism as their ecumenical partner. The sum of this historical investigation is that Pentecostals no longer beg for their inclusion in ecumenical spaces but are expected to exercise leadership.

Pentecostal ecumenical leadership can develop pneumatology for the whole church, beyond merely increasing Pentecostal engagements with other churches. In conclusion, the unique gift of the "poor" of Pentecostalism provides a model of serving and leading inter-church engagements. This comes as a bit of a surprise, but it has foundational value. This gift keeps Pentecostalism securely grounded for a healthy theological and spiritual future, in both global and regional (East and Southeast Asia) contexts.

Pentecostals in Ecumenism

Development

David du Plessis (1905-1987), originally from South Africa, was responsible for the birth and development of the PWF.[2] His legacy is his pioneering engagement with mainline churches.

---

[1]Wonsuk Ma, "Pentecostal Gift to Christian Unity: Its Possibility in the New Global Context," *International Review of Mission* 107, no. 1 (July 1, 2018): 33-48, https://doi.org/10.1111/irom.12207.

[2]Wilson, "The Pentecostal World Fellowship," 155.

He first addressed the International Mission Council meeting in Willingen, West Germany, in 1952. He widened his ecumenical involvement as a Pentecostal observer at the WCC in 1954 and 1961, and at the Second Vatican Council. He gained a reputation as "Mr. Pentecost" among the mainline churches, but his denomination (the USA Assemblies of God) defrocked him in 1962.[3]

The establishment of the Christian Unity Commission by the Pentecostal World Fellowship in 2019 marks a significant development in Pentecostal ecumenism,[4] although this does not remove restrictions set by denominations.[5] Until then, all Pentecostal delegates in the dialogues did so as individual members of Pentecostalism. Meanwhile, their counterparts sat around the dialogue table by their church's formal appointment.

The subsequent development of Pentecostal ecumenical engagement owes a great debt to Cecil M. Robeck's sustained involvement in the ecumenical spaces and his passionate advocacy among Pentecostals over many decades.[6] During his years in another "Mr. Pentecost" role, he recruited many peers and younger Pentecostal "ecumenists" to active participation in dialogues and interchurch gatherings.

---

[3]The USA Assemblies of God reinstated him 18 years later, in 1980.

[4]David R. Wells, "The Development and Role of the Christian University Commission," *Pentecostal Education* 7, no. 2 (Fall 2022): 165-71.

[5]The USA Assemblies of God maintained its formal position prohibiting ecumenical engagements until 2009. See the original Bylaws of the General Council of the Assemblies of God, Article IX. Doctrines and Practices Disapproved, Section 11. The Ecumenical Movement, reading, "The General Council of the Assemblies of God disapproves of ministers or churches participating in any of the modern ecumenical organizations on a local, national, or international level in such a manner as to promote the ecumenical movement. . . ." The revision now retitled the section to "Interdenominational or Ecumenical Relationships." The revised statement now reads: "The General Council of the Assemblies of God encourages ministers or churches to fellowship with other Christians of like precious faith . . . and urges its ministers and churches to avoid entanglement with such interdenominational or ecumenical organizations." Its attitude of suspicion continues.

[6]An extremely detailed and analytical work on Robeck's role is Josiah Baker, *A Visible Unity: Cecil Robeck and the Work of Ecumenism* (Lanham, MD: Lexington Books, 2024).

Some Pentecostal groups, especially in the Global South, actively joined ecumenical bodies. In 1996, David Yonggi Cho of Yoido Full Gospel Church, Seoul, Korea, decided that the Korean Assemblies of God would join the National Council of Churches of Korea. He courageously withstood the pressures from a Western sister denomination. The Apostolic Faith Mission of South Africa has long been a member of the WCC.

The 2000 count revealed that over 150 Pentecostal denominations hold membership with regional or national ecumenical bodies.[7] During the 2013 WCC General Assembly in Busan, Korea, Korean Assemblies of God leaders led a lively Pentecostal evening prayer for the delegates. It was a dramatic display of Pentecostal dynamics among the world's Christians.

My Ecumenical Journey

My own ecumenical involvement as a member of the Asia Pacific Theological Seminary illustrates the growing awareness of and engagement of Asian Pentecostals with other churches. I began as a typical Pentecostal, uninterested in other churches. When the entire Evangelical mission world convened in Manila for the second Lausanne Congress in 1989, none at the Seminary attended. Later, we read that some Evangelical delegates walked out of the conference when a Pentecostal speaker began his presentation. Thus, the hesitation in Pentecostal ecumenical involvement had two sides.

My wife Julie's and my first formal ecumenical participation was with the Reformed-Pentecostal Dialogue in 1997, thanks to the invitation of Cecil Robeck, the Pentecostal co-chair of the Dialogue. This seven-year involvement demanded a commitment

---

[7]Cecil M. Robeck, Jr., "Christian Unity and Pentecostal Mission: A Contradiction?" in *Pentecostal Mission and Global Christianity*, ed. Wonsuk Ma, Veli-Matti Kärkkäinen, and J. Kwabena Asamoah-Gyadu, Regnum Edinburgh Centenary Series 20 (Oxford: Regnum Books, 2014), 182-206. For a historical overview of the PWF's ecumenical engagement, see Cecil M. Robeck, Jr., "An Account of Ecumenism and the Pentecostal World Fellowship," *Pentecostal Education* 10, no. 1 (Spring 2025): 29-44.

of time (for a full-time teacher and administrator) and finances (for a struggling missionary). However, our involvement dramatically strengthened our ecumenical and global awareness and understanding. It also brought Asian Pentecostal voices to the table as we represented the Seminary.

In 1998, two important internal structures emerged for Asian Pentecostalism. The first was the formation of the Asian Pentecostal Society (APS) at the Pentecostal World Conference (PWC) at Yoido Church. About half a dozen scholars traveled to Daejon for the International Symposium on Global Pentecostalism. As a pre-PWC program, the APS-planned international gathering continued in Los Angeles (2001) and Johannesburg (2004). The second was the launch of the *Asian Journal of Pentecostal Studies* by the Seminary. Global ecumenical circles have noticed its enduring presence and unique contribution. The publication of the *International Dictionary of Pentecostal and Charismatic Movements* (2002) was another significant venue where Asian Pentecostals added Asian entries to this international project. The editors were almost desperate towards the close of the editorial work to identify Asian Pentecostal scholars who could add Asian voices. Selected faculty members of the Seminary demonstrated academic maturity to the world readers.

Around that time, Julie Ma, an Asian faculty member of APTS, was invited to present a study to the Joint Consultative Committee of the WCC. In 2004, the newly organized Global Christian Forum rolled out an ambitious plan to create a new and more conducive ecumenical "space" for all the major streams of world Christianity. For its 2004 Asian Consultation in Hong Kong, Hubert van Beek, the founding general secretary, approached me (as the representative of APS) to nominate Pentecostal delegates. Selected members of the APTS faculty served as well. This engagement led me to deliver the plenary speech at its first international gathering in Kenya (2007).[8]

---

[8]See Julie C. Ma and Wonsuk Ma, *Mission in the Spirit: Towards a Pentecostal/Charismatic Missiology* (Oxford: Regnum Books, 2010), especially chap. 17: "Spirit, Mission, and Unity: A Personal Journey." Later,

The year 2005 was a special year for Asian Pentecostals. The WCC's Commission on World Mission and Evangelism made a historic decision to invite Evangelical and Pentecostal delegates to its 2005 gathering near Athens, Greece. The Commission recognized APS as a suitable and credible representative of Asian Pentecostals. Surrounded by four seminary faculty members, I delivered the plenary speech.[9] This was followed in the same year by another ecumenical mission conference organized by the Church of Scotland to prepare for the centennial celebration of the 1910 Edinburgh Mission Conference. Two Seminary faculty members attended this exclusive twenty-member consultation, another sign of the representative position of APS and the Seminary for Asian Pentecostal voices.

Pentecostal Ecumenical Leadership

These two historical overviews illustrate the growing ecumenical understanding among Pentecostals. A shift is detectable where global interchurch networks and events want to include voices from the second-largest Christian family, which is also the fastest growing. The typical list of qualifications for those from the Global South includes men and women with academic qualifications and ministry involvement, giving preference to younger members. A desire for "acceptance" lies in the past for Pentecostals. The Global Christian Forum includes Pentecostals in its four pillars with Catholics, the World Council of Churches, and the World Evangelical Alliance, including them also. However, being sought after does not naturally lead to ecumenical leadership. It takes intentionality and commitment.

One recent example may illustrate this. In December 2022, William Wilson (Empowered21) and Rick Warren (Finishing the

---

I led the Theology Task Force to draft an official document: GCF, "Our Unfolding Journey with Jesus Christ: Reflections on the Global Christian Forum Experience," 2013, https://globalchristianforum.org/wp-content/uploads/2018/07/GFC-Our-Unfolding-Journey-ENG.pdf.

[9]Wonsuk Ma, "'When the Poor are Fired Up,'" 28-34.

Task) convened an exclusive strategy meeting with two dozen global Christian Evangelical leaders. Its press release, entitled "Ministry leaders united on fulfilling the Great Commission by 2033," listed Michael Oh (Lausanne Movement), Thomas Schirrmacher (World Evangelical Alliance), Nick Perryman (Alpha), Doug Clay (USA Assemblies of God), Bobby Gruenewald (YouVersion), and James Hwang (Billion Soul Harvest), among the participants.[10] They signed a covenant document at the end of the two-day high-powered meeting. Their commitment set the year 2033, the 2,000th anniversary of the church, as the common target point for all-out evangelism. The organizers did not hide their Spirit-empowered language.

In Amsterdam in 2023, Empowered21 launched a global evangelization movement called the EveryONE campaign. It marked the start of "a defining decade, a decade in which it is possible for every person on earth to hear the gospel."[11] The Covenant document ends with a solid ecumenical commitment: "We dedicate our lives to obeying Christ's command and call for the global Church to unite with us in making the next ten years the greatest decade of Great Commission effort in history." Unlike other annual gatherings among "Spirit-empowered" leaders, Empowered21's Amsterdam conference was unmistakably ecumenical. It drew speakers and participants from a large range of churches and mission communities. This demonstrates Pentecostalism's leadership and convening capability to bring different church traditions together for a common purpose.

Before moving to the next discussion, I will include the trending mode of ecumenical meetings. Pentecostals have played a significant role in the formation and development of the Global Christian Forum (GCF). Unlike the WCC mode of theological (or

---

[10]A. Larry Ross Communications, "Ministry Leaders Unite on Fulfilling the Great Commission by 2033," *Religion News Service*, December 8, 2022, sec. RNS Press Releases, https://religionnews.com/2022/12/08/ministry-leaders-unite-on-fulfilling-the-great-commission-by-2033/.

[11]Empowered21, "Amsterdam 2023."

academic) ecumenical dialogues, GCF's purpose statement and its ethos in fulfilling it can be summed up in "relationships."

> The efforts of the GCF to initiate relationships and to promote their broadening and deepening offer distinctive new ways of coming together, journeying together and witnessing together. . . . The primary purpose of the Forum has always been to encourage new relationships among those who do not otherwise meet one another.[12]

The GCF has adopted the Pentecostal practice of testimony-sharing as its *modus operandi* for every gathering. The same practice is now replicated in other global networks, such as the Global Forum of Theological Educators:

> The most important practice in the development of the GCF and in its meetings is the telling of faith stories. It was discovered that this approach enabled the full participation of those Christian communities in which sharing testimonies occurs regularly, including notably Pentecostal, Evangelical and African Instituted churches whose experience the GCF has sought especially to include. In these communities, the stories are a means to spread the Gospel, seeking through one's own story of conversion and God's continuing faithfulness to encourage and strengthen the faith of others in their praise and service of God. All members are recognized to have a story; testimonies are not reserved to those with special position.[13]

---

[12]"Experience," section 2, https://globalchristianforum.org/wp-content/uploads/2018/07/GCF-Our-Unfolding-Journey-ENG.pdf (accessed January 23, 2023).

[13]GCF, "Our Unfolding Journey with Jesus Christ," section 2.2.

These cases indicate the growing significance of Pentecostal churches in convening, influencing, and leading the world church for ecumenical matters.

One Theological Contribution: Charismatic Pneumatology

So far, my argument on the unique Pentecostal contribution to the future of global Christianity has been on growth, democratization of ministry, Spirit-empowerment, upward social mobility, and the like. They are all rooted in unique Pentecostal theological traditions. Following the Pentecostal epistemology, theological inquiries only follow the experience as an afterthought. The importance of experience makes the Pentecostal phenomenon dynamic and vibrant. The result of this process is the utilitarian motivation of Pentecostal theology. Extreme cases include the prosperity gospel and hyper-grace advocacy. With the expectation of the emerging leadership of Pentecostalism in the global ecumenical spaces, Pentecostals are now called to consider a substantial theological contribution. The following section explores one theological discipline for consideration.

Charismatic Pneumatology So Far

Pneumatology is the natural priority of Pentecostal theology. To begin with, among the traditional themes of systematic theology, pneumatology has remained underdeveloped since the Great Schism of 1054 over the process of the Holy Spirit.[14] Since the *filioque* controversy between the East and Western churches, an underdeveloped state of pneumatology is best seen in the historic creeds. The Apostle's Creed reveals the theological developmental nature of the Trinity. Two lines (in the Church of England version)

---

[14]For a more detailed discussion, especially in the Asian context, see Wonsuk Ma, "Lord and Giver of Life: The Holy Spirit among the Spirits in Asia," in *Christian Theology in Asia: Evangelical Perspectives*, ed. Timoteo D. Gener and Stephen T. Pardue (Carlisle, UK: Langham Global Library, 2019), 119-38.

on the Father assume the "settled" consensus, and ten lines on the Son indicate the immediate theological agenda, ongoing debates, and priority. Just one line on the Holy Spirit, however, "And I believe in the Holy Spirit," suggests a "tabled" and developing nature for future development. The Nicene-Constantinopolitan Creed (381 CE) added the following to the brief line of the Creed of Nicaea (325 CE): ". . . the Lord, and Giver of Life, Who proceeds from the Father, Who with the Father and the Son together is worshipped and glorified, Who spoke by the Prophets."

Thus, the primary attention of Pentecostal theology to pneumatology is historically valuable and ontologically natural. Pentecostalism traces its birth to the modern outpouring of the Holy Spirit in several parts of the world around the turn of the twentieth century. Pentecostal theologians have developed the "charismatic" aspect of pneumatology based on Luke-Acts. Roger Stronstad and Robert Menzies represent this movement.[15] The definition of "Pentecostal" is rooted in the empowering presence of the Holy Spirit. Max Weber proposed this concept in his groundbreaking sociological study on leadership.[16] His definition is primarily based on the leader's personality and charm. To test the "hottest" AI response, I asked ChatGPT, "What are the characteristics of charismatic leadership by Max Weber?" The following are its top five responses:

- A strong sense of personal magnetism or charm.
- The ability to inspire and motivate followers through personal charisma and enthusiasm.

---

[15]Stronstad, *The Charismatic Theology of St. Luke*; Robert P. Menzies, *The Development of Early Christian Pneumatology: With Special Reference to Luke-Acts*, *Journal for the Study of the New Testament Supplement Series* 54 (Sheffield: JSOT Press, 1991). I also divided the work of God's Spirit in the Old Testament into two categories: Charismatic and non-Charismatic, e.g., Wonsuk Ma, *Until the Spirit Comes: The Spirit of God in the Book of Isaiah*, *JSOT Supplement Series* 271 (Sheffield: Sheffield Academic Press, 1999).

[16]Maximillan Weber, *Theory of Social and Economic Organization*, trans. A. R. Anderson and Talcott Parsons (New York: Free Press, 1947, from the 1922 German original).

- A vision or mission that appeals to followers' values and aspirations.
- The ability to create a sense of community and shared purpose among followers.
- A willingness to take bold and decisive action.

In exploring a holistic pneumatology with Pentecostal distinctives for the whole church, redefining "charismatic" may be the first step. I want to move the definition from a sociological to a theological concept based on scriptural evidence. I again asked ChatGPT, "What are the characteristics of Charismatic leadership according to the Bible?" Surprisingly, the list is quite different:

- Humility: A leader should be humble and willing to serve others, rather than seeking power or prestige for themselves.
- Integrity: A leader should be honest, trustworthy, and of good character.
- Vision: A leader should have a clear vision for the future and be able to inspire and guide others towards it.
- Wisdom: A leader should have wisdom and understanding and be able to make sound decisions.
- Faith: A leader should have strong faith in God and be guided by biblical principles.

This AI-based software noted, "Many of these characteristics are exemplified by Jesus Christ, who is described as the ultimate leader in the Bible."[17]

---

[17]For an analysis of the charismatic leadership model, see Wonsuk Ma, "Toward Spirit-Empowered Leadership: An Old Testament Foundation," in *Voice Loud and Clear: Understanding the Spirit's Movement Worldwide*, ed. Kong Hee, Byron Klaus, and Doug Petersen (Oxford: Regnum Books, 2024), 33-44.

Charismatic Spirit Redefined

My study of the Spirit of God in the Old Testament and the Holy Spirit in the New Testament, especially in the life and work of Christ, notes that Charismatic leadership includes the following elements: 1) The leader is elected and called by God; 2) God places his Spirit upon the leader as a sign of his election and for empowerment; 3) As a result, the leader receives a special status with an intimate relationship with God; 4) The leader's God-given task or mission is aimed toward another person or group of people; and 5) Thus, he represents God through the presence of his Spirit.

The earliest "Charismatic" call is found in the first two chapters of the Bible, the creation of humanity. Shaped in the image of God (Gen 1:26) and animated by God's "breath" (Gen 2:7; the word "breath" is often translated interchangeably with the "Spirit"), humans exercised a God-given task to God's creation while enjoying a special status from and relationship with the Creator. God intended this charismatic call and gift for the whole of humanity. This intention was disrupted by human sin.

The decisive fulfillment of this disrupted plan came through the life and work of Christ. Born of the life-giving Holy Spirit, the same Spirit empowered Jesus to perform miracles, heal, confront the power of the devil, do good works (Acts 10:38), and carry the cross (Heb 9:14).[18] And the same Spirit raised him from the dead (Rom 8:11). If the life and work of Christ served as the archetype of the Spirit's Charismatic work, the widespread perception of charismatic leadership can be misleading.

A Charismatic call is issued to execute God's plan for the benefit of someone or a group. For instance, God elected Gideon and endowed him with his Spirit to call for an inter-tribal army to deliver Israel from the Midianite invasion (Judg 6-7). The beneficiary of Gideon's Charismatic call and equipment was Israel. However, the common image of a charismatic entity is a high-

---

[18]Frank D. Macchia, *Jesus the Spirit Baptizer: Christology in Light of Pentecost* (Grand Rapids: Eerdmans, 2021), 248-56.

profile "anointed" leader, thanks to the secular usage of the term (as in Weber[19]).

A biblical exploration of charismatic leadership should include communities as God-elected "servants." The election of Israel is an exceptional case. God called the nation to be his special people (or "treasured possession," Exod 19:5) from the nations. Israel was to enjoy a special relationship with its covenant God ("holy nation") and to fulfill God-given tasks toward the nations (as a "kingdom of priests," Exod 19:6). God brought his people out of Egypt, crossing the Red Sea through the "blast (or Spirit) of his nostril" (Exod 15:8). His Spirit was present among them in the wilderness (Isa 63:11), and the same Spirit completed their journey ("they were given rest," Isa 63:14). The nation was a charismatic servant of the Lord to be a light to the nations (e.g., Isa 51:4). In the New Testament, the church repeated the same pattern, born of the Holy Spirit on the day of Pentecost (Acts 2), to be God's chosen people, and to be God's faithful witness to the world.

Consequently, Charismatic work focuses more on the faithful fulfillment of God-given tasks than the awe-evoking display of God's wonder. For example, the Servant's perseverance over obstacles to bring God's justice to the nations (Isa 42:1-4) is more "Charismatic" than Samson's killing of a lion, which threatened his life (Judg 14:6). For the latter, the beneficiary was Samson himself; thus, he was not qualified to be "Charismatic," according to our criteria. Indeed, the "Charismatic" call of Israel was to enjoy the special status as God's own possession, and this faithfulness was the primary means to fulfill God's call: for the nations to come to the sovereign rule of Yahweh (e.g., Isa 44:5). The climax of Christ's life and work was carrying the cross and rising from the dead, both by the Holy Spirit. As human minds naturally gravitate to the external mode of superhuman behaviors, it is a theological call for Pentecostals to reiterate the primary characteristics of being Charismatic.

---

[19]Weber, *Theory of Social and Economic Organization.*

Charismatic and Non-Charismatic

What is the ultimate work of the Spirit? I struggled with the two categories of the Spirit's work in the Old Testament: Charismatic (including Spirit-endowed leaders and prophets) and non-Charismatic (including the Spirit in creation and wisdom). After closely examining the work of the Spirit in the book of Isaiah, I concluded that the restoration of "life" as God intends brings both the charismatic and non-charismatic work of the Spirit.[20] Isaiah presents several elected servants who were empowered by the Spirit. The future Davidic king will uphold justice and righteousness by strengthening the weak and purging the wicked (Isa 11:1-5). His rule will culminate in a restored paradise (11:6-9). The anointed prophet will focus his message and ministry to the poor, hurt, captives, and imprisoned (61:1). As suggested in Isaiah 11, the climax of the Spirit's presence upon God's people is the restoration of the fortune of God's people in the restored creation:

> . . . till the Spirit is poured on us from on high,
> and the desert becomes a fertile field,
> and the fertile field seems like a forest.
>
> The LORD's justice will dwell in the desert,
> his righteousness lives in the fertile field.
>
> The fruit of that righteousness will be peace;
> its effect will be quietness and confidence forever.
>
> My people will live in peaceful dwelling places,
> in secure homes,
> in undisturbed places of rest (Isa 32:15-18).

This "life" is more than a state of being animated: as God granted his own "breath," the human became a "living soul" (Gen 2:7). The word used does not distinguish between human and animal life. However, the presence of God's breath (or "Spirit," and

[20]Wonsuk Ma, "Isaiah," in *A Biblical Theology of the Holy Spirit*, ed. Trevor J. Burke and Keith Warrington (London: SPCK, 2014), 34-45.

also "image") signals the extraordinary nature of humans. Aubrey Johnson defines this "God-matter" as the "extension of God's personality."[21] The core of the totality of human life is to be his own possession, to relate intimately, to undertake a God-given mission, and to care for God's creation with care and responsibility. This summation of God-shaped life is what he planned to restore, yes, by his Spirit. Then, Charismatic individuals are called to serve this purpose, sometimes with signs and wonders, but more importantly, with relentless dedication.

The benefits of expanded pneumatology with Pentecostal distinctives are numerous, but a few deserve our attention. The restoration of life as the goal of pneumatology resonates with the recent focus of the mainline Christian churches on the "flourishing of life" through the Spirit. The WCC's new statement on mission exemplifies this trend.[22] Titled *Together Towards Life*, this is a heavily pneumatological document. It defines Christian mission as the WCC envisioned, highlighting the life-giving, sustaining, and restoring work of the Holy Spirit. One can easily suspect sufficient Pentecostal input as the document went through a lengthy editorial process, including the 2012 Commission on World Mission and Evangelism conference in Manila. At the same time, by placing the charismatic aspect of Pentecostal pneumatology in the context of life, its distinctives are preserved. This also challenges establishing a holistic view of life, from physical and material to community well-being and eternal life. In this way, the theology of blessing (aka the "prosperity gospel") finds a meaningful place in Pentecostal pneumatology.

Concluding with One Attitudinal Note: The "Poor"

Through my ecumenical engagement, I have learned several attitudinal virtues for mutual respect and constructive

[21]Aubrey R. Johnson, *The One and the Many in the Israelite Conception of God,* 2nd ed. (Cardiff: University of Wales Press, 1961), 22.

[22]Jooseop Keum, ed., *Together Towards Life: Mission and Evangelism in Changing Landscapes* (Geneva: WCC Publications, 2013).

engagement. The first is our own knowledge of and appreciation for Pentecostal Christianity. I regularly remind myself that each Christian tradition responded to a specific historical circumstance, hence we have differences. As I approach other Christian families with an open and learning mind, I should be able to present the Pentecostal faith, life, and theology to my ecumenical friends. This knowledge includes the strengths ("gifts") and weaknesses ("un-gifts") of our faith.

Thus, humility is the rule of successful ecumenical engagement. We draw a historical resource from the Pentecostal identity of the "poor."[23] This descriptor applies immediately to the lower social strata, where most adherents are drawn to the Pentecostal message. At the turn of the twentieth century, "Pentecostal" breakouts took place among the socially marginalized: the Welsh revival among coal miners in Wales, the Mukti revival among orphaned children and women, the Pyongyang revival under the Japanese annexation of Korea, and the Azusa Street revival among the "colored," the poor, and immigrants. The souls of desperation met radical divine encounters and empowerment. This combination has produced unprecedented passion, commitment, and zeal. The exponential growth of the movement attests to this. Understandably, this attitudinal and lifestyle change results in upward social mobility, as David Martin carefully observed among Latin American Pentecostal believers.

Interestingly, the downward cycle of the "serial movement" of Christianity is also experienced among Pentecostal churches and believers that have grown out of the "poor" state. Consider the current struggle of Korean Pentecostalism. Martin noticed that those Pentecostals who have obtained a level of economic progress tend to "forget" their "poor" roots and lose their ability to minister to the struggling population in their societies.[24] Worse

---

[23]Similar expressions have been used, e.g., Robert Mapes Anderson, *Vision of the Disinherited: The Making of American Pentecostalism* (New York: Oxford University Press, 1979). Also Ma, "'When the Poor Are Fired Up,'" 28-34.

[24]Martin, *Tongues of Fire,* 233, as one example.

yet, the obsession with material prosperity has led to half a dozen prosperity preachers in Africa with their private jets.[25]

We need to learn to handle prosperity for Pentecostal Christianity to remain cutting-edge, constantly innovating, and spiritually vibrant. Pentecostals should heed what God urged his people, "Remember that you were slaves in Egypt, and the LORD your God redeemed you" (Deut 15:15). How about Jesus? He emptied himself of the form of, or equality with God, and took the form of a slave in the likeness of a human, becoming obedient unto death (Phil 2:6-8). This voluntary "downward mobility" as our identity of the "poor" is not something we need to leave behind, but an identity to keep and treasure. Our Charismatic brothers and sisters who started with a higher socioeconomic status can help us handle prosperity well.

This chapter of reflection ends with a lesson learned through my engagement with other churches, in this case, from African brothers and sisters who are African Presbyterians: "If you want to go fast, go alone; if you want to go far, go together."

---

[25]See, U. Onyekachi, "List of Nigerian Pastors with Private Jets," *The Nigerian Info.com*, September 24, 2022, https://thenigerianinfo.com/list-of-nigerian-pastors-with-private-jets/.

CHAPTER 9

Serving the World: Mission in the Spirit

God's people are sent to the world (e.g., John 17:18; 20:21) to live out and proclaim Christ's good news to all. We were originally in and of the world. After being redeemed through the atoning work of Christ, we are now in the world but not of the world. This makes our existence in the earthly life missional: we have been sent to the world for a specific "mission."

Pentecostals from the beginning have taken this missional nature seriously, resulting in the close connection between their spiritual experience called the "baptism in the Holy Spirit" and mission. Also, early Pentecostals understood the outpouring of the Holy Spirit as a clear sign of the imminent return of Christ. All these theological elements—Spirit baptism, eschatology, and mission—resulted in Pentecostalism as a powerful mission movement. Three distinct dimensions of Pentecostal mission can be applied to the Asian setting.

Three Ripples of Mission in the Spirit

I developed this imagery to illustrate Pentecostal mission, which was further refined.[1] As the title suggests, they are:

[1]This section is a summary of Wonsuk Ma and Julie C. Ma, "Missiology: Evangelization, Holistic Ministry, and Social Justice," in *Routledge Handbook*

preaching the gospel (evangelization and church planting), caring for the suffering (holistic mission), and addressing the root causes of injustice (justice mission).

Saving Souls

The first ripple, evangelism, was a natural development of the Spirit's advent around the turn of the twentieth century. This passion for saving souls has been the mother of Pentecostal mission. This category includes all related activities that facilitate and enhance evangelism. Pentecostals sent evangelists and missionaries, established training programs for evangelism and training institutions, produced evangelistic tracts and material, organized public evangelistic gatherings, and used various media such as printing, radio, TV, Internet, and many more.

Passion for saving souls is a common characteristic of most revivals. All four revivals at the turn of the twentieth century—the Welsh Revival (1904), the Mukti Revival (1905), the Azusa Street Mission (1906), and the Pyongyang Revival (1907)—contained repentance, regeneration, and zeal for evangelism. The Pyongyang revival of Korea broke into spontaneous and emotionally charged public confessions of sin, where participants asked for the forgiveness of God and neighbors and dedicated their lives anew to God's work. This revival spread quickly throughout the Korean peninsula with mass evangelization. Between 1906 and 1907, the Presbyterian Church grew from 54,987 to 73,844, or a 34% increase. The Methodist Church recorded even higher growth: from 18,107 to 39,613, or a 118% increase.[2] Subsequently, the whole Korean church launched a 10-million-person evangelization campaign.

The Pentecostal-Charismatic movement is mainly known for the significant role of evangelists. In large cities and small towns, global and local Pentecostal evangelists organize and conduct

of Pentecostal Theology, ed. Wolfgang Vonday (London: Routledge, 2020), 279-89.

[2]Younghoon Lee, *The Holy Spirit Movement in Korea: Its Historical and Theological Development* (Oxford: Regnum Books, 2009), 31.

healing "crusades." The list of global Spirit-empowered evangelists would be long.[3] In the late 1940s, Oral Roberts pitched large tents for his healing and evangelistic meetings in large cities in the United States. Drawing thousands of people to the message of healing and salvation, hundreds repeated the prayer of salvation.[4] When he pivoted his evangelistic efforts to TV in the early 1950s, his message of healing and salvation reached millions of American living rooms.[5] Reinhard Bonnke was another global Pentecostal evangelist. It is claimed that close to 80 million Africans accepted Christ as their Savior through his five-decade evangelistic ministry.[6] Throughout his ministry, he also trained countless numbers of national evangelists.

Equally critical is the mass of "nameless" evangelists, beyond "local" evangelists. In Pentecostal understanding, "everyone" is "empowered" to be witnesses (based on Acts 1:8), and theologically, this makes every Spirit-filled believer a witness or evangelist. The well-known cell group system of Yoido Full Gospel Church, Seoul, South Korea, is an example of organized lay evangelists. When David Yonggi Cho simultaneously experienced rapid numerical growth in his church and serious health challenges in 1964, he launched the ground-breaking cell group system. He initially faced two challenges: first, people were not willing to be led by another lay person, indicating the clergy-laity binary; and second, people, including female members, preferred a male leader, signifying the deep-rooted gender value of the society. Cho convinced the reluctant female lay leaders and the whole church that the Lord

---

[3]For example, see Global Evangelist Alliance, *The Spirit Empowered Evangelist* (Tulsa: Global Evangelist Alliance, 2023) for the new breed of Spirit-empowered evangelists.

[4]David Edwin Harrell, Jr., *Oral Roberts: An American Life* (Bloomington, IL: Indiana University Press, 1985), 88, 91.

[5]Ibid., 120-21. For original comments by Oral Roberts on winning one million souls to Christ through his media platform, see Oral Roberts, "A Master Plan," *Abundant Life* (Oct. 1956): 3-5, 18-22.

[6]Charles Morara Obara, "A Critical Analysis of Reinhard Bonnke's Charismatic Leadership Paradigm," *Spiritus: ORU Journal of Theology* 7, no. 2 (Fall, 2022): 246.

had called, empowered, and commissioned everyone, male and female, as well as clergy and laity, for God's work.[7] The system revolutionized church life: the largest church in the world was indeed the collection of the smallest churches meeting in homes. The weekly cell group meeting throughout the metropolis became the most effective evangelistic space, inviting and reaching out to neighbors. Many cell leaders brought their sick members or neighbors to the church's prayer mountain for prayer and fasting. The church also shared testimonies of divine healing and salvation through cell groups.

This grassroots presence of Christian witness is also observed in the Pentecostal ethos of church planting. Earlier, I compared the presence of Pentecostal congregations and Catholic churches in Burkina Faso and Brazil. In 2010, 1.1 million Assemblies of God members were in 7,100 local churches. The average number of people per church was 155. The Catholic Church had 1.9 million members in 2,420 churches, translating to 785 believers per church. Similarly, a Catholic church in Brazil had an average of 11,221 members, while the Assemblies of God had 135.[8] This comparison explains why Catholic churches are full in cities and towns, while there are seldom churches in smaller communities. In contrast, Pentecostal congregations are relatively smaller (although there are megachurches), but are found in towns and villages. This saturated presence of Pentecostal churches suggests active grassroots evangelism.

Caring for the Needy

The second ripple is an extension of evangelism expressed in various terms, such as mercy mission, compassion mission, holistic mission, and more. Pentecostals almost intuitively gravitate

---

[7]For the beginning of the Cell Group System, see Cho, *Dr. David Yonggi Cho*, 83-96.

[8]Wonsuk Ma, "Pentecostal Gift to Christian Unity: Its Possibility in the New Global Context," *International Review of Mission* 107, no. 1 (July 1, 2018): 38.

to those who are suffering, much as the Pentecostal message of miracle and empowerment draws the downtrodden. A daily newspaper ridiculed the Azusa Street Mission with derogatory headlines and subtitles. It first described the congregation as consisting of "colored people and a sprinkling of whites" and meeting "in a tumble-down shack." They were ". . . the devotees of the weird doctrine [who] practice the most fanatical rites, preaching the wildest theories and work themselves into a state of mad excitement in their peculiar zeal."[9]

The Mukti Mission of Pandita Ramabai began among orphans and widows on social margins. She provided holistic care to the orphans: physical care with food and shelter, mental care through education and Christian love, and spiritual care through the preaching of the gospel. In this setting, evangelism and care were fully integrated. For this reason, many Pentecostal missionaries provide care as a means of evangelism.

Recently, there has been a tendency among Pentecostals to understand care ministry as a valid mission category. This is part of the broader Evangelical development of missional thinking, anchored in the Lausanne Covenant, which identified evangelism and social service as two pillars of mission. Increasingly, Christians, including Spirit-filled believers, take social action as part of kingdom mission. Jesus is the role model who feeds the hungry, heals the sick, raises the dead, and gives hope to the hopeless. With the rapid growth of the Pentecostal faith in the Global South, churches began robust social programs to address community issues and challenges.

Two Evangelical social scientists, Donald Miller and Tetsunao Yamamori, launched a multi-year study on Christian social engagement. The results of their research surprised them. They looked for churches in the Global South that were growing and actively addressing social issues with no external assistance, and discovered that 85 percent of them were Pentecostal and Charismatic![10] This finding proves that Pentecostals have not only

[9]"Weird Babel of Tongues," *Los Angeles Daily Times*, April 19, 1906.
[10]Miller and Yamamori, *Global Pentecostalism*, 5.

intuitively undertaken this second layer of mission but have also articulated caring as an authentic part of mission.

This growing understanding among Pentecostals is expressed in various ways. They range from disaster relief, responding to community needs, and caring for the homeless to more organized operations such as homes for orphans and the elderly, vocational schools for underprivileged youths, and establishing non-governmental organizations (NGOs) to carry out compassion ministries systematically.

Justice Mission

The third ripple is justice mission, for lack of a better expression. It is closely related to the second ripple, as both tackle issues threatening human well-being. The two ripples often overlap, but the two still warrant separate treatments. If the second ripple attempts to meet the immediate needs of suffering people, the third ripple seeks to identify and address the root of suffering. The former serves suffering victims of injustice, while the latter traces and attempts to resolve the root of injustice. It also stretches deeper into public spaces, including advocacy, public policy, legislation, and more.

One case study is Philippe Ouedraogo. This Pentecostal minister in Burkina Faso wrestled with the issue of inequality in education in the country. He specifically observed that far fewer girls from Muslim homes enrolled for elementary education than boys from the same Muslim homes and Christian children. He organized an inter-church body to roll out an accelerated nine-month education program in two northern states with dense Muslim populations. The program mobilized local churches as classrooms and church leaders as facilitator-teachers. Through the eleven-year pilot program, more than five thousand children aged nine to twelve had a second chance at education. In conclusion, the children were tested to be placed in public schools. A large portion of the children and their families became believers. The government has taken over the program and expanded it to the whole nation. Also, two neighboring Muslim countries have adopted the program for their settings, utilizing Christians.

Philippe identified not only the problem (the lack of educational opportunities for Muslim girls) but also its root causes (poverty and religious orientation). His approach was to set up an educational system designed explicitly for this young population. However, he took further steps: he explored the government's assistance. The Ministry of Education responded by creating a special desk to aid the program. Through its success, the Ministry adopted accelerated education as part of the nation's education system.

Ultimately, Christians sent a strong message to the public that God has his answer to human problems, even in this Muslim-majority nation. The prime minister hailed the program as "the role played by the Evangelical churches and Christian NGOs in improving the lives of women in Burkina Faso." He observed its contribution to the country's effort to "meet the Millennium Development Goals."[11] Through the process, the program brought different churches together: ecumenism.

These areas of influence go beyond caring for those who are suffering. Due to the complexity and magnitude of the program, Christians must move outside of their familiar "church" world. They exercise their "citizenship" responsibilities, addressing the chronic problems of the nation and offering Christian solutions.

The argument for the validity of justice mission for Pentecostals comes with formidable challenges. First, it takes Christian mission to public spaces. By nature, addressing the root of suffering forces believers to confront political, economic, and social injustices, often waging a "holy war" against powerholders and brokers of society.

Second, Pentecostals have only recently articulated the second layer of mission, exemplified by the addition of a mercy mission to the bylaws of the USA Assemblies of God.[12] Understandably,

---

[11]Titius Zongo, "Forewords" for Philippe Ouedraogo, *Female Education and Mission: A Burkina Faso Experience* (Oxford: Regnum Books, 2014), xiii.

[12]See Richard L. Schoonover, "Introduction, Compassion Ministry Expressing the Heart of God," *Enrichment* 17, no. 1 (Winter 2012): 24. The magazine's entire issue is dedicated to "Compassion Ministry: Expressing the

Pentecostals have not yet discussed this openly, let alone moved toward a consensus about theological grounds, the range of engagement, and the limits of justice mission.

The initial commitment is advocacy. A more radical response is activism, which includes active political involvement wherein Pentecostals might run for public offices, including the presidency. There is a divided response to this approach among various Pentecostal churches. An extreme expression may even include armed resistance. This has often been headed by religious leaders, as happened in South America and the Philippines during the dictatorship era.

Third, the expansion of the second layer may be a valid starting point, as demonstrated by Philippe's experimental education program. Without confronting educational injustice, he offered a charitable solution in collaboration with other churches and the government. His approach resulted in the educational policy change by the government's positive adoption of the program.

Another area, despite contentions, is the promotion of church unity. An increasing number of Pentecostal denominations are members of the National Council of Churches and the WCC.[13] Pentecostals have fully participated in the GCF from its inception.[14]

Reflections on Serving the "World" in the Asian Context

As Asian Pentecostal churches wish to serve the world, I have tried to identify common challenges facing Asia. The 2024 Asia and Pacific Regional Report of the United Nations Development Program sets the well-being of the people as the goal of human development. It identifies four areas of disparities and five

---

Heart of God."

[13]For the 2000 list of Pentecostal churches in the WCC network, see Cecil M. Robeck, Jr., "Christian Unity and Pentecostal Mission: A Contradiction?" in *Pentecostal Mission and Global Christianity*, ed. Wonsuk Ma, Veli-Matti Kärkkäinen, and J. Kwabena Asamoah-Gyadu, Regnum Edinburgh Centenary Series 20 (Oxford: Regnum Books, 2014), 201-06.

[14]GCF, "Who We Are," https://globalchristianforum.org/about-us/who-we-are/, accessed January 2, 2025.

widespread disruptions challenging human development in the region. The disruptions include a declining Human Development Index (HDI), rising financial pressures, backsliding on gender equality, weakening climate commitments, and the erosion of democratic liberty.[15] The three areas of HDI are helpful: healthcare, education, and economy. These are expressed as "long and healthy life, being knowledgeable, and having a decent standard of living."[16]

Ground mapping was also explored through an AI facility. When I asked for five top social issues in Asia, ChatGPT produced the following list: poverty and economic inequality, gender inequality, environmental degradation, human rights violations, and healthcare access and public health.[17] These needs largely overlap with the UN report regarding equality in basic human sustenance and flourishing.

However, neither list included religious issues, which often trigger social unrest, regional conflicts, and human rights violations. This is obvious in the plight of the Rohingya Muslims in Buddhist-majority Myanmar. Media attention quickly subsided, but their plight reminds us of the critical role religions play in Asian life.[18]

A recent book edited by Amos Yong and Mark Lamport identifies five primary issues facing Asian Christianity, including Pentecostalism. These include engaging with other religions, oppressive political systems such as totalitarianism and dictatorship, diaspora/migration, marginalization, and the

---

[15]United Nations Development Programme, "2024 Regional Human Development Report: Making Our Future: New Directions for Human Development in Asia and the Pacific" (New York: UNDP, 2024).

[16]UNDP, "Human Development Index (HDI)," https://hdr.undp.org/data-center/human-development-index#/indicies/HDI/ (accessed February 8, 2024).

[17]https://chat.openai.com/c/cf97677d-ad8e-4b14-8957-7ef64a1ee4b6/, February 8, 2024.

[18]See Grant Peck, "Indonesia's Rescue of Rohingya Refugees at Sea Is a Reminder of an Ordeal that Began in Myanmar," March 21, 2024, https://apnews.com/article/rohingya-refugees-bangladesh-malaysia-aceh-indonesia-boats-9fa83728f999b28d87803066578a9755/.

reorientation of the Christian world.[19] This list considers religious matters but conspicuously excludes basic economic struggles.

I identify primary areas of concern for Asian Pentecostal churches and believers to contemplate as they engage with the "world." Pentecostals must be conscious of the religious contexts, work to reduce human suffering, address various issues of inequality, and bring together a fragmented society for the common good (peacemaking). Religion is an integral part of one's identity (both individual and corporate) that pervades every aspect of human existence. Thus, religious contexts will not be treated as a free-standing, single issue but as a transversal, bringing the impact of religion upon the remaining three areas. For each area, I will illustrate Pentecostal possibilities with helpful examples.

Addressing Human Suffering

As discussed earlier, Pentecostals have an inherent sympathy for those suffering various life problems, whether physical, economic, or social. Pentecostal responses are broad, ranging from immediate action to relieve pain and suffering to institutionalized and large-scale programs. Many Malaysian Pentecostal churches have provided care for the elderly and orphaned, tutoring for children of low-income households, and free or affordable medical services. One may argue that these are creative avenues of "evangelism" that churches are forced to explore in the face of strict laws prohibiting proselytism in this Islamic society. Similarly, many Pentecostal churches initiate and manage small-scale community development projects such as clinics, drug rehabilitation programs, education initiatives, etc.

Pentecostal missionaries from the West often demonstrate their commitment to eliminating human suffering. Mark and Huldah Buntain, USA Assemblies of God missionaries, began by helping urban children in Calcutta, India, through feeding and orphanage programs. Their ministries gradually expanded

---

[19]Amos Yong and Mark A. Lamport, ed., *Uncovering the Pearl: The Hidden Story of Christianity in Asia* (Eugene, OR: Wipf & Stock, 2023).

to include education (including a nursing and medical school), church, ministerial training (a Bible school), medical services (hospital), and many more.[20]

Although these examples are churches or Christian NGOs, the core vision and commitment of leaders and community members is to do something about the suffering of their neighbors. Mentioned above, the Miller and Yamamori study discovered that most of the growing Christian communities in the Global South that engaged with local issues and used local resources were Pentecostal churches.[21] These two Evangelical scholars studied and analyzed the community-transforming ministries of these Pentecostal churches. Their research demonstrated the unique potential of Pentecostalism in improving lives, challenging the common perception that Pentecostals are more oriented toward afterlife matters, e.g., evangelism.

Sometimes, a community-level ministry becomes a national-scale institutional project. The community assistance program of the Church of Pentecost in Ghana soon developed into an NGO.[22] Similarly, Yoido Full Gospel Church (Seoul, South Korea) began to provide vocational training to youths of underprivileged families. This grew and expanded into establishing an NGO called The Good People, which serves a broad range of human needs, including disaster relief and children's adoption programs throughout the world.

Pentecostal denominations, churches, and institutions increasingly engage with issues relating to human suffering as part

---

[20]For more discussion, see below—also, Julie C. Ma, *The Holy Spirit, Women and Mission* (Eugene, OR: Wipf & Stock, 2025 forthcoming), the chapter titled "Touching the Lives of People through the Holistic Mission Work of the Buntains (Mark and Huldah) in Calcutta, India."

[21]Miller and Yamamori, *Global Pentecostalism*, especially 4-5.

[22]For a full treatment of the church's social service, see David D. Daniels III, "Progressive Pentecostalism, Pentecostal Philanthropy: The Church of Pentecost," in *African Pentecostal Missions Maturing: Essays in Honor of Apostle Opoku Onyinah*, ed. Lord Elorm Donkor and Clifton R. Clarke (Eugene, OR: Pickwick, 2018), 50-63.

of their mission practices.[23] Poverty is the top social agenda that Pentecostals embrace.[24] More Pentecostal academics are studying the Pentecostal potential of social services. The recent Global Pentecostal Summit in Singapore (November 2023) gathered two dozen Pentecostal scholars to map the contemporary state of Pentecostalism. Its book, *Voices Loud and Clear*, included eight studies that addressed various human challenges and Pentecostal responses to them.[25]

Issues of Inequality: Education

Most international institutions measure inequalities in terms of household income. The keywords of the Asia Development Bank's report on inequality identify the key areas of inequality: economics, education, gender equality, health, inclusive growth, etc.[26] A casual observation immediately reveals that issues of inequality are complex, requiring far more than "helping the victims." They involve culture, religion, social structure, governance, policies, and corruption. Amidst many challenges, Christianity has brought modern education, medical services, and literacy to many Asian countries. Among them, education has a lasting impact on nation-building, especially among nations that gained independence in the middle of the last century.

---

[23]For example, see Joel A. Tejedo, "Pentecostal Civic Engagement in the Squatter Area" and Doreen Benavidez and Edwardneil Benavidez, "The War on Drugs in the Philippines and the Image of Healing and Restoration in Mark 5:1-20," both in Wonsuk Ma and Opoku Onyinah, ed., *Good News to the Poor: Spirit-Empowered Responses to Poverty* (Tulsa: ORU Press, 2022), 321-343, and 345-362, respectively.

[24]For example, Empowered21's 2019 Scholars Consultation was held in Bogota, Colombia, which resulted in a book, Wonsuk Ma and Opoku Onyinah, ed., *Good News to the Poor: Spirit-Empowered Responses to Poverty* (Tulsa: ORU Press, 2021).

[25]Kong Hee, Byron D. Klaus, and Douglas Petersen, ed., *Voices Loud and Clear* (Oxford: Regnum Books, 2024).

[26]Asian Development Bank, Inequality in Asia and the Pacific: Trends, Drivers, and Policy Implications (Manila: Asian Development Bank, 2014).

Pentecostal educational ministries have far-reaching influences. The first example was briefly mentioned above: the Calcutta Mercy, founded in 1954 by Mark and Huldah Buntain, an American Pentecostal couple. This multifaceted ministry includes educating children of poor families in this metropolis of over 14.5 million people. It has established its own schools, including a Bible college and a nursing university. The Calcutta Mercy website summarizes its education ministry: "We provide education to impoverished children who lack access to quality and affordable schools. We support 100+ schools with an enrollment of 32,000 students."[27]

Along with feeding and healthcare, the ministry identified education as the third urgent and strategic areas of human flourishing. Calcutta Mercy argues that: first, India has the largest illiterate population in the world with 237 million illiterate adults; second, "Literacy is key to the health of a country;" third, about 9 percent (or 35 million) of 400 million children do not receive education; and fourth, close to 90 percent of unschooled children, a large number of whom are in child labor and prostitution, can be brought back by affordable and reliable education programs.[28] These students are also the beneficiaries of Calcutta Mercy's massive feeding program.

A second example is ChildHope (formally known as Latin America ChildCare). Founded by John Bueno, a USA Assemblies of God missionary to Latin America in 1963, the ministry has provided education to close to 100,000 children of poor families in twenty countries of Latin America and the Caribbean.[29]

---

[27]Calcutta Mercy, "Educate," https://www.calcuttamercy.org/education-projects (accessed December 27, 2024).

[28]Calcutta Mercy, "Why Educate?" https://www.calcuttamercy.org/why-educate (accessed December 27, 2024).

[29]ChildHope, "About Us," https://childhopeonline.org/our-mission/about-us/ (accessed December 29, 2024); Mary Kathleen Mahon, "*Todo lo Puedo*: The Empowerment of Children Born into Poverty through ChildHope," in *Good News to the Poor*, 207-25. This powerful ministry also has a "rescue" dimension for children at risk, Mary Mahon, "Spirit-Empowered Global Christianity: The Pathway to Agency for Children at Risk," in *Voices Loud and*

Although these two examples are well-structured and large-scale education ministries, Miller and Yamamori observed that Pentecostals offer many small-scale education programs.[30] A few observations are helpful:

- Education is universally valued, as seen in the case of Burkina Faso. Muslim parents did not hesitate to send their children to Speed Education classes in local churches.
- Educational excellence in Christian education systems raises the general education level, often prized by well-to-do families.
- Education by Christians results in the significant evangelization of children and their families.

Promoting Common Good: Healthcare

Despite the complex nature of social challenges, this exploration illustrates the church's vital role in promoting the common good of the given community or nation. The lack of adequate healthcare in Asia has been a key contributor to poverty, suffering, and inequalities. Three Pentecostal examples show potential approaches to affordable and effective healthcare for those who cannot afford the public healthcare system.

Zambia is a landlocked country in Southern Africa. The HIV pandemic has been the most serious healthcare challenge in the country. The 2023 UNAIDS report provides the following grim data:[31]

Clear, 245-256.

[30]Miller and Yamamori, *Global Pentecostalism*. Also, see Makonen Getu, "Empowering Christian Low-Fee Independent Schools: Edify's Response to Poverty," in *Good News to the Poor*, 279-299.

[31]UNAIDS, "Zambia 2023," https://www.unaids.org/en/regions countries/countries/zambia (accessed December 29, 2024).

- Adults and children living with HIV: 1,300,000
- Adult aged 15 to 49 HIV prevalence rate: 9.8%
- Adults and children newly infected with HIV: 23,000
- Adult and child deaths due to AIDS: 17,000
- Orphans due to AIDS aged 0 to 17: 390,000

Joshua Banda, a Pentecostal bishop of Zambia, is pastor of the megachurch Northmead Assembly of God Church in Lusaka. In 1999, he initiated an all-out Christian response to the HIV pandemic. The culmination of his campaign was the opening of the Circle of Hope Clinic in 2003. He encourages his male members to test for HIV at the church's clinic, provides education on prevention, and offers Antiretroviral therapy and care for the HIV-infected. The church also established an orphanage cum elementary school for HIV orphans.[32]

Soon, many churches followed Northmead's example to address this national pandemic, adopting the Circle of Hope as their Christian HIV program. In 2007, the president appointed Banda to chair the National Aids Council, which he led for seven years. During his leadership, he advocated fidelity in marriage as a lifestyle countermeasure to the HIV-AIDS pandemic.

Similarly, many churches in Malaysia provide free or affordable medical services for low-income families. On January 23, 2024, *The Star* newspaper featured Eagles Dialysis Centre in Subang Jaya, a community outreach ministry of Full Gospel Tabernacle. Established in 2013, it aims to "serve the less fortunate in our society, namely end-stage kidney failure patients from the lower income group, so they can obtain affordable and quality hemodialysis treatment."[33] The center can serve forty-eight patients with a staff

[32]Joshua Banda, "Engaging with the Community, the Fight against AIDS," in *Good News from Africa: Community Transformation through the Church*, ed. Brian Woolnough (Oxford: Regnum Books, 2013), 48-49. Also, Wonsuk Ma, "Circle of Hope for Tackling AIDS," *Sojourners: Faith in Action for Social Justice* (January 2017), 33.

[33]Ming Teao, "Subsidised Kidney Dialysis Treatment for the Poor," *The Star,* January 23, 2024, https://www.thestar.com.my/lifestyle/family/2024/01/23/subsidised-kidney-dialysis-treatment-for-the-poor.

of three doctors, two nephrologists (kidney specialists), six nurses, and dialysis assistants. It treats eligible patients regardless of race or religion. The Center's challenge is securing qualified volunteer doctors and nurses and financial donations to sustain this lifeline service for many.

Calcutta Mercy also provides a large-scale healthcare service to those who cannot afford established medical facilities. In 1977, Calcutta Mercy Hospital was established to address these urgent needs. With 173 beds, it currently serves around 100,000 patients each year. Again, the context is dire: the public healthcare system is inadequate, with understaffed doctors and a shortage of beds. To worsen the situation, gender and caste keep many away from healthcare services. Poor sanitation exposes the urban poor to diseases; diarrhea is the number one killer of children in India.[34]

The healthcare ministry of Calcutta Mercy notes two important areas that challenge healthcare inequalities in India. The first is an urban-rural disparity: "70% of India's health care resources are located in India's cities, yet nearly 70% of the population lives in rural India." The Red District of Calcutta is another sector of society with little medical service. To meet these needs, Calcutta Mercy has developed 12 rural clinics and one Red District clinic since 1970. They serve 40,000 people each year in 14 cities and villages. They aim to add 10 more clinics by 2025.[35]

The second challenge is inequality for socio-cultural reasons. The Calcutta Mercy website briefly includes serious inequalities in healthcare services:

> Some of the neediest people in Calcutta are refused treatment due to their gender, caste, or economic status. It is not uncommon for hospitals to turn away the dying poor who cannot pay or the prostitute's daughter who carries a social stigma. Parents abandon their deformed

[34]Calcutta Mercy, "Why Medically Assist?" https://www.calcuttamercy.org/why-medically-assist/ (accessed December 27, 2024).

[35]Calcutta Mercy, "Medical Projects," https://www.calcuttamercy.org/medical-projects/ (December 28, 2024).

> toddlers in trash heaps because they can't bear the shame of the "curse" they had birthed. A widespread preference for male children means daughters are often delayed or refused treatment for treatable illnesses.[36]

This statement identifies that caste, gender, occupation, poverty, social stigma, and religious belief contribute to inequality. Calcutta Mercy's healthcare services fight discrimination by offering fair treatment for the improvement of living standards. Indeed, the Ministry aspires to transform societies through the Christian values of every life.

Spiritual Capital and Social Capital

The ministries introduced above epitomize the Pentecostal potential for social transformation. Miller and Yamamori also discovered that Pentecostals are the best prepared for such a task, calling them "Progressive Pentecostals." We need to ask at least two questions: what is the Pentecostal spiritual capital, and how can it expand to the societal level?

Examining Pentecostal Spiritual Capital

My continuing inquiry into Pentecostal uniqueness was motivated by my missionary work among struggling tribal groups in the Philippines. Like many Pentecostals, my desire for evangelism was accompanied by what may be termed holistic mission. It included healthcare, education assistance, etc. The 2005 conference of the Commission on World Mission and Evangelism of the WCC was held in Athens under the theme, "Come Holy Spirit, Heal and Reconcile." My plenary address presented five cases of life-transformative work and elucidated the spiritual and theological assets unique to Pentecostals.[37]

---

[36]Calcutta Mercy, "Why Medically Assist?"

[37]Wonsuk Ma, "'When the Poor Are Fired Up:' The Role of Pneumatology in Pentecostal-Charismatic Mission," in *Come Holy Spirit, Heal and Reconcile:*

This journey continued through several research works, identifying, for example, the two theological bases found in this book.[38] However, a more elaborate list has nine (which includes the two) in two categories:[39]

Hermeneutical Values—or how Pentecostals are spiritually "wired:"

- "People of the Book:" Scripture and Life
- Restorational Impulse: Apostolic Vision
- Participatory Process: Place of Community
- Experience: Lived-out Spirituality
- People of the Spirit(s)

Theological Assets—or what they believe and how they behave:

- Baptism in the Spirit
- The Prophethood of All Believers
- Eschatology
- The Primacy of "Soul" Matter

With an activism-oriented orientation and a faith larger than life-size, I conclude that Pentecostals have proven to be the best soul-winners. They also hold the best promise as change agents for troubled lives. Then, what keeps many Pentecostals settled within the first mission circle: saving souls?

Report of the WCC Conference on World Mission and Evangelism, Athens, Greece, May 2005 ed. Jacques Matthey (Geneva: WCC Publications, 2008), 159-167.

[38]Chapter 6, especially the section above on "Two Theological and Spiritual Dynamics;" and Wonsuk Ma, *Mission in the Spirit: Formation, Theology and Praxis* (Oxford: Regnum Books, 2023), 59-69, the chapter entitled "'When the Poor are Fired Up:' Pneumatology in Pentecostal Mission."

[39]Wonsuk Ma, *Mission in the Spirit: Formation, Theology and Praxis* (Oxford: Regnum Books, 2023), 89-102, chap. 8, "The Theological Motivation for Pentecostal Mission."

Taking the Spiritual Capital to the Social Domain

In an email conversation with Michael Cassidy of African Enterprise, he poignantly challenged, "How can Pentecostals translate their spiritual capital into social capital?" While celebrating the heroic work of "Progressive Pentecostals," why do a large number of Pentecostal and Charismatic churches consider that helping neighbors is a theologically "progressive" or liberal agenda? This discussion will only be a starter, identifying several directional suggestions.

First, there is an organic relationship between proclamation and social service. Pentecostals can learn valuable lessons from the intense debate within the Lausanne movement about the relationship between these two "pillars" of Christian mission.[40] How can the two motivate and enrich each other instead of existing as two separate mission agendas? The outer ripples should move inward so that justice mission is actualized in serving the suffering, while the latter also results in saving souls. This ultimate telos of soul-saving makes Christian social engagement different from secular NGOs. In the same way, love for the lost prompts one to care for the needy and to address the roots of suffering. The conversation has been active and encouraging in academic circles since the last quarter of the previous century.[41]

Second, Pentecostal social services should be rooted in their unique pneumatological missiology. This unique theology includes both the theology itself and the theologizers, as it has much to do with who Pentecostals are. The first Christians were characterized as "Galileans," or people from the margins; Pentecostals are often called "the poor." When the poor are "fired up," their theological

---

[40]For example, see Al Tizon, *Transformation after Lausanne: Radical Evangelical Mission in Global-Local Perspective* (Oxford: Regnum Books, 2008).

[41]For a recent discussion, see Jerry M. Ireland, *The Missionary Spirit: Evangelism and Social Action in Pentecostal Missiology* (Maryknoll, NY: Orbis, 2021).

intensity and life-out expressions can be different from the same fired-up of the "not-so-poor."

Third is a practical question. With existing historical and theological resources, how can Pentecostal believers and communities be encouraged and prepared to become aware of the pressing needs of their surroundings, and train their members to find small ways to address them? Learning from "good practices" is a good start. There are exemplary cases in addition to the Miller-Yamamori book.[42]

Fourth, there is a powerful ecumenical potential when churches in the area combine resources to address their common issues. Such collaboration reduces unnecessary duplication, enhances effectiveness, builds bridges among the churches, and ultimately bears a stronger witness to the Christian faith.

Summary

Engaging society and its difficulties is the most challenging aspect of Christian mission. The church has been divided by its mission focus between "life before death" and "life after death."[43] Equally challenging is the complexity and enormity of each community's problems. Their overwhelming sense and meager resources could easily dwarf a small church's desire to address them.

Most of the cases we have studied so far suggest several helpful tips, including:

- Churches can begin their responses in small ways in line with their resources. This bite-size approach includes addressing the hardships of their own members.
- As churches gain experience and confidence, they explore collaborations with local government, charities, and churches in the same area.

---

[42]See Ma and Onyinah, ed., *Good News to the Poor*.
[43]Ma and Ma, *Mission in the Spirit*, 264-65.

- Churches also expand their ministry from immediate relief for urgent needs to long-term capacity-building projects such as education.
- Large churches and experienced communities often establish legal bodies (NGOs) to "professionalize" their social service.

Such an approach has been criticized as caring only for the victims rather than tracing and addressing the root of the problems. This "one-person-at-a-time" approach is also considered inadequate as it only makes a dent in the problem. Another criticism is the spiritualization of challenges, which requires another critical engagement.

There are clear limitations to a Christian community serving the needy. The root problem is often complex and beyond a church's capacity. Challenges include civil unrest, poor medical and social infrastructure, religious values, cultural traditions, corruption, ethnic conflict, and many more. Despite evident limitations, the viability of the Pentecostal way of social service is well-established, especially compared with approaches inspired by liberation theology.

The mounting sense is that much work remains to be done on academic and practical fronts. Pentecostals have unique spiritual and theological assets and sufficient practical experiences. Therefore, they are uniquely prepared to serve their communities.

However, some explosive landmines lie ahead. Due to complex social challenges, Pentecostals may eventually find themselves in uneasy positions. For example, a hot debate is whether Pentecostals should run for public office, including the presidency. Each community needs to set its focus and limitations in social engagement.

Social science has proven to be extremely useful for academic reflection. While Pentecostals were active in transforming lives in Latin America, a sociological study by Martin, a non-Pentecostal, offers a helpful insight. His *Tongues of Fire* positively presents the transformational outcome of the Pentecostal faith, ranging from personal life, work habits, and family life, to the positive effect on community. However, he also shares a troubling observation that the transformational effect stays only within the individual and family levels. Indeed, many who achieved social upward mobility through the Pentecostal faith tend to pay little attention to the fellow "poor," forgetting their past.[44] In this context, when several Latin American countries elected Pentecostal presidents, hope for higher moral standards was high. However, the expectation soon proved to be false, as they were marred by the allegation of corruption. On the other hand, Miller-Yamamori's study, expanded to a global scope, provides many useful cases of community transformation. A distinct feature of their analysis was the grassroots nature of the transformative ministries.[45]

---

[44]Martin, *Tongues of Fire.*
[45]Miller & Yamamori, *Global Pentecostalism.*

Personal Postscript

This book is the fruit of my long quest to understand the role of Asian Pentecostalism, first as a missionary and then as an academic researcher. As in other continents, Asia holds unique possibilities and challenges in the development of Christianity. There is no Christianity without Christ and his followers; I approached this subject with a great conviction that Asia needs to rise to overcome its poor performance in evangelization throughout church history. At the same time, many argue that the twenty-first century will see Asian Christianity play a significant role while Africa continues its sustained growth as in the twentieth century. I even argue that this may become the century of Asian Christianity. The potential presented in this book offers the challenging proposition that Asian Pentecostalism will lead the growth of Asian Christianity and beyond.

For the sustained growth of Asian Pentecostalism and Christianity to contribute to the continuing growth and expansion of global Christianity, a firm theological foundation is essential. The five theological chapters in this book only "sample" the wide expanse of theological inquiries. My two previous books contain about a dozen theological explorations, especially in the Asian context.[374] As many of these studies illustrate, the constantly

[374]*Mission in the Spirit: Towards a Pentecostal/Charismatic Missiology*

changing socio-cultural context poses a challenge, while making the theologization process live, relevant, and dynamic. Ongoing evolution is also found in the movement itself. These two variables make the task of Pentecostal theology always "under construction," refusing to be "settled" once and for all. For this reason, I am blessed to be an Asian Pentecostal theologian.

The gracious foreword of Dr. Billy Wilson states that Pentecostalism is the largest active Christian family, and it is endowed with a powerful and unique missiology. Is the largeness, then, sufficient to lead Asian Christianity into a season of sustained growth? Recent history suggests this possibility. The second foreword by Malaysian Methodist Bishop Hwa Yung points out the need for theologization, especially ecclesiology for the Charismatic and Neo-Charismatic segments of global Pentecostal Christianity.

Which areas should Pentecostal church leaders and researchers focus on to ensure that this possibility becomes a living reality? I previously identified specific topics requiring further exploration. I now propose four overarching guidelines for the furtherance of Pentecostal dynamics, especially in the context of global Christianity:

First, we need faithful inculcation of Pentecostal theological distinctives and spirituality. The most distinct theological tenet is that baptism in the Holy Spirit empowers believers to be active witnesses. There are various interpretations of this spiritual experience: Classical Pentecostals believe that speaking in tongues is its distinct physical evidence, while Charismatics treat it as one of many spiritual gifts. The core, however, is the missional intention of Holy Spirit baptism.

This core theology can be weakened by various factors. A changing or waning emphasis on imminent eschatological expectation in second and third-generation Pentecostals results in a change in focus. Korean Pentecostalism, exemplified by David Yonggi Cho, replaced the missional urge of earlier Pentecostals

(2010, co-authored with Julie C. Ma) contains six studies, and *Mission in the Spirit: Formation, Theology and Praxis* (2023) contains seven theological chapters.

with church growth as well as other-worldly orientation to this-worldly expectations of God's blessing.[375] This illustrates the critical role of context in forming a revised local theology. It suffices here to note that the Pentecostal movement must identify its primary distinctives carefully, ensuring they are continued in the next generation while discerning the secondary ones.

Second, Pentecostal spirituality is experiential. The extraordinary dynamism demonstrated in Pentecostal life and mission is primarily attributed to believers' encounters with the reality of God. These range from hearing God's voice to divine healing and supernatural intervention. However, baptism in the Holy Spirit is the most commonly held experience, often with speaking in tongues as the sign. The manifestation of spiritual gifts has a strong experiential aspect. This layer of Pentecostal spirituality reinforces theological distinctives and turns beliefs into an actionable lifestyle. This is how the movement has become the most potent mission movement today.

At the same time, Pentecostals need to be alert in at least two areas to put their spiritual experiences in the right place. One is the observable decline in spiritual experiences among believers with improved education and social status. A 2006 Pew Research survey of Pentecostal-Charismatics in ten countries reported that at least 40% of Pentecostals responded that they did not pray in tongues.[376] The receding trend is also found in the 10-year comparison of Spirit-baptisms: a decrease of 3.1% between 2013 and 2023.[377] This disturbing trend has become widespread. In South Korea, once-crowded prayer mountains experience fewer visitors; many are closing.

The other area for vigilance concerns criticism that Pentecostalism has built its theology on experiences. This is not

---

[375]Ma, *Mission in the Spirit: Formation, Theology and Praxis*, ch. 9, "Eschatology and Mission: What Happened When the Wave Hit the West End of the Oceans?"

[376]Pew Research Center, "Spirit and Power—A 10-Country Survey of Pentecostals" (Oct. 2006).

[377](USA) Assemblies of God, "Index to 2023 AG Statistical Reports," https://ag.org/ (accessed April 10, 2025).

entirely groundless. For instance, a placard for a Pentecostal evangelistic gathering may read, "Bring all the sick," implying a promise. Similarly, the doctrine of healing in Christ's atonement may suggest a promise that requires a careful and nuanced theological presentation. The prosperity gospel is definitely an overreach of the Pentecostal belief in God's goodness and his power to meet the needs of his people. Excessive claims and promises are morally and theologically wrong.

Most issues surrounding spiritual experiences may be a matter of equilibrium. Spiritual experiences should come under the judgment of biblical evidence and sound theology. The urgent need for discipleship is also mentioned by Hwa Yung in his foreword. Revival, both individual and corporate, requires a careful process of discipleship to mature its fruits for a prolonged period. Pentecostal leaders should encourage and promote spiritual experiences. At the same time, theological literacy and ongoing discipleship should be improved among believers. The movement should seek a proper balance to manage the relationship and tensions between Pentecostal practice and theology.

Third, it is vital to maintain the Pentecostal identity of the "poor." This notion of marginality has several layers, which scholars have studied from within and without. Pentecostalism began as a "religion of the poor," attracting people from lower social strata. The Azusa Street Mission of Los Angeles received the first local media attention, titled "Weird Babel of Tongues: New Sect of Fanatics Is Breaking Loose. . . ." The *Los Angeles Daily Times* described the meeting as "colored people and a sprinkling of whites" under the leadership of "an old colored exhorter, blind in one eye." The newspaper report described the chaotic prayer meeting where "pandemonium breaks loose."[378] Early Pentecostals were immigrants, ethnic minorities, and people from social and economic margins. This profile of Pentecostalism is widely shared worldwide.

The "poor" also expresses the Pentecostal bias for the suffering. This part of Pentecostal identity is not something to "graduate

---

[378] "Weird Babel of Tongues," *Los Angeles Daily Times*, April 19, 1906.

from" but a value that strengthens their theological and practical life. Pentecostals know the pain of poverty and marginalization and yearn for God's mercy, strength, and grace to persevere with his gracious provision. This important motivation engages Pentecostals with social challenges, as Miller and Yamamori studied.

The last layer is attitudinal: Pentecostals are called to serve others with humility. Sociological studies affirm the Pentecostal trend for upward social mobility. Pentecostalism has recorded outstanding numerical growth, with megachurches in every part of the world. Yet the prosperity gospel is an undesirable response to the "poor" life, requiring profound and self-critical theologizing. The report of private jets owned by Pentecostal preachers is the opposite of the life of Jesus; his Spirit-empowered life *par excellence* should be our model.

Fourth, a close partnership between practitioners and academicians is fundamental. The gap between theological education and the church provides a long-standing challenge. The church and the academy must work in tandem to faithfully preserve the unique theological gift of Pentecostalism, to mobilize every believer to evangelize the world, and hand the latter down to the next generation. In doing so, both communities are called to identify social and cultural forces that hinder the full realization of this distinctiveness in Pentecostal life and mission. Given the grassroots nature of Pentecostal theological development, safeguarding measures are critical to counter any unwarranted theological spinoffs, such as the prosperity gospel.

There are encouraging examples of close partnership between the church and academia. In 2023, City Harvest Church in Singapore organized the Global Pentecostal Summit in partnership with two US Pentecostal scholars. The three-day conference brought over twenty Pentecostal academics from around the world, which is no small feat for a local church. The most significant feature of the conference, however, was its setting: this highly academic gathering took place in the context of regular church life. At least two sessions were held in the church's main hall with thousands of lay members registered for the conference. Within the celebratory worship, a study was presented. This was followed by a long period of prayer when the scholars prayed for those who came forward. Although this setting posed some challenges to the presenting scholars and participants, the conference presented a possibility that could narrow the gap between theology and ministry.

Equally encouraging is the ongoing commitment of City Harvest Church to the development of Pentecostal theology to enrich the global Pentecostal movement. In 2025, the church held a European-Asian Pentecostal Symposium and an Asian Pentecostal Summit. More events are expected in the coming years. The program showcases the unique leadership and contribution that a large church or megachurch can make to hold an academic program. The organizing church has since created a mechanism to share valuable studies with the public through its website (www.gpvoices.org) and open-access publications.[379] This new initiative could be a significant model for other large Pentecostal churches worldwide.

Pentecostalism is a young Christian movement that must refuse to "age." It must keep its youthful spirit! In this way, it will fulfill the biblical mandates given to each location and each generation. Asian Pentecostalism, especially, now has a unique call for Asia and the world "for such a time as this" (Esth 4:14)!

[379]The 2023 Summit resulted in *Voices Loud and Clear* (Regnum), and the book will become the church's gift through open access.

References Cited

A. Larry Ross Communications. "Ministry Leaders Unite on Fulfilling the Great Commission by 2033." *Religion News Service*, December 8, 2022, sec. RNS Press Releases. https://religionnews.com/2022/12/08/ministry-leaders-unite-on-fulfilling-the-great-commission-by-2033/.

Acoba, E. "A Locus for Doing Theology: Theological Stories at the Front Line of Grassroots Missions Engagement." In *Doing Theology in the Philippines,* edited by John Suk, 24-36. Mandaluyong City, Philippines: OMF Lit., 2005.

Adeney, Miriam, and Sadiri Joy Tira. *Wealth, Women & God: How to Flourish Spiritually and Economically in Tough Places.* Pasadena, CA: William Carey Library, 2016.

Aikman, David. *Jesus in Beijing: How Christianity is Transforming China and Changing the Global Balance of Power.* Washington, DC: Regnery, 2003.

Anderson, Allan H. *An Introduction to Pentecostalism.* Cambridge: Cambridge University Press, 2004.

______, and Edmond Tang, eds. *Asian and Pentecostal: The Charismatic Face of Christianity in Asia*, 2nd ed. Oxford: Regnum Books, 2011.

Anderson, Neil T. *Victory over the Darkness: Realize the Power of Your Identity in Christ*, 2nd ed. Bloomington: Bethany House, 2000.

Anderson, Robert Mapes. *Vision of the Disinherited: The Making of American Pentecostalism.* New York: Oxford University Press, 1979.

Archdiocesan Office for Research and Development. *Guidelines of the Catholic Charismatic Renewal Movement in the Archdiocese of Manila.* Manila, 1983.

Asamoah-Gyadu, J. Kwabena. *African Charismatics: Current Developments within Independent Indigenous Pentecostalism in Ghana*. Studies of Religion in Africa 27. Leiden, Netherlands: Brill, 2004.

Asian Development Bank. *Inequality in Asia and the Pacific: Trends, Drivers, and Policy Implications.* Manila: Asian Development Bank, 2014.

Assemblies of God. "Fundamental Truth of the (US) Assemblies of God." http://ag.org/top/beliefs/truths.cfm# I.

Austin, Denise A., and John F. Carter. "Asia Pacific Theological Association: Three Decades of Contribution toward Pentecostal Research and Ministry Training." *International Bulletin of Mission Research* 46, no. 4 (Oct. 2022): 505-15.

Austin, Denise A. Jacqueline Grey, and Paul W. Lewis, eds. *Asia Pacific Pentecostalism.* Leiden: E. J. Brill, 2019.

Baker, Josiah. *A Visible Unity: Cecil Robeck and the Work of Ecumenism.* Lanham, MD: Lexington Books, 2024.

Banda, Joshua. "Engaging with the Community, the Fight against AIDS." In *Good News from Africa: Community Transformation through the Church*, edited by Brian Woolnough, 41-54. Oxford: Regnum Books, 2013.

Barrett, David B., George Thomas Kurian, and Todd M. Johnson, eds. *World Christian Encyclopedia: A Comparative Survey of Churches and Religions in the Modern World*, 2nd ed., 2 vols. Oxford: Oxford University Press, 2001.

Bartleman, Frank. *Azusa Street.* South Plainfield, NJ: Bridge Publishing, 1980.

______. *How Pentecost Came to Los Angeles: The Story Behind the Azusa Street Revival.* Edited by Cecil M. Robeck, Jr. Springfield, MO: Gospel Publishing House, 2017.

Bays, Daniel H. *A New History of Christianity in China.* Malden, MA: Wiley-Blackwell, 2012.

Bennett, Dennis J. *Nine O'Clock In The Morning.* Newberry, FL: Bridge-Logos, 1970.

Bird, Warren. "Global Megachurches: World's Largest Churches." Leadership Network. https://leadnet.org/world/.

Borgall, Saheb John. *The Emergence of Christ Groups in India: The Case of Karnataka State.* Oxford: Regnum, 2016.

Bray, Gerald. *The Church: A Theological and Historical Account.* Grand Rapids: Baker Academic, 2016.

Bruner, Frederick Dale, and William Horden. *The Holy Spirit: Shy Member of the Trinity.* Eugene, OR: Wipf & Stock, 2001.

Bulatao, Jaime. *Split-Level Christianity: Christian Renewal of Filipino Values.* Manila: Ateneo de Manila University, 1966.

Calcutta Mercy. "Educate." https://www.calcuttamercy.org/education-projects.

______. "Medical Projects." https://www.calcuttamercy.org/medical-projects.

Carter, John F., et al. "Advancing the Vision for Pentecostal Theological Education Worldwide: The Origins and Development of the World Alliance for Pentecostal Theological Education." *Pentecostal Education* 7, no. 2 (Fall 2022): 241-60.

Chambon, Michel. "Are Chinese Christians Pentecostal? A Catholic Reading of Pentecostal Influence on Chinese Christians." In *Global Chinese Pentecostal and Charismatic Christianity*, edited by Fenggang Yang, Joy K. C. Tong, and Allan H. Anderson, 181-99. Leiden: Brill, 2017.

Chan, Simon. *Grassroots Asian Theology: Thinking the Faith from the Ground Up.* Downers Grove: InterVarsity Press, 2014.

China for Jesus. "Statement Faith of Chinese House Churches." http://www.chinaforjesus.com/StatementOfFaith.htm.

Cho, David Yonggi. "An Interview: Pastoring with the Holy Spirit" [in Korean]. In *Charis and Charisma: Church Growth of Yoido Full Gospel Church*, edited by Sung-boon Myung and Yong Hong, 14. Seoul: Institute for Church Growth, 2003.

______. *Dr. David Yonggi Cho: Ministering Hope for 50 Years.* Alachua, FL: Bridge-Logos, 2008.

Chong, Terence. "Megachurches in Singapore: The Faith of an Emergent Middle Class." *Pacific Affairs* 88, no. 2 (June 2015): 215–35.

Cox, Harvey. *Fire from Heaven: The Rise of Pentecostal*

Spirituality and the Reshaping of Religion in the Twenty-First Century. Reading, MA: Addison-Wesley, 1995.

Daniels, David D., III. "Progressive Pentecostalism, Pentecostal Philanthropy: The Church of Pentecost." In *African Pentecostal Missions Maturing: Essays in Honor of Apostle OpokuOnyinah*, edited by Lord Elorm Donkor and Clifton R. Clarke, 50-63. Eugene, OR: Pickwick, 2018.

Eim, Yeol-soo. "South Korea." In *New International Dictionary of Pentecostal and Charismatic Movements*, edited by Stanley M. Burgess, et al, 241. Grand Rapids: Zondervan, 2003.

Empowered21. "Amsterdam 2023: EveryONE, A New Era of Evangelism." https://amsterdam2023.com/.

Engcoy, Dynnice Rosanny D. "A Reflection of a Missionary to the Philippines: Gary A. Denbow Interview." *Asian Journal of Pentecostal Studies* 8, no. 2 (July 2005): 307-326.

_______. *Pentecostal Pioneer: The Life of Legacy of Rudy Esperanza and the Early Years of the Assemblies of God in the Philippines.* Eugene, OR: Wipf & Stock, 2017.

England, John C., and Archie C. C. Lee. *Doing Theology with Asian Resources: Ten Years in the Formation of Living Theology in Asia.* Auckland: Programme for Theology and Cultures in Asia, 1993.

Ewing, Jeannie. "Golden Jubilee Year for Catholic Charismatic Renewal." *Today's Catholic,* December 11, 2017. https://todayscatholic.org/golden-jubilee-year-catholic-charismatic-renewal/.

Fielder, Caroline. "The Growth of the Protestant Church in Rural China." *China Study Journal* 23 (Spring/Summer 2008): 42-55.

Fulton, Brent. *China's Urban Christians: A Light that Cannot Be Hidden.* Eugene, OR: Wipf and Stock, 2015.

Garcia, César. "Beyond Liberation and Prosperity Gospel: A Third Way." In *Good News to the Poor: Spirit-Empowered Approaches to Poverty*, edited by Wonsuk Ma and Opoku Onyinah, 141-155, Tulsa: ORU Press, 2022.

Global Christian Forum. "Taking Shape: Global Christian Forum." http://www.wcc-coe.org/wcc/news/press/00/25pre.html.

Global Evangelist Alliance. *The Spirit Empowered Evangelist.* Tulsa: Global Evangelist Alliance, 2023.

Harper, George W. "Philippine Tongues of Fire? Latin American Pentecostalism and the Future of Filipino Christianity." *Journal of Asian Mission* 2, no. 2 (2000): 225-59.

Harrell, David Edwin, Jr. *Oral Roberts: An American Life.* Bloomington, IL: Indiana University Press, 1985.

Hartford Institute for Religion Research. "Database of Megachurches in the US." http://hirr.hartsem.edu/megachurch/database.html.

______. "Megachurches." http://hirr.hartsem.edu/megachurch/megachurces.html.

Hee, Kong, Byron D. Klaus, and Douglas Petersen, eds. *Voices Loud and Clear.* Oxford: Regnum Books, 2024.

Hollenweger, Walter J. *Pentecostalism: Origins and Developments Worldwide.* Peabody, MA: Hendrickson, 1997.

Hong, Young-gi."The Backgrounds and Characteristics of the Charismatic Mega-churches in Korea." *Asian Journal of Pentecostal Studies* 3, no. 1 (2000): 99-118.

Hwa Yung. *Mangos or Bananas? The Quest for an Authentic Asian Christian Theology*, 2nd ed. Oxford: Regnum, 2014.

Ireland, Jerry M. *The Missionary Spirit: Evangelism and Social Action in Pentecostal Missiology.* Maryknoll, NY: Orbis, 2021.

Irianto, Sulistyowati. "Indonesia." In *Christianity in East and Southeast Asia*, edited by Kenneth R. Ross, Francis D. Alvarez SJ, and Todd M. Johnson, 200-11. Edinburgh: Edinburgh University Press, 2020.

Jin, Mingri. *Back to Jerusalem with All Nations: A Biblical Foundation.* Oxford: Regnum, 2016.

Johnson, Aubrey R. *The One and the Many in the Israelite Conception of God*, 2nd ed. Cardiff: University of Wales Press, 1961.

Johnson, Dave. *Led by the Spirit: The History of the American Assemblies of God Missionaries in the Philippines.* Pasig City, Philippines: ICI Ministries, 2009.

Johnson, Todd M., and Gina A. Zurlo. *Introducing Spirit-Empowered Christianity: The Global Pentecostal & Charismatic Movement in the 21st Century.* Tulsa: ORU Press, 2023.

______, and Gina A. Zurlo. *World Christian Encyclopedia*, 3rd ed. Edinburgh: Edinburgh University Press, 2020.

______, and Kenneth R. Ross, eds. *Atlas of Global Christianity.* Edinburgh: Edinburgh University Press, 2009.

Kaiser, Sigurd. "The Kingdom and Power: Elements of Growth in Chinese Christianity: Some Personal Insights." *Religions & Christianity in Today's China* 2, no. 2 (2012): 42-44.

Kang, Chang-soo. "The Analytical Study of the Life of Woon-mong Na, Indigenous Korean Pentecostal." Th.M. thesis, Asia Pacific Theological Seminary, Philippines, 2002.

Kärkkäinen, Veli-Matti. *An Introduction to Ecclesiology: Ecumenical, Historical and Global Perspectives.* Downers Grove: IVP Academic, 2002.

______. *Pneumatology: The Holy Spirit in Ecumenical, International, and Contextual Perspective.* 2nd ed. Grand Rapids: Baker Academic, 2018.

Kay, William K., and Robin Parry, eds. *Exorcism and Deliverance: Multi-Disciplinary Studies.* Milton Keynes: Paternoster, 2011.

Khodr, Georges. "Christianity in the Pluralist World: The Economy of the Holy Spirit." In *Orthodox Perspectives on Mission*, edited by Petros Vassiliadis, 114-22. Regnum Edinburgh Centenary Series 17. Oxford: Regnum, 2013.

Kim, Sebastian C. H., and Kirsteen Kim. *A History of Korean Christianity.* New York: Cambridge University Press, 2015.

King, Johnny Loye. *Spirit and Schism: The History of Oneness Pentecostalism in the Philippines.* N.p.: Johnny Loye King Publishing (Kindle, 2020).

Kitano, Koichi. "Socio-religious Distance between Charismatics and Other Religious Group Members: A Case Study of the Philippines in the 1980s." *Journal of Asian Mission* 5, no. 2 (2003): 231-42.

_____. "Spontaneous Ecumenicity between Catholics and Protestants in the Charismatic Movement: A Case Study." Ph.D. diss., Centro Escolar University, Philippines, 1981.

Lausanne Movement. "The Cape Town Commitment." https// www.lausanne.org/content/ctc/ctcommitment.

Lee, Younghoon. "Yoido Full Gospel Church: A Case Study in Expanding Mission and Fellowship." In *Called to Unity for the Sake of Mission*, edited by John Gibaut and Knud Jorgensen, 275-84. Oxford: Regnum, 2014.

_____. *The Holy Spirit Movement in Korea.* Oxford: Regnum Books, 2009.

Life Church. "Locations." https://www.life.church/locations/.

_____. "What Is Open Network?" https://open.life.church/.

Lim, David S. "A Critique of Modernity in Protestant Missions in the Philippines." *Journal of Asian Mission* 2 no. 2 (2000): 149-177.

Liu, Yi. "The 'Galilee of China:' Pentecostals without Pentecostalism." In *Global Chinese Pentecostal and Charismatic Christianity*, edited by Fenggang Yang, Joy K. C. Tong, and Allan H. Anderson, 200-15. Leiden: Brill, 2017.

Lord, Andrew M. "The Holy Spirit and Contextualization." *Asian Journal of Pentecostal Studies* 4, no. 2 (2001): 201-213.

_____. *Spirit-Shaped Mission: A Holistic Charismatic Missiology.* Bletchley, UK: Paternoster, 2005.

Ma, Julie C. "Growing Churches in Manila." *Asia Journal of Theology* 11 (1997): 324-42.

_____. "Pentecostals and Charismatics." In *Christianity in East and Southeast Asia*, edited by Kenneth R. Ross, Francis D. Alvarez SJ, and Todd M. Johnson, 336-338. Edinburgh: Edinburgh University Press, 2020.

_____. *The Holy Spirit, Women and Mission.* Eugene, OR: Wipf & Stock, 2025.

_____. *When the Spirit Meets the Spirits: Pentecostal Ministry among the Kankana-ey Tribe in the Philippines.*
Frankfurt am Main: Peter Lang, 2000.

_____, and Wonsuk Ma. *Mission in the Spirit: Towards Pentecostal/Charismatic Missiology.* Oxford: Regnum Books, 2010.

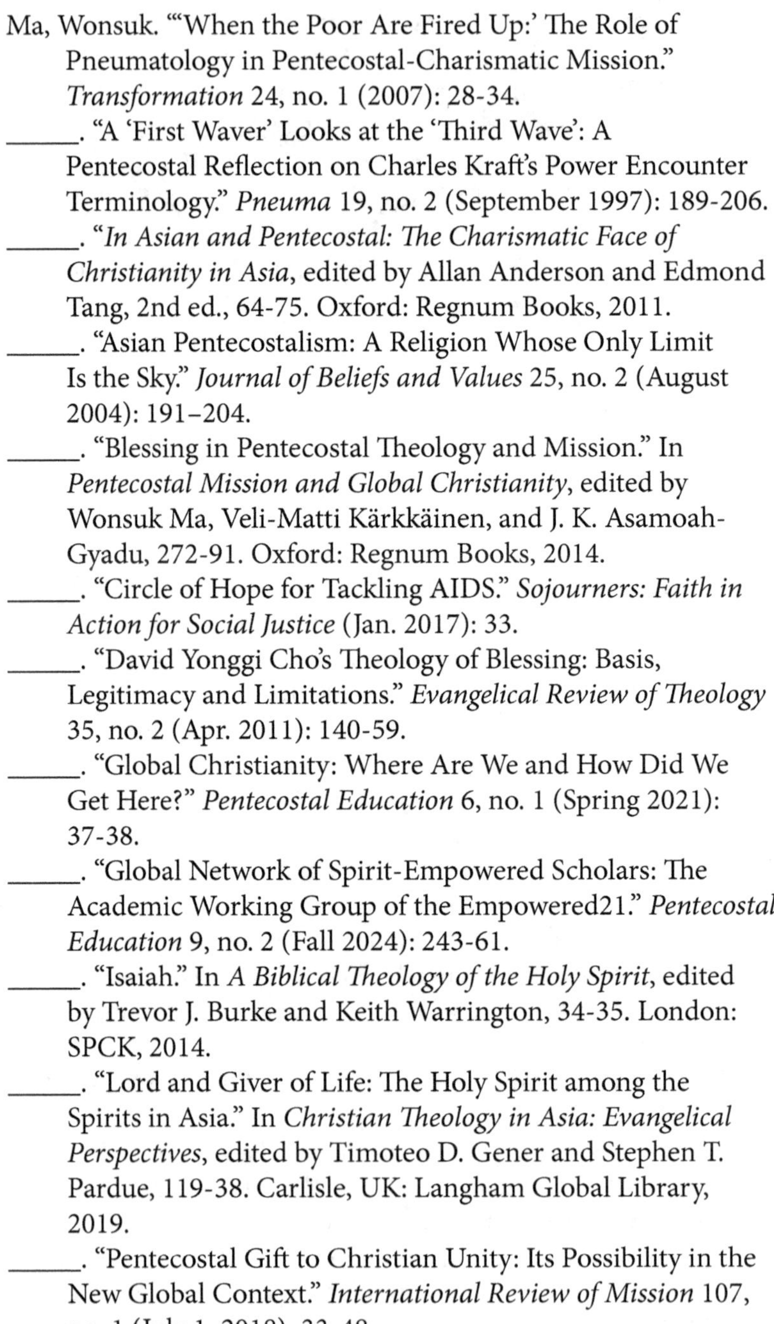

Ma, Wonsuk. "'When the Poor Are Fired Up:' The Role of Pneumatology in Pentecostal-Charismatic Mission." *Transformation* 24, no. 1 (2007): 28-34.

_____. "A 'First Waver' Looks at the 'Third Wave': A Pentecostal Reflection on Charles Kraft's Power Encounter Terminology." *Pneuma* 19, no. 2 (September 1997): 189-206.

_____. "*In Asian and Pentecostal: The Charismatic Face of Christianity in Asia*, edited by Allan Anderson and Edmond Tang, 2nd ed., 64-75. Oxford: Regnum Books, 2011.

_____. "Asian Pentecostalism: A Religion Whose Only Limit Is the Sky." *Journal of Beliefs and Values* 25, no. 2 (August 2004): 191–204.

_____. "Blessing in Pentecostal Theology and Mission." In *Pentecostal Mission and Global Christianity*, edited by Wonsuk Ma, Veli-Matti Kärkkäinen, and J. K. Asamoah-Gyadu, 272-91. Oxford: Regnum Books, 2014.

_____. "Circle of Hope for Tackling AIDS." *Sojourners: Faith in Action for Social Justice* (Jan. 2017): 33.

_____. "David Yonggi Cho's Theology of Blessing: Basis, Legitimacy and Limitations." *Evangelical Review of Theology* 35, no. 2 (Apr. 2011): 140-59.

_____. "Global Christianity: Where Are We and How Did We Get Here?" *Pentecostal Education* 6, no. 1 (Spring 2021): 37-38.

_____. "Global Network of Spirit-Empowered Scholars: The Academic Working Group of the Empowered21." *Pentecostal Education* 9, no. 2 (Fall 2024): 243-61.

_____. "Isaiah." In *A Biblical Theology of the Holy Spirit*, edited by Trevor J. Burke and Keith Warrington, 34-35. London: SPCK, 2014.

_____. "Lord and Giver of Life: The Holy Spirit among the Spirits in Asia." In *Christian Theology in Asia: Evangelical Perspectives*, edited by Timoteo D. Gener and Stephen T. Pardue, 119-38. Carlisle, UK: Langham Global Library, 2019.

_____. "Pentecostal Gift to Christian Unity: Its Possibility in the New Global Context." *International Review of Mission* 107, no. 1 (July 1, 2018): 33-48.

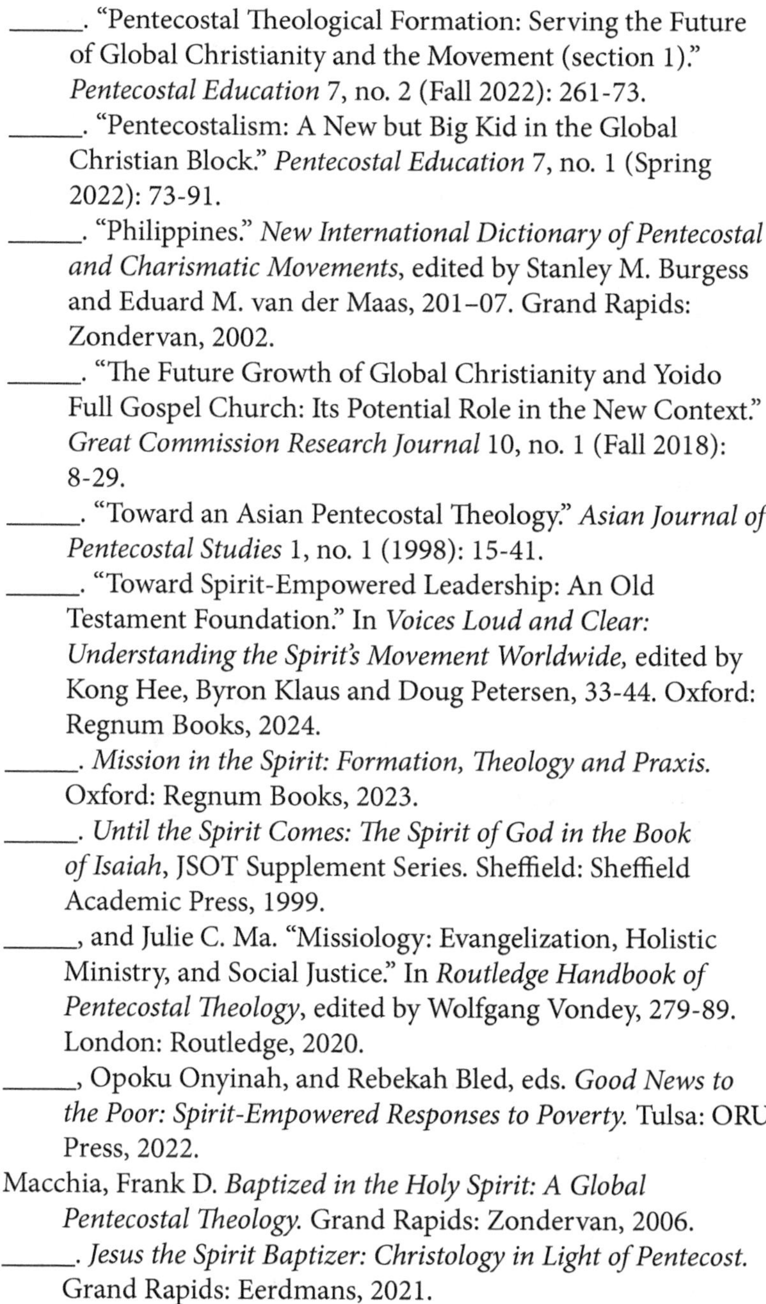

______. "Pentecostal Theological Formation: Serving the Future of Global Christianity and the Movement (section 1)." *Pentecostal Education* 7, no. 2 (Fall 2022): 261-73.

______. "Pentecostalism: A New but Big Kid in the Global Christian Block." *Pentecostal Education* 7, no. 1 (Spring 2022): 73-91.

______. "Philippines." *New International Dictionary of Pentecostal and Charismatic Movements*, edited by Stanley M. Burgess and Eduard M. van der Maas, 201–07. Grand Rapids: Zondervan, 2002.

______. "The Future Growth of Global Christianity and Yoido Full Gospel Church: Its Potential Role in the New Context." *Great Commission Research Journal* 10, no. 1 (Fall 2018): 8-29.

______. "Toward an Asian Pentecostal Theology." *Asian Journal of Pentecostal Studies* 1, no. 1 (1998): 15-41.

______. "Toward Spirit-Empowered Leadership: An Old Testament Foundation." In *Voices Loud and Clear: Understanding the Spirit's Movement Worldwide,* edited by Kong Hee, Byron Klaus and Doug Petersen, 33-44. Oxford: Regnum Books, 2024.

______. *Mission in the Spirit: Formation, Theology and Praxis.* Oxford: Regnum Books, 2023.

______. *Until the Spirit Comes: The Spirit of God in the Book of Isaiah*, JSOT Supplement Series. Sheffield: Sheffield Academic Press, 1999.

______, and Julie C. Ma. "Missiology: Evangelization, Holistic Ministry, and Social Justice." In *Routledge Handbook of Pentecostal Theology*, edited by Wolfgang Vondey, 279-89. London: Routledge, 2020.

______, Opoku Onyinah, and Rebekah Bled, eds. *Good News to the Poor: Spirit-Empowered Responses to Poverty.* Tulsa: ORU Press, 2022.

Macchia, Frank D. *Baptized in the Holy Spirit: A Global Pentecostal Theology.* Grand Rapids: Zondervan, 2006.

______. *Jesus the Spirit Baptizer: Christology in Light of Pentecost.* Grand Rapids: Eerdmans, 2021.

Mahon, Mary Kathleen. "*Todo lo Puedo*: The Empowerment of Children Born into Poverty through ChildHope." In *Good News to the Poor: Spirit-Empowered Responses to Poverty*, edited by Wonsuk Ma, Opoku Onyinah, and Rebekah Bled, 207-25. Tulsa: ORU Press, 2022.

Martin, David. *Tongues of Fire: The Explosion of Pentecostalism in Latin America.* Oxford: Blackwell, 1990.

Martin, Larry. *The Life and Ministry of William J. Seymour.* Joplin, MO: Christian Life Books, 1999.

Menzies, Robert P. "Simultaneous Prayer: A Pentecostal Perspective." In *The Holy Spirit, Spirituality and Leadership: Essays in Honour of Younghoon Lee*, edited by Wonsuk Ma and Robert P. Menzies, 89-103. Oxford: Regnum Books, 2024.

______. *Empowered for Witness: The Spirit in Luke-Acts.* London: T. & T. Clark, 2004.

______. *The Development of Early Christian Pneumatology: With Special Reference to Luke-Acts.* Journal for the Study of the New Testament Supplement Series 54. Sheffield: JSOT Press, 1991.

Miller, Donald, and Tetsunao Yamamori. *Global Pentecostalism: The New Face of Christian Social Engagement.* Berkeley: University of California Press, 2007.

Moreau, Scott, ed. *Deliver Us from Evil: An Uneasy Frontier in Christian Mission.* Monrovia, CA: World Vision International, 2002.

Morgan, Timothy C. "A Tale of China's Two Churches." *Christianity Today* 42 (July 13, 1998): 30-39.

New Wine. "About Us." https://www.new-wine.org/about/.

Newberry, Warren. "Contextualizing Indigenous Church Principles: An African Model." *Asian Journal of Pentecostal Studies* 8, no. 1 (2005): 110-14.

Nguyen, Thao. "A New Way of Being Church for Mission: Asian Catholic Bishops and Asian Catholic Women in Dialogue: A Study of the Documents of the Federation of Asian Bishops' Conference (FABC)." Ph.D. diss., Graduate Theological Union, Berkeley, 2013.

Noll, Mark A. *The New Shape of World Christianity: How American Experience Reflects Global Faith.* Downer's Grove, IL: IVP Academic, 2009.

Obara, Charles Morara. "A Critical Analysis of Reinhard Bonnke's Charismatic Leadership Paradigm." *Spiritus: ORU Journal of Theology* 7, no. 2 (Fall 2022): 243-255.

Onnuri Community Church. *Onnuri Community Church: The First 30 Years.* Seoul: Onnuri Community Church, 2017.

"One Token. . . ." *The Apostolic Faith* (Los Angeles). (Feb.–Mar. 1907): 7.

Onyekachi, U. "List of Nigerian Pastors with Private Jets." *The Nigerian Infor.com*, September 24, 2022. https://thenigerianinfo.com/list-of-nigerian-pastors-with-private-jets/.

Organization of African Instituted Churches. "About Us." https://www.oaic.org/about-us/.

Ouedraogo, Philippe. "Transforming Communities through Education." In *Good News from Africa: Community Transformation through the Church*, edited by Brian Woolnough, 82-83. Oxford: Regnum Books, 2013.

______. *Female Education and Mission: A Burkina Faso Experience.* Oxford: Regnum Books, 2014.

Park, Myung Soo. "Globalization of the Korean Pentecostal Movement: The International Ministry of Dr Yonggi Cho." In *Korean Church, God's Mission, Global Christianity*, edited by Wonsuk Ma and Kyo Seong Ahn, 228-41. Oxford: Regnum, 2015.

______. "Korean Pentecostal Spirituality as Manifested in the Testimonies of Members of Yoido Full Gospel Church." In *David Yonggi Cho: A Close Look at His Theology and Ministry*, edited by Wonsuk Ma, Hyeon-sung Bae, and William W. Menzies, 43-67. Baguio, Philippines: APTS Press, 2004.

Peck, Grant. "Indonesia's Rescue of Rohingya Refugees at Sea is a Reminder of an Ordeal that Began in Myanmar." https://apnews.com/article/rohingya-refugees-bangladesh-malaysia-aceh-indonesia-boats-9fa83728f999b28d87803066578a9755.

Pentecostal Education 9, no. 1 (Spring 2024), a special issue featuring "Movements and Associations for Pentecostal Theological Education."

Pew Research Center. "Global Christianity: A Report on the Size and Distribution of the World's Christian Population." http:/ www.pewforum.org/2011/12/19/global-christianity-exec/.

_____. "Tolerance and Tension: Islam and Christianity in Sub-Saharan Africa." Washington, DC: Pew Research Center, 2010. https://www.pewresearch.org/religion/2010/04/15/ executive-summary-islam-and-christianity-in-sub-saharan-africa/.

Poloma, Margaret M. *The Assemblies of God at the Crossroads: Charisma and Institutional Dilemmas.* Knoxville: University of Tennessee Press, 1989.

Publication Committee of the 60-Year History. *With the Holy Spirit: A 60-Year History of the Korean Assemblies of God* [in Korean]. Seoul: Assemblies of God Korea, 2013.

Ro, David L. "A Study of an Emerging Missions Movement in Urban China: Fron the Perspective of Four Beijing Pastors." Ph.D. diss., Oxford and London, Oxford Centre for Mission Studies / Middlesex University, 2023.

_____. "Mainland China (House Churches)." In *Christianity in East and Southeast Asia*, edited by Kenneth R. Ross, Francis D. Alvarez SJ, and Todd M. Johnson, 63-73. Edinburgh: Edinburgh University Press, 2020.

Robeck, Cecil M., Jr. "Christian Unity and Pentecostal Mission: A Contradiction?" In *Pentecostal Mission and Global Christianity*, edited by Wonsuk Ma, Veli-Matti Kärkkäinen, and J. Kwabena Asamoah-Gyadu, 182-206. Regnum Edinburgh Centenary Series 20. Oxford: Regnum Books, 2014.

_____. "Growing Opportunities for Pentecostal Ecumenical Engagement." *Pentecostal Education* 7, no. 2 (Fall 2022): 173-190.

_____. "Pentecostals and the Apostolic Faith: Implications for Ecumenism." *Pneuma: The Journal of the Society for Pentecostal Studies* 9, no. 1 (Spring 1987): 61-84.

______, Sotiris Boukis and Ani Ghazaryan Drissi, eds. *Towards a Global Vision of the Church*, Volume I: *Explorations on Global Christianity and Ecclesiology*. Faith and Order Paper No. 234. Geneva, Switzerland: WCC Publications, 2022.

Roberts, Oral. "A Master Plan." *Abundant Life* (October 1956): 3-5, 18-22.

Satyavrata, Ivan. *Pentecostal and the Poor: Reflections from the Indian Context.* Baguio City, Philippines: APTS Press, 2017.

Schoonover, Richard L. "Introduction, Compassion Ministry Expressing the Heart of God." *Enrichment* 17, no. 1 (Winter 2012): 24.

Seleky, Trinidad E. "Six Filipinos and One American: Pioneers of the Assemblies of God in the Philippines." *Asian Journal of Pentecostal Studies* 4, no. 1 (2001): 119-29.

Seo, Dongjun. "Testing the Spirits? The Theological Controversy Surrounding David Yonggi Cho and the World's Largest Church, 1983-1994." Studies in World Christianity 31, no. 2 (2025): 151-170.

Shin, Chang-sup. "Assessing the Impact of Pentecostalism on the Korean Presbyterian Church in Light of Calvin's Theology." *Chongshin Theological Journal* 3, no. 1 (1998): 115-31.00

Steinfels, Peter. "Beliefs." *New York Times*, March 16, 1991. https://www.nytimes.com/1991/03/16/us/beliefs-385491.html.

Stronstad, Roger. *The Charismatic Theology of St. Luke: Trajectories from the Old Testament to Luke-Acts*, 2nd ed. Grand Rapids: Baker Academic, 2012.

______. *The Prophethood of All Believers: A Study in Luke's Charismatic Theology.* Sheffield: Sheffield Academic Press, 1999.

Sugirtharajah, R. S. *Asian Biblical Hermeneutics and Postcolonialism: Contesting the Interpretations.* Sheffield: Sheffield Academic Press, 1998.

Suico, Joseph R. "Institutional and Individualistic Dimensions of Transformational Development: The Case of Pentecostal Churches in the Philippines." Ph.D. thesis, University Wales, 2003.

_____. "Pentecostalism in the Philippines." In *Asian and Pentecostal: The Charismatic Face of Christianity in Asia*, edited by Allan Anderson and Edmond Tang, 350-56. Oxford: Regnum Books, 2005.

Synan, Vinson, and Billy Wilson. *As the Waters Cover the Sea: The Story of Empowered21 and the Movement It Serves.* Tulsa: Empowered Books, 2021.

_____. *Where He Leads Me: The Vinson Synan Story.* Franklin Springs, GA: LifeSprings Resources, 2019.

Tan Jin Huat. *Planting an Indigenous Church: The Case of the Borneo Evangelical Mission.* Oxford: Regnum, 2011.

Tang, Edmond. "'Yellers' and Healers: Pentecostalism and the Study of Grassroots Christianity in China." In *Asian and Pentecostal: The Charismatic Face of Christianity in Asia*, edited by Allan Anderson and Edmond Tang, 2nd ed., 379-94. Oxford: Regnum Books, 2011.

Teao, Ming. "Subsidised Kidney Dialysis Treatment for the Poor." *The Star*, January 23, 2024. https://www.thestar.com.my/lifestyle/family/2024/01/23/subsidised-kidney-dialysis-treatment-for-the-poor.

Timenia, Lora Angeline Embudo, *Third Wave Pentecostalism in the Philippines: Understanding Toronto Blessing Revivalism's Signs and Wonders Theology in the Philippines.* Eugene, OR: Wipf & Stock, 2021.

Tizon, Al. *Transformation after Lausanne: Radical Evangelical Mission in Global-Local Perspective.* Oxford: Regnum Books, 2008.

Transparency International. "Corruption Perceptions Index 2023." https://www.transparency.org/en/cpi/2023.

UNAID. "Zambia 2023." https://www.unaids.org/en/regionscountries/countries/zambia.

Underwood, B. E. "Memphis Miracle." *Legacy* 4 (Summer 1997): 3-6.

United Nations Development Programme. "2024 Regional Human Development Report: Making Our Future: New Directions for Human Development in Asia and the Pacific." New York: UNDP, 2024.

Wagner, C. Peter. *Signs and Wonders Today: The Story of Fuller Theological Seminary's Remarkable Course on Spiritual Power*, expanded edition. Alamonte Springs, FL: Creation House, 1987.

Währisch-Oblau, Claudia. "Power Evangelism in a Protestant Context? Reflections after a Workshop in Samosir/ Indonesia." *International Review of Mission* 107, no. 1 (June 2018): 142-58.

Walls, Andrew F. "Christianity across Twenty Centuries." In *Atlas of Global Christianity*, edited by Todd M. Johnson and Kenneth R. Ross, 48-49. Edinburgh: Edinburgh University Press, 2009.

______. "Mission History as the Substructure of Mission Theology." *Swedish Missiological Themes* 93, no. 3 (2005): 367-78.

Wang, Kwok Nai. *The Local Church.* Hong Kong: Christian Conference of Asia, 2005.

Weber, Maximillan. *Theory of Social and Economic Organization.* Translated by A. R. Anderson and Talcott Parsons. New York: Free Press, 1947.

"Weird Babel of Tongues: New Sect of Fanatics Is Breaking Loose; Wild Scene Last Night on Azusa Street; Gurgle of Wordless Talk by a Sister." *Los Angeles Daily Times*, April 18, 1906.

Wells, David R. "The Development and Role of the Christian University Commission." *Pentecostal Education* 7, no. 2 (Fall 2022): 165-71.

Wenk, Matthias. *Community-Forming Power: The Socio-Ethical Role of the Spirit in Luke-Acts.* Sheffield: Sheffield Academic Press, 2000.

Wesley, Luke. *The Church in China: Persecuted, Pentecostal and Powerful.* Baguio City, Philippines: AJPS Books, 2004.

Wiegele, Katharine L. *Investing in Miracles: El Shaddai and the Transformation of Popular Catholicism in the Philippines.* Honolulu: University of Hawaii Press, 2006.

Wilkerson, David R. with John and Elizabeth Sherrill. *The Cross and the Switchblade.* New York: B. Geis, 1968.

Wilson, William M. "The Pentecostal World Fellowship: Its Past, Present, and Future." *Pentecostal Education* 7, no. 2 (Fall 2022): 153-64.

"Word and Spirit, Church and World: The Final Report of the International Dialogue between Representatives of the World Alliance of Reformed Churches and Some Classical Pentecostal Churches and Leaders 1996-2000." *Asian Journal of Pentecostal Studies* 4, no. 1 (2001): 41-72.

World Council of Churches. *The Church: Toward a Common Vision*, Faith and Order Paper no. 214. Geneva: WCC Publications, 2023.

_____. *Together Towards Life: New Affirmation on Mission and Evangelism.* Geneva: WCC, 2013.

Wostyn, Lode. "Catholic Charismatics in the Philippines." In *Asian and Pentecostal: The Charismatic Face of Christianity in Asia*, edited by Allan Anderson and Edmond Tang, 363-83. Oxford: Regnum Books, 2005.

Xin, Yalin. "Deborah Xu: The Story of a Catalytic Leadership in the Chinese House Church Movement." In *Evangelical and Frontier Mission: Perspectives on the Global Progress of the Gospel*, edited by Beth Snodderly and A. Scott Moreau, 138-42. Oxford: Regnum Books, 2011.

_____. *Inside China's House Church Network: The Word of Life Movement and Its Renewing Dynamic.* Lexington, KY: Emeth Press, 2009.

Xu Yongze. "Preface" to Brother Yun and Paul Gattaway. *The Heavenly Man.* Peabody, MA: Hendrickson, 2002.

Yang, Fenggang, Joy K. C. Tong, and Allan H. Anderson, eds. *Global Chinese Pentecostal and Charismatic Christianity.* Global Pentecostal and Charismatic Studies 22. Leiden, Netherlands: E. J. Brill, 2017.

Yong, Amos. "I Believe in the Holy Spirit: From the Ends of the Earth to the Ends of Time." In *The Spirit over the Earth: Pneumatology in the Majority World*, edited by Gene L Green, Stephen T. Pardue, and K. K. Yeo, 13-33. Carlisle: Langham Global Library, 2016.

_____, and Mark A. Lamport, eds. *Uncovering the Pearl: The Hidden Story of Christianity in Asia.* Eugene, OR: Wipf & Stock, 2023.

Yoo, Boo-woong. *Korean Pentecostalism: Its History and Theology.* Frankfurt: Peter Lang, 1988.

YouVersion. "YouVersion reports Verse of the Year and Ukrainian movement." https://www.youversion.com/press/youversion-reports-verse-of-the-year-and-ukrainian-movement/.

Yun, Koo Dong. The Holy Spirit and Ch'i (Qi): *A Chiological Approach to Pneumatology.* Eugene, OR: Pickwick, 2012.

Zhu, Rachel Xiaohong. "The Catholic Charismatic Renewal in Mainland China." In *Global Chinese Pentecostal and Charismatic* Christianity, edited by Fenggang Yang, Joy K. C. Tong, and Allan H. Anderson, 264-85. Leiden: Brill, 2017.

Zurlo, Gina A. "A Demographic Profile of Christianity in East and Southeast Asia." In *Christianity in East and Southeast Asia,* edited by Kenneth R. Ross, Francis D. Alvarez SJ, and Todd M. Johnson, 3-14. Edinburgh: Edinburgh University Press, 2020.

"심장병 수술 4000명 돌파 감사예배" [Thanksgiving Service Celebrating 4000 Beneficiaries of the Children's Heart Surgery Program]. *The Full Gospel Family Newspaper* April 18, 2008.

Index

N

O

P

U

V

W

X-Z

www.ingramcontent.com/pod-product-compliance
Lightning Source LLC
LaVergne TN
LVHW050620100826
845148LV00011B/1660

* 9 7 9 8 3 8 5 2 7 6 1 9 6 *